Praise for INTO THE TEMPEST

"This book is a treasury of big-picture insight from our leading theorist of the emerging system of global capitalism. Robinson's project—to understand the political economy in order to change it—stands as the preeminent successor to Marx's project from an earlier epoch. For readers perplexed about our changing world and apprehensive about its future, here is your primer and call to action."
—**Paul Raskin**, author of *Journey to Earthland*

"William Robinson's *Into the Tempest* is a timely account of global gentrification. While most scholars concentrate on the city, Professor Robinson covers its global impact that has resulted in environmental destruction, social inequalities, and displacement of billions of people around the world. This has led to forced mass migrations. As in the case of micro-gentrification, society is entering the final stages of inequality accelerating a global collapse of modern civilization. Few realize that the state after gentrification is a Blade Runner world—a dystopian society devoid of human emotion and a collective historical memory."
—**Rodolfo F. Acuña**, professor emeritus, Chicana/o Studies Department, California State University, Northridge

"'Know your enemy and know yourself . . .' is how the iconic Sun Tzu began his famous command. William Robinson offers those engaged in the struggle against global capitalism a remarkable and compelling insight and framework in order to both understand our opponents as well as better grasp the strengths and weaknesses of the oppressed and dispossessed. This is the book for which I have been waiting and I could not put it down."
—**Bill Fletcher, Jr.**, former president of TransAfrica Forum; coauthor of *Solidarity Divided,* and author of *They're Bankrupting Us: And Twenty Other Myths About Unions*

"*Into the Tempest* challenges us to look at the big picture, to examine without blinders the dramatic changes that have reshaped twenty-first-century capitalism and led to a true crisis of human civilization. Without flinching, it goes on to present theoretical and political analyses that help inform our quest for strategic clarity as we fight for a different world."
—**Max Elbaum**, author of *Revolution in the Air: Sixties Radicals Turn to Lenin, Mao and Che*

"Robinson has by now accumulated an extraordinary mix of knowledges about global capitalism. Having worked in very diverse areas of the world, he brings to it a kind of wisdom, and this enables the reader to grasp the breadth of instances of the global in today's world."
—**Saskia Sassen**, Columbia University, author of *Expulsions*

"Robinson's brilliant and courageous research has culminated in this pathfinding work of political reconnaissance that traces capitalism's virulent history, exposes its contradictions, locates its capacity to reorganize and digitally reconfigure itself as the fulcrum upon which the survival of the transnational ruling elite rests, and presents an alternative social logic and transgressive strategies for transcending the proliferation of injustices wrought by the existing social order. A masterpiece!"

—**Peter McLaren**, distinguished professor in critical studies, Chapman University; chair professor, Northeast Normal University, China

"Robinson's *Into the Tempest* is a collection of his essays on the emergence of a global police state and the nature of twenty-first-century fascism. It applies a trenchant structural analysis of the world system with a Gramscian effort to theorize and mobilize liberatory social movements that challenge the reactionary forces emerging during the contemporary period of crisis. Robinson is one of the best macrosociologists of his generation. His comparative and temporally deep perspective drives a synthesis of global capitalism and world-system perspectives in a way that allows us to see through the fog of globalization."

—**Chris Chase-Dunn**, University of California, Riverside

PRAISE FOR *GLOBAL CAPITALISM AND THE CRISIS OF HUMANITY:*

"In this thoughtful and informative study, William I. Robinson carries forward the theory of global capitalism that he has presented in earlier works, applying it to the severe crises of an unprecedented moment of human history when decisions directly affect the prospects for decent survival. The perspective that he develops is a most valuable one, broadly researched and carefully analyzed, addressing issues of utmost importance."

—**Noam Chomsky**

INTO THE TEMPEST

ESSAYS ON THE NEW GLOBAL CAPITALISM

WILLIAM I. ROBINSON

Haymarket Books
Chicago, Illinois

Published in 2019 by
Haymarket Books
P.O. Box 180165
Chicago, IL 60618
773-583-7884
www.haymarketbooks.org
info@haymarketbooks.org

ISBN: 978-1-60846-546-0

Distributed to the trade in the US through Consortium Book Sales and
Distribution (www.cbsd.com) and internationally through Ingram
Publisher Services International (www.ingramcontent.com).

This book was published with the generous support
of Lannan Foundation and Wallace Action Fund.

Special discounts are available for bulk purchases by organizations
and institutions.
Please call 773-583-7884 or email info@haymarketbooks.org
for more information.

Cover design by Ricky Chan.

Printed in the United States.

Library of Congress Cataloging-in-Publication data is available.

10 9 8 7 6 5 4 3 2 1

Educate yourselves because we will need all your intelligence.
Be excited because we will need all your enthusiasm.
Organize because we will need all your strength.

— Antonio Gramsci

CONTENTS

FOREWORD

During the First Ministerial Conference of the World Trade Organization in Singapore in 1996, representatives of the International Monetary Fund, World Bank, various corporations, and the governments of the North toasted the WTO as the "jewel" in the crown of multilateralism and the cutting edge of the high tide of globalization that was then sweeping the world. It had barely been seven years since the socialist governments of Eastern Europe and the Soviet Union had collapsed, and there no longer seemed to be any significant barriers remaining to the creation of a borderless world integrated by global capital. There was an air of triumphalism, as speaker after speaker proclaimed that removing the barriers to trade, investment, and finance would bring about the best of all possible worlds by allowing the market to work its magic to bring about prosperity for all.

They were wrong.

Barely a year later, a massive financial crisis swept East Asia, putting the world on notice that financial liberalization was not the force for good that Wall Street had trumpeted. Then in December 1999, the collapse of the WTO Third Ministerial Conference in Seattle opened the ears of even neoclassical economists like Jeffrey Sachs and Joseph Stiglitz to the voices of globalization's critics that free trade, structural adjustment, and other neoliberal policies were leading in the opposite direction from what its partisans claimed. But it took the 2008 global financial crisis that ravaged the economies of the Global North to convince most people in the United States and Europe of a truth people in the Global South had been shouting from the rooftops for years: globalization was leading to greater crises and insecurity for the vast majority of people on the planet and threatened the planet itself.

Throughout this whole period, William Robinson stood out as an uncompromising critic of globalization, exposing its myths, exploring its contradictions, and warning about the perils of unleashing uncontrolled capital on the world . His intellectual leadership was an inspiration to many in the Anti-Globalization Movement, World Social Forum, and Occupy Movement. Even those who did not agree with all of his propositions had to acknowledge that they were put forward with brilliance, bravery, and intellectual rigor.

In this volume, William brings together ten essays that sum up his thoughts on various aspects of globalization, ranging from his theory of the global capitalist class to the effects of globalization on class, gender, and racial inequalities and the future of globalization. This is an indispensable guide for anyone interested in understanding globalization and the resistance to it, written by an indispensable thinker.

Walden Bello
Bangkok, August 23, 2018

ACKNOWLEDGMENTS

Intellectual labor is no different than any other form of work: it is collective, part of the social labor process. Intellectuals like myself and others are able to study the world and reflect theoretically on it only because others are producing the food, clothing, and shelter that allows us to withdraw from laboring to produce these basic necessities of life. Beyond the mass of toiling humanity, the more immediate collective labor behind this study includes hundreds of people who have contributed to my own intellectual and political development since I came of age in the late 1970s. The most I can do here is to acknowledge the people that most directly and personally provided me with invaluable encouragement or inspiration in the development of my ideas on global capitalism over the past three decades, who supported my (second) career as a university professor, who assisted in my research during this time, and those I had the privilege of mentoring as graduate students.

I cannot possibly list them all, but I want to acknowledge at least some of them: the late Giovanni Arrighi, Yousef Baker, Mario Barrera, Walden Bello, Christopher Chase-Dunn, Noam Chomsky, Roberto Danipour, Richard A. Falk, David Feldman, Bill Fletcher Jr., Felipe Gonzalez, Jamella Gow, Maryam S. Griffin, Jerry Harris, Peter McLaren, Veronica Montes, Abelardo Morales, Craig Murphy, Hoai-An Nguyen, Kent Norsworthy, Steven Osuna, Salvador Rangel, Paul Raskin, Marielle Robinson-Mayorga, Cesar "Che" Rodiguez, Manuel Rozental Amandeep Sandhu, Juan Manuel Sandoval (and all my colleagues and comrades from the *Red Mexicana Frente al Libre Comercio* and the *Seminario Permanente de Estudios Chicanos y de Fronteras* of the National Institute of Anthropology and History of Mexico), Xuan Santos, Leslie Sklair, David A. Smith, Oscar Soto, Jeb Sprague, Martin Vega, and

Immanuel Wallerstein. My apologies to those I have inadvertently omitted. A very affectionate thanks to my wife, Venus Yinman Leung, and my brother, Kevin Robinson-Avila. And a very special and affectionate thanks to my stepson, Ricky Chan, for the brilliant cover he designed for this book. I am indebted to Haymarket Books' reviewer, Ashley Smith, for his painstakingly detailed and invaluable comments and suggestions on the entire manuscript. Thanks as well to Anthony Arnove and Nisha Bolsey of Haymarket Books, and to Ida Audeh for her careful and professional copy and style editing. I gratefully acknowledge research grants from the Academic Senate of the University of California at Santa Barbara that helped fund portions of this study. I also thank the journal *Social Justice* for permission to reproduce "Global Capitalism and the Restructuring of Education" and *Global Transition Initiative* for permission to reproduce "Reflections on a Brave New World.

INTRODUCTION

THEORY FOR A RADICAL PRAXIS

Humanity stands at a crossroads. Global warming and environmental destruction, unprecedented social inequalities, the increasingly difficult struggle for survival of billions of people around the world, escalating social strife, military conflict, and the growing threat of nuclear war—all of these threaten the collapse of global civilization and even our annihilation and mass extinction. We truly face a crisis of humanity. Our very survival depends on us at the very least curbing the excesses of the out-of-control system of global capitalism, if not its outright overthrow. The good news is that mass struggles against the ravages of global capitalism are breaking out everywhere. Waves of resistance, often followed by repression and co-optation, have been spreading, especially since the global financial collapse of 2008.

But we cannot change a system that we do not understand. More than academic debate, how we understand the world of the twenty-first century is a burning political question. We cannot develop our own projects for a just, democratic, and sustainable future without an accurate understanding of the dominant project—its agents, its structure, and its logic. Social and political struggle, in order to be effective, requires *praxis*, or the unity of theory and practice. The lives of peoples everywhere have been fundamentally shaped by capitalist globalization—the "master process" of our age. Analysis and theoretical reflection on the structural changes brought about by capitalist globalization is the indispensable prerequisite to understanding the current global moment of unprecedented crisis and to working out viable projects of struggle.

1

Karl Marx and Frederick Engels famously declared in *The Communist Manifesto* that "all that is solid melts into air" under the dizzying pace of change wrought by capitalism. It is the most dynamic system that humanity has ever seen, in a constant and never-ending process of transformation. As such, capitalism is a moving target. It never lands and stabilizes in any one place. The dynamics internal to capitalism such as outward expansion and cycles of crisis lead to the clash of social forces and ongoing restructuring. It is a moving target in the political sense, insofar as billions of people struggle against the depredations of a system that is in constant flux. But it is also a moving target in an intellectual sense, insofar as we must constantly update our understanding of how the system is functioning at any given moment and in what ways it is experiencing transformation. The problem of many intellectuals, including regrettably many Marxist critics of my theory of global capitalism, is that analyses get frozen in a particular moment of capitalism rather than developing in concert with the dynamic changes underway in the system. If this is troubling in the academy, it is as much or more of a problem for those engaged in social justice struggles, for we cannot change what we do not understand.

THE NEED FOR THEORETICAL RENEWAL

If globalization has brought us to a new epoch in the world capitalist system, then we require new forms of anti-capitalist and emancipatory struggle. I do not claim to have the answers with regard to the way forward in emancipatory struggles. The agents engaged in those struggles forge these answers in the actual heat of mass struggles. My goal in this book is decidedly more modest: to offer a theoretical framework and analytical inputs into understanding the nature of the new global capitalism *as a critical requisite for us to engage effectively in struggle against it*. Confronting global capitalism requires a new paradigmatic perspective. Yet I have come up against objections to new perspectives on global capitalism in the three decades that I have been writing about it. Much of the older Marxist-inspired Left is amazingly resistant to new paradigms, no matter how grounded they are in a rigorous historical materialist analysis and empirical exposition. On the other hand, I have found that many of the younger generation of activists in mass social movements shy away from theoretical engagement beyond what can be supplied in a tweet or a Facebook post.

I have had thousands of students over the years whose commitment to social justice and activist engagement never ceases to inspire me. Yet I don't know how many times student activists who are open to radical, anti-capitalist, and even socialist ideas have told me that they do not see the need for theoretical engagement. Perhaps even more troubling, many of these young people on whom the future depends have a hard time with abstractions and with critical thinking. *Conscientization*—the process of learning to perceive social, political, and economic contradictions and to take action against the oppressive elements of reality—must involve theoretical engagement. Yet dulling the ability to deal with abstraction and critical thinking is just how global capitalist hegemony is intended to work. As global capitalism penetrates ever deeper into the cultural systems and social relations, it colonizes the very "life world" of our consciousness, numbing the ability to think critically and to challenge the system *from outside of its logic.*

There is a biographical segue here to the origins of this book. I took a nontraditional route to the academy. I first became politically active as a teenager in New York and then discovered revolutionary Marxism while studying in East and West Africa and a time when the continent was still embroiled in anti-colonial and immediate post-colonial struggles. From there I traveled to Central America to participate in the revolutionary movements then engulfing that region. For the next decade I practiced journalism and worked with the Sandinista government in Nicaragua, until I was forced out with the triumph of counterrevolution in 1990. It was then that I turned to graduate school and became immersed in historical and theoretical study. It was not until 2001 that I definitively settled into US academia.

But if my academic experience has been incredibly enriching, I came to realize a few years back when my students were unable to understand some of my more dense writings that I was losing the ability to communicate in a way I had previously done as a journalist so as to be accessible to the layperson. It was time to get back to writing for a broader intellectually and politically engaged public audience. I began to write for Internet magazines and blogs and to open my own Facebook blog (www.facebook.com/WilliamIRobinsonSociologist), where I now post regular commentaries and news analyzes. I was thrilled when, in 2017, Haymarket offered me a contract for the present book. If intellectuals must be able to communicate in such ways that make accessible their intellectual production to a larger public audience, this does not mean "dumbing down" to the point that there is all description and simplistic analysis but no theory. The reader will be the judge as to whether I have achieved my goal in this book. Yet there is just so much that can be accomplished in a single book. I have expounded at great length in earlier books on ideas discussed here in briefer form. The reader who wants a more expansive exposition of those ideas and the debates they have generated may read my other works, some of which are listed at the end of this book. Many of my articles are available on my website, at www.soc.ucsb.edu/faculty/robinson/.

A word on the title I have chosen, *Into the Tempest*. This title points to the unprecedented crisis that humanity faces—a period of great upheavals, momentous changes, and uncertainties, that is, the storm that is upon us. It is a draw on Shakespeare's play, *The Tempest*. That play is seen as an allegory for social upheaval, the breakdown of the reigning social order, and the stormy period into which humanity had been thrust at the time that Shakespeare wrote it in 1623, when the capitalist system was emerging with all its violence, colonial pretensions, and contradictions.

TEN ESSAYS AND AN APPENDIX

While I encourage readers to engage the entire book, it has been designed so that one can pick it up and read each essay on its own. There are common themes that run through each one and some intentional redundancy, precisely so that each essay can stand alone. Earlier versions of these essays were published between 1996 and 2017. Each has been thoroughly revised and updated for this book, except for the essays that form Chapters 7 and 10; they are reproduced here with only minor modifications to the original text published in 2017. The essays in Chapters 3 and 4 are virtually new, cobbled out of numerous scattered writings over the past twenty-five years and combined with entirely new data and material. Chapter 9, "Global Police State," is entirely new, written specifically for this book, although it draws on material and ideas I have been writing about over the past decade.

Those who want to get a sweeping overview of the new global capitalism can read the two essays that form the "bookends." An earlier version of the first, "Globalization: Nine Theses on Our Epoch," was originally published in 1996 and has been updated for this collection.

It lays out a snapshot of the "forest" as an introduction to the book by identifying the most imperious "trees" of global capitalism and their interconnections, in accordance with what I believe should be the key theoretical and practical concerns of intellectuals and activists. It was shortly after this essay was published that tens of thousands of activists from around the world descended on Seattle, in 1999, to protest the ministerial meeting of the World Trade Organization in what was referred to at that time as the opening salvo of an "anti-globalization movement." Yet, as I argue in that essay, a transnational counterhegemonic project would not entail resisting globalization—alas, we cannot simply demand that historic processes be halted to conform to our wishes. We would do better to understand how we might influence and redirect those processes into a "globalization from below."

The website Great Transition Initiative published in 2017 the other bookend, "Reflections on a Brave New World" (Chapter 10). It briefly summarizes the theory of global capitalism and then focuses on a core theme of all the essays, the worldwide crisis in which humanity finds itself as we step into the unknown. Great Transition Initiative (greattransition.org) defines its goal as follows:

> an online forum of ideas and an international network for the critical exploration of concepts, strategies, and visions for a transition to a future of enriched lives, human solidarity, and a resilient biosphere. By enhancing scholarly discourse and public awareness of possibilities arising from converging social, economic, and environmental crises, and by fostering a broad network of thinkers and doers, it aims to contribute to a new praxis for global transformation.

I published an earlier version of Chapter 2, "Critical Globalization Studies," in 2003 at a time when the concept of globalization had become popularized among academics, journalists, and the general public. Despite the rise of an anti-globalization movement a few years earlier, globalization was still seen by many in the popular imagination as the harbinger of a new harmonious global civilization, especially among mainstream commentators. But at that time, global capitalism was already frayed and descending into crisis. The United States has recently invaded Iraq and the dot-com bust of 2000 threw the world into a major recession. Nonetheless, the "end of history" thesis—the idea that liberal global capitalism was the joyous end of the line for the development of human society—was still in vogue. At the time (and to this day), a dilettante postmodernism that rejected Marxism and socialism as "oppressive narratives" reigned hegemonic in the social sciences and humanities. The essay discusses the critical role that intellectuals must play in the face of capitalist globalization. It challenges the notion of the "neutral" intellectual and stresses that practice without theory and theory without practice are self-deception.

Chapters 3 and 4, "The New Global Economy and the Rise of a Transnational Capitalist Class" and "The Nation-State and the Transnational State," explore in detail two central components of the new global capitalism, the rise of a transnational capitalist class and a transnational state. While they can also be read individually, I recommend that they be read in conjunction, as the two are really flip sides of the very same coin. These essays, especially the one on the transnational state, contain a few dense passages on theory; I repeat my conviction that effective action in favor of progressive social change can only be accomplished with the aid of theory. The twin concepts of the transnational capitalist class and the transnational state are essential for understanding the contemporary world and for developing effective strategies of struggle against global capitalism. As the reader will discover in subsequent essays, these concepts can be applied to a great range of topics and shed light on current debates.

Chapter 5, "Beyond the Theory of Imperialism," was first published in 2007 as the debate over the 2003 US invasion and occupation of Iraq continued to rage. At the time, that invasion was almost universally interpreted as an effort by the United States to shore up its world empire against imperial rivals. My view that, to the contrary, the United States undertook the invasion to shore up and advance a crisis-ridden global capitalism on behalf of a transnational ruling class was met with derision among more than a few on the Left. Here I have revised and updated the essay to sharpen the argument and take into account world developments since that essay was first published.

Chapters 6 and 7 apply the tools of global capitalism theory to look at two contemporary matters, the immigrant justice struggle and the worldwide restructuring of education. "Global Capitalism, Migrant Labor, and the Struggle for Social Justice" weaves together major excerpts of an article I published in 2014 (with the assistance of Xuan Santos) with my earlier and more recent writings on this topic. "Global Capitalism and the Restructuring of Education: Producing Global Economy Workers and Suppressing Critical Thinking," published in 2017, argues that transnational capital faces the challenge of imposing a system of global education that imparts just enough skills to supply the labor needed for the farms, factories, and offices of the global economy and at the same time transmits a political and ideological content that compels conformity and undercuts critical thinking. It observes that the coupling of educational systems with those of mass social control appears to be reaching depths hitherto unseen.

Chapter 8, "Davos Man Comes to the Third World: The Transnational State and the BRICS," first published in 2014 and here revised, takes up another raging debate. Do the BRICS countries (Brazil, Russia, India, China, and South Africa) and the increasingly prominent role they play in the international system represent a progressive and anti-imperialist alternative for the peoples of the former Third World? While many of us respond with a resounding no, I argue in this essay that global capitalism theory is best able to make sense of the BRICS phenomenon.

Chapter 9 warns that a global police state is emerging as world capitalism descends into an unprecedented crisis. *Global police state* refers to three interrelated developments. First is the ever more omnipresent systems of mass social control, repression and warfare promoted by the ruling groups to contain the real and the potential rebellion of the global working class and surplus humanity. Second is how the global economy itself is based increasingly on the development and deployment of these systems of warfare, social control, and repression simply as a means of making profit and continuing to accumulate capital in the face of stagnation. And third is the increasing move toward political systems that can be characterized as twenty-first-century fascism, or even in a broader sense, as totalitarianism.

The appendix provides a reprint of an interview that the journal *E-International Relations* conducted with me in fall 2017; I include it here as a biographical synopsis and statement on the development of my ideas.

ONE

GLOBALIZATION

NINE THESES ON OUR EPOCH

The left and progressives around the world have been struggling for several decades now to come to terms with the fundamental dynamic of our epoch: capitalist globalization. The globalization of capitalism, and the transnationalization of social, political, and cultural processes it entails, is the world-historic context of developments as the twenty-first century progresses. The debate on globalization continues to play out in the academy, and more important, among diverse social and political movements worldwide. These movements have run up against globalizing processes that are redefining the very terrain of social action, including the deep constraints, as well as real opportunities, that the new global environment presents for popular change. In my view, however, activists and scholars alike have tended to understate the *systemic* nature of the changes involved in globalization, which is redefining the fundamental reference points of human society and social analysis, and requires a modification of existing paradigms.[1]

Capitalist globalization denotes a world war. This war was brewing for four decades following World War II, concealed behind a whole set of secondary contradictions tied up with the Cold War and the East–West conflict. It was incubated with the development of new technologies and the changing face of production and of labor in the capitalist world and with the incubation of transnational capital out of former national capitals in the North. The opening salvos date back to the early 1980s, when class fractions representing transnational capital gained effective control of state apparatuses in the North and set about to capture these apparatuses in the South. (I return to this argument later in this chapter and elsewhere in this book.) This war has proceeded with the liberation of transnational capital from any constraint to its global activity that came with the demise of the former Soviet bloc and with the increasing achievement by capital of total mobility and of access to every corner of the world. It is a war by a global rich and powerful minority against the global poor, dispossessed, and outcast majority. Casualties already number in the hundreds of millions and threaten to mount into the billions. I refer to this figuratively as a world war, in that the level of social conflict and human destruction has reached bellicose proportions. But I also mean so literally, in that the conflict bound up with capitalist globalization is truly *world* war: it involves all peoples around the world and none can escape involvement.

Describing the current state of affairs as a *world war* is a dramatic statement, intended to underscore the extent to which I believe humanity has entered a period that could well rival or even surpass the colonial depredations of past centuries. However, I do not mean to be apocalyptic and disarming. As I discuss below, capitalist globalization is a *process*, not so much completed as in motion. It confronts major contradictions that present the possibilities of altering its course. A more precise reading of capitalist globalization is therefore required as a guide to our social inquiry and our action. What follows is a modest attempt to take stock of the principal contours of our epoch. It is intended to present a holistic snapshot of the globalization "forest" as an introduction to the essays in this book by identifying its most imperious trees and their interconnections, in accord with what I believe should be key theoretical and practical concerns of intellectuals and activists. The following theses are presented here as open-ended summary statements that present complex phenomena in simplified form. Subsequent chapters will explore each in more depth.

First, the essence of the process is the replacement for the first time in the history of the modern world capitalist system of all residual pre(or non)capitalist production relations with capitalist ones in every part of the globe.

Activists and scholars have noted that globalization involves the hastened internationalization of capital and technology, a new international division of labor, economic integration processes, a decline in the importance of the nation-state, and so on. The world has been moving in the past few decades to a situation in which nations have been linked through capital flows and exchange in an integrated international market to the globalization of the process of production itself.[2] In turn, economic globalization is bringing with it the material basis for the transnationalization of political processes and systems and civil societies and the global integration of social life. Globalization has increasingly eroded national boundaries and made it structurally impossible for individual nations to sustain independent, or even autonomous, economies, polities, and social structures. Nation-states are no longer appropriate units of analysis.

These are all important features. But the core of globalization, theoretically conceived, is the near culmination of a process that began with the dawn of European colonial expansion and the modern world system over 500 years ago: the gradual spread of capitalist production around the world and its displacement of all precapitalist relations.[3] From a world in which capitalism was the dominant mode within a system of "articulated modes of production," globalization is bringing about a world integrated into a single capitalist mode (thus *capitalist* globalization).[4] This involves all the changes associated with capitalism, but changes that are *transnational* rather than national or *inter*national in character. It includes the transnationalization of classes and the accelerated division of all of humanity into just two single classes, global capital and global labor, although both remain embedded in segmented structures and hierarchies, as discussed below.

Global capitalism is tearing down all nonmarket structures that have in the past placed limits on the accumulation—and the dictatorship—of capital. Every corner of the globe, every nook and cranny of social life, is becoming commodified. This involves breaking up and commodifying nonmarket spheres of human activity, namely public spheres managed by states, and private spheres linked to community and family units (local and household economies). This complete commodification of social life is undermining what remains of democratic control by people over the conditions of their daily existence, above and beyond that involved with private ownership of the principal means of production. As James O'Connor has noted, we are seeing the maturation of the capitalist *economy* into capitalist *society*, with the penetration of capitalist relations into all spheres of life.[5]

Commodification involves the transfer to capital of both formerly public spheres and formerly noncapitalist private spheres such as family and cultural realms. All around the world, the public sphere, ranging from educational and health systems to police forces, prisons, utilities, infrastructure and transportation systems, is being privatized and commodified. The juggernaut of exchange value is also invading intimate private spheres of community, family, and culture. None of the old precommodity spheres provide a protective shield from the alienation of capitalism. In every aspect of our social existence, we increasingly interact with our fellow human beings through dehumanized and competitive commodity relationships.

Second, a new "social structure of accumulation" is emerging, which for the first time in history is global.

A social structure of accumulation refers to a set of mutually reinforcing social, economic, and political institutions and cultural and ideological norms that fuse with, and facilitate a successful pattern of capital accumulation over specific historic periods.[6] A new global social structure of accumulation is becoming superimposed on, and transforming, existing national social structures of accumulation. Integration into the global system is the causal structural dynamic that underlies the events we have witnessed in nations and regions all around the world over the past few decades. The breakup of national economic, political, and social structures is reciprocal to the gradual breakup, starting in the latter decades of the twentieth century, of a preglobalization nation-state-based world order. New economic, political and social structures emerge as each nation and region becomes integrated into emergent transnational structures and processes.

The agent of the global economy is transnational capital, organized institutionally in global corporations and in supranational economic planning agencies and political forums, such as the International Monetary Fund, the Trilateral Commission, the Group of 7 (G7) forum, and the World Economic Forum, and managed by a class-conscious transnational elite based in the centers of world capitalism but increasingly present outside of these centers. This transnational elite has put forth an integrated global agenda of mutually reinforcing economic, political, and cultural components that, taken together, comprise a new global social structure of accumulation.[7]

The economic component is *hyperliberalism*, which has come to be known as neoliberalism, and that seeks to achieve the conditions for the total mobility and unfettered worldwide activity of capital.[8] Hyperliberalism includes the elimination of state intervention in the economy and the regulation by individual nation-states over the activity of transnational capital in their territories. It is putting an end to the state's earlier ability to interfere with profit making by capturing and redistributing surpluses. In the North, hyperliberalism, first launched by the Reagan and Thatcher governments, takes the form of deregulation and the dismantling of Keynesian welfare states. In the South, it involves neoliberal structural adjustment programs. These programs seek macroeconomic stability (e.g., price and exchange rate stability) as an essential requisite for the activity of transnational capital, which must harmonize a wide range of fiscal, monetary, and industrial policies among several nations if it is to be able to function simultaneously, and often instantaneously, among numerous national borders.

The political component, at least up until the first decade of the twenty-first century, has been the development of political systems that operate through consensual rather than through direct, coercive domination. As globalization unfolded, consensual mechanisms of social control tended to replace dictatorships, authoritarianism and repressive colonial systems that characterized much of the world's formal political authority structures right up to the post-Cold War period. The transnational elite refers to these political systems as "democracy," although there is little or no authentic democratic content. The "democratic consensus" in the new world order is a consensus among an increasingly cohesive global elite on the type of political system most propitious to the reproduction of social order in the new global environment. This component is discussed in more detail below, and as I discuss later in the book, escalating political instability and social conflict around the world make it increasingly difficult to maintain "democratic" systems. Indeed, as global crisis deepens, we are already seeing a reversion to dictatorships and openly authoritarian systems.

The culture/ideological component is consumerism and cutthroat individualism. Consumerism proclaims that well-being, peace of mind, and purpose in life are achieved through the acquisition of commodities.[9] Competitive individualism legitimizes personal survival, and whatever is required to achieve it, over collective well-being. Consumerism and individualism imbue mass consciousness at the global level. They channel mass aspirations into individual consumer desires, even though induced wants will never be met for the vast majority of humanity. The culture and ideology of global capitalism thus works to depoliticize social behavior and preempt collective action aimed at social change by channeling people's activities into a fixation on the search for individual consumption and survival.

Globalization, therefore, has profound consequences for each nation of the world system. Productive structures in each nation are reorganized reciprocal to a new international division of labor, characterized by the concentration of finances, services, technology, and knowledge in the North and the labor-intensive phases of globalized production in the South. However, as I suggest below and will argue later in this book, this new international division of labor has been giving way to a global division of labor as the great North–South divide (what used to be called the First World–Third World divide) begins to erode. As each national economy is restructured and subordinated to the global economy, new activities linked to globalization come to dominate. Pre-globalization classes, such as national peasantries, small-scale artisans, and domestic bourgeoisies linked to national capital and internal markets, are weakened and are threatened with disintegration. New groups linked to the global economy emerge and become dominant, both economically and politically. States are externalized. Political systems are shaken and reorganized. The dominant global culture penetrates, perverts, and reshapes cultural institutions, group identities, and mass consciousness.[10]

Third, this transnational agenda has germinated in every country of the world under the guidance of hegemonic transnationalized fractions of national bourgeoisies.

Global capitalism is represented in each nation-state by in-country representatives, who constitute transnationalized fractions of dominant groups. The *international class alliance* of national bourgeoisies into the post-World War II period has mutated into a *transnationalized bourgeoisie* in the post-Cold War period and had become by the 1990s the hegemonic class fraction globally. This denationalized bourgeoisie is both class conscious and conscious of its transnationality. At its apex is a managerial elite that controls the levers of global policymaking and which responds to transnational finance capital as the hegemonic fraction of capital on a world scale.

In the 1970s and 1980s, incipient transnationalized fractions set out to eclipse national fractions in the core capitalist countries of the North and to capture the "commanding heights" of state policymaking. From the 1980s into the 1990s, these fractions became ascendant in the South and began to vie for (and in many countries to capture) state apparatuses.[11] By the *fin de siècle*, the transnational agenda was embryonic in some countries and regions (e.g., much of sub-Saharan Africa). It had incubated and was ascendant in others regions, including in major portions of Asia. It became fully consolidated elsewhere (e.g., in much of Latin America). Given the structures of North–South asymmetry, transnationalized fractions in the Third World are "junior" partners. At the local level, and under the tutelage of their "senior" counterparts in the North, in the late twentieth and early twenty-first centuries they oversaw sweeping economic, political, social, and cultural changes involved in globalization, including free-market reform, the fomenting of "democratic" systems in place of dictatorships, and the dissemination of the culture/ideology of consumerism and individualism.

Fourth, observers search for a new global "hegemon" and posit a tripolar world of European, American, and Asian economic blocs. But the old nation-state phase of capitalism has been superseded by the transnational phase of capitalism.

In his master study, *The Great Transformation*, Karl Polanyi summed up the previous historic change in the relationship between the state and capital, and society and market forces, that took place with the maturation of national capitalism in the nineteenth century and the first half of the twentieth.[12] We have been witness since the late twentieth century to another unfolding "great transformation," the maturation of *transnational capitalism*.

But activists and scholars still cling on to an outdated nation-state framework of analysis that reifies the state, with a consequent misreading of events and the danger of misdirected social action. The momentary fluxes, conflicts, and contradictions bound up with the transition from national to transnational capitalism should not be confused with the historic tendency itself. Globalization changes the relationship between capitalism and territoriality, and with it the relationship between classes and the nation-state. As I discuss later on, the structural power of mobile transnational capital has been increasingly superimposed over the direct power of nation-states as the "commanding heights" of state decision-making shift toward webs of supranational institutions.[13] The historic relation between nation-states and formerly nation-based classes, and between class power and state power, has been modified and requires redefinition.

The transnational bourgeoisie seeks to exercise its class power through two channels. One is a dense network of supranational institutions and relationships that increasingly bypass formal states, and that should be conceived as an emergent transnational state that has not acquired any centralized institutional form, is still very much in formation, and is subject to all sorts of contradictory pressures. The other is the utilization of national governments as territorially bound juridical units (the interstate system) are transformed into transmission belts and filtering devices for the imposition of the transnational agenda. At the same time, transnational capitalists and elites in each country have captured their respective national states, or at least key ministries in these states, from where they promote the transnational agenda, so that national states become *proactive agents* of globalization. Transnational capital requires that nation-states perform three functions: (a) adopt fiscal and monetary policies, which assure macroeconomic stability; (b) provide the basic infrastructure necessary for global economic activity (highways, telecommunications systems, educational systems for training global workers, and so on); and (c) provide social control, order, and stability. (The transnational elite assessed in the late twentieth century that "democracy" is better able than dictatorship to perform this social order function, as discussed below, but this may be changing as the global crisis deepens.) In a nutshell, we are not witnessing "the death of the nation-state," but rather its transformation into neoliberal states.

It is true, therefore, as many scholars and activists have pointed out, that capital still needs state power. However, state power and the nation-state are not co-equivalent, and the interests of transnational capital do not correspond to any "national" interest or any nation-state. The confusion is in equating capital's need for the services provided by neoliberal states, and the use it makes of the lingering interstate system, with some type of organic affinity between transnational capital and specific nation-states, as existed in the national stage of capitalism. If major concentrations of transnational capital are no longer associated with any particular nation-state, on what material and class basis should interstate conflict be interpreted? What theoretical rationale exists for predicting rivalry and competition between nation-states as an expression of the competition of national capitals?

The spatial decentralization of the power of transnational capital has been confused with a growing "strength" and "independence" of "US rivals," and with geopolitical shifts in power conceived in terms of nation-states. In fact, transnational capital and its principal institutional agent, the global corporation, are able to exploit an antiquated nation-state/interstate system to wring further concessions from global labor. The continued separation of the world into nation-states creates a central condition for the power of transnational capital.

As I discuss throughout this book, an outdated nation-state framework can lead to a faulty reading of events. Although it was the Reagan government of the 1980s that first launched neoliberal globalization in the United States, at the time many commentators interpreted Reaganism as a trenchant right-wing project opposed to a more "liberal" program. Since then all US administrations and the core of both the Democratic and Republican parties have pushed capitalist globalization. The differences among these administrations have not represented a fundamental clash between distinct capitalist fractions or projects, but differences over the pace, timing, and secondary aspects (e.g., social policy) of advancing the transnational agenda in the United States. The fundamental restructuring of social policies that began under Reaganism and Thatcherism in the North was not the product of conservative movements and right-wing political inclinations, per se, despite appearances. Rather, they represented the logical concrete policy and ideological adjuncts of globalization as it has applied to the particular conditions of each country.

Similarly, tactical differences between national governments of core countries over how to advance transnational interests—tactical differences often originating in the particulars of local and regional histories and conditions—take on the appearance of fundamental contradictions between rival "national capitals" and "national interests." Events may *appear* as contradictions between nation-states when in *essence* they are often contradictions internal to global capitalism. The need for neoliberal states to secure legitimacy as part of their social order function often entails a discourse of "national interests," "foreign competition," and so on, at the ideological and the mass public levels. Suffice it to recall that the hallmark of good social analysis is to distinguish appearance from essence.

The Trump government that came to power in 2017, for instance, put forth a nationalist and populist discourse, yet the actual content of its policies represented an intensification of neoliberalism in the face of an increasingly severe global crisis, as I discuss later in the book. In fact, the Trump election reflected precisely a far-right response, tinged by twenty-first-century fascist currents, to the crisis of global capitalism. As with other "right-wing populist" and far-right movements in recent years, Trumpism was a response to the crises of state legitimacy in the face of the extreme polarization of wealth unleashed by globalization and the increasing insecurity, downward mobility, and even immiseration of major sectors of the US working class. The crisis of state legitimacy has resulted in an increase in *inter*national tensions, which however, have to be understood in a different light than earlier national rivalries based on competing national capitalist classes.

Fifth, the "brave new world" of global capitalism is profoundly anti-democratic.

Global capitalism is predatory and parasitic. In today's global economy, capitalism is less benign, less responsive to the interests of broad majorities around the world, and less accountable to society than ever before. At the end of the twentieth century, some 400 transnational corporations had come to own 66 percent the planet's fixed assets and control 70 percent of world trade. With the world's resources controlled by a few hundred global corporations, the lifeblood and the very fate of humanity is in the hands of transnational capital, which holds the power to make life and death decision for millions of human beings. Such tremendous concentrations of economic power leads to tremendous concentrations of political power at the global level. Any discussion of "democracy" under such conditions becomes meaningless.

The paradox of the demise of dictatorships, "democratic transitions," and the spread of "democracy" around the world that took place in the late twentieth and early twenty-first centuries was to be explained by new forms of social control, and the misuse of the concept of democracy, the original meaning of which (the power, *cratos*, of the people, *demos*), has been disconfigured beyond recognition. What the transnational elite calls democracy is more accurately termed *polyarchy*, to borrow a concept from academia.[14] Polyarchy is neither dictatorship nor democracy, at the level of the political system. It refers to a system in which a small group actually rules, on behalf of capital, and participation in decision-making by the majority is confined to choosing among competing elites in tightly controlled electoral processes. This "low-intensity democracy" is a form of *consensual domination*. Social control and domination is *hegemonic*, in the sense meant by the great Italian socialist thinker Antonio Gramsci. It is based less on outright repression than on diverse forms of ideological co-optation and political disempowerment made possible by the structural domination and "veto power" of global capital.

Starting in the 1980s and coinciding with the onslaught of capitalist globalization, polyarchy was promoted around the world ("democracy promotion") by the transnational elite in the South as part of parcel of its agenda, and in tandem with the promotion of neoliberalism, in distinction to the earlier global network of civilian–military regimes and outright dictatorships (e.g., the Somozas, the Duvaliers, the Marcos, the Pinochets, white minority regimes), and before them, repressive colonial states, that the Northern capitalist countries promoted and sustained for much of modern world history. Authoritarian systems tended to unravel as globalizing pressures broke up embedded forms of coercive political authority, dislocated traditional communities and social patterns, and stirred masses of people to demand the democratization of social life. Disorganized masses pushed for a deeper popular democratization, while organized elites push for tightly controlled transitions from authoritarianism and dictatorships to elite polyarchies.

This issue is crucial, because much of the left worldwide was not democratic in the twentieth century, both within its own organizations and in state practices in those countries where it came to power. The left's historic democratic failings have made some hesitant to denounce polyarchy for what it is—a mockery of democracy. The left must be committed to democracy in society and in its own institutions—a popular, participatory democracy from the grassroots up that empowers popular classes at the local level, subordinates states to civil society, holds leaders accountable, and so on. But polyarchy has as little to do with democracy as did the Stalinist political system in the former Soviet bloc.

The trappings of democratic procedure in a polyarchy do not mean that the lives of the mass of people become filled with authentic or meaningful popular democratic content, much less that social justice or greater economic equality is achieved. The new polyarchies ("the new democracies" in the lexicon of the transnational elite) of emergent global society did not, and were not intended to, meet the authentic aspirations of repressed and marginalized majorities for political participation, for greater socioeconomic justice, and for cultural realization.[15] As the twenty-first century progressed, the contradictions of global capitalism became ever more explosive, and it was not clear if the fragile polyarchies that still characterized the political systems of most countries around the world could absorb mounting crises of social control and legitimacy. There may be a return to dictatorial and authoritarian forms of control. In subsequent chapters, I discuss the danger of what I refer to as twenty-first-century fascism.

Sixth, "poverty amidst plenty," the dramatic growth under globalization of socioeconomic inequalities and of human misery in nearly every country and region of the world, is a consequence of the unbridled operation of transnational capital.

The concentration of wealth among a privileged strata encompassing some 20 percent of humanity, in which the gap between rich and poor is widening *within* each country, North and South alike, is occurring at the same time as inequalities *between* the North and the South are increasing sharply. The worldwide inequality in the distribution of wealth and power is a form of permanent structural violence against the world's majority. This is a widely noted phenomenon, but it needs to be linked more explicitly to globalization.

In 1992, the United Nations Development Program (UNDP) began publishing its annual *Human Development Report*, which chronicles levels of social development (or underdevelopment), poverty, and inequality worldwide. The report that year indicated that the wealthiest 20 percent of humanity received 82.7 percent of the world's wealth.[16] Fast-forward to 2015: according to a report released that year by the international development agency Oxfam, the richest 20 percent of humanity owned 94.5 percent of the world's wealth, while the remaining 80 percent had to make do with just 5.5 percent of that wealth.[17] According to a 2010 UNDP report, 1.5 billion people worldwide lived in extreme poverty that year, defined as making less than $1.25 dollars a day, while another 900 million were at risk of slipping into extreme poverty.[18] In other words, some 35 percent of humanity lived on the verge of life and death.

In all, 3 billion people earned less than $2.50 a day, 1 billion were without access to health service, 1.3 billion had no access to safe water, and 1.9 billion were without access to adequate sanitation.

Global poverty and inequality is often measured as the gap between rich and poor countries, or North and South. There is indeed an abyss between the rich and poor nations when measured in in terms of nation-states, and it continues to widen. In 1960, the wealthiest twenty of the world's nations were thirty times richer than the poorest 20 percent. Thirty years later, in 1990, it was sixty times richer, according to the 1994 UNDP report. The report noted, however (and as I discuss in more detail later in the book), that "these figures conceal the true scale of injustice since they are based on comparisons of the average per capita incomes of rich and poor *countries*. In reality, of course, there are wide disparities within each country between rich and poor *people*."[19] Adding the maldistribution within countries, the richest 20 percent of the world's people got at least 150 times more than the poorest 20 percent. In other words, the ratio of inequality between the global rich and the global poor seen as social groups in a highly stratified world system was 1:150.

In Chapter 5, "Beyond the Theory of Imperialism," I challenge readers to move beyond the classical and more contemporary theories of imperialism, world-systems theory, and international political economy theories, in our understanding of global inequalities. These theories emphasize the outward drainage of surplus from the South to the North. The 1994 UNDP report noted that in 1992, the outflow in debt service charges alone (a figure that therefore does not include profit repatriation and other forms of surplus transfer from South to North) on the Third World's combined debt of $1.5 trillion was 2.5 times the amount of Northern development aid and $60 billion more than total private flows to developing countries. These "open veins" through which wealth continues to flow from South to North suggests that transnational capital operates in such a way that it still requires strategic rearguards in the core of world capitalism, where global management, the store of capital, and the centers of technology and finances have concentrated within a changing global division of labor.

But the perpetuation of the North–South or Center–Periphery divide does not translate into continued prosperity for majorities in the North. Simultaneous with the widening of the North–South divide, there has been a widening gap between rich and poor in the United States and the other developed countries, along with heightened social polarization and political tensions. Between 1973 and 2015, real wages stagnated for 80 percent of the US population and rose for the remaining 20 percent. In 2015, some 50 million people in the United States lived in poverty, and tens of millions more lived near the poverty level.[20] The top quintile in the United States increased its share of income from 41.1 percent in 1973 to 51 percent in 2015, while the lowest quintile earned only 3.1 percent of national income,[21] and the richest 1 percent had more income than the bottom 90 percent.[22] The concentration of wealth (which includes income and wealth) was even more pronounced. Already in 1991, the top .05 percent of the population owned 45.4 percent of all assets, excluding homes. The top 1 percent owned 53.2 percent of all assets, and the top 10 percent owned 83.2 percent. The United States *belonged* to a tiny minority. The pattern is similar in other developed countries of the Organization of Economic Cooperation and Development.

The Occupy Wall Street movement of 2011–12 brought to worldwide attention the concentration of the world's wealth in the hands of the 1 percent with its famous rallying cry, "We are the 99 percent!" Indeed, according the Oxfam report mentioned above, the top 1 percent of humanity owned an incredible 50 percent of the planet's wealth in 2015. However an equally if not more significant division of the world's population with regard to political and sociological analysis is between that better off—if not necessarily outright wealthy—20 percent of humanity whose basic material needs are met, that enjoys the fruits of the global cornucopia and that generally enjoy conditions of security and stability, in contrast to the bottom 80 percent of the world's people who face escalating poverty, depravation, insecurity, and precariousness.

The North–South divide is growing and should not be understated. However, humanity is increasingly stratified along transnational class lines. Given the accelerated creation under globalization of lakes of wealth in Third World countries and seas of poverty in First World countries, as well as the rise of new centers of global management, technology, and finance in places such as China and India, it makes more sense to see the world as increasingly divided along class lines than along national lines. There are important empirical processes such as downward "global leveling" and theoretical issues that these processes raise, which I take up in later chapters.

Seventh, this escalating global poverty and inequality have deep and interwoven racial, ethnic, and gender dimensions.

As global capital concentrates, it disproportionately locks out women and racially and ethnically oppressed groups, in particular, the working class and poor majority within these groups. As transnational capital moves to the South of the world it does not leave behind in the North, or encounter in the South, homogenous working classes, but ones which are historically stratified and segmented along racial, ethnic, and gender lines. In the North, for instance, labor of color, drawn originally (and often by force) from the periphery to the core as menial labor, is disproportionately excluded from strategic economic sectors, relegated to the ranks of the growing army of "supernumeraries," made the most vulnerable sectors in a racially segmented labor market (which is becoming *more*, not less, rigid under globalization), and subject to a rising tide of racism, including the dismantling of affirmative action programs and repressive state measures against immigrant labor pools.[23] Although globalizing processes are undermining the existence of precapitalist classes, they are also intensifying stratification among labor, often along racial/ethnic lines, in both North and South. However, I suggest that such hierarchies of labor are becoming spatially organized *across* the North–South axis, given global integration processes, new migration patterns, and increased concentrations of Third World labor in the First World, as well as the increasing impoverishment of once-privileged "labor aristocracies" of European origin.

The roots of the subordination of women—unequal participation in a sexual division of labor on the basis of the female reproductive function—is exacerbated by globalization, which increasingly turns women from reproducers of labor power required by capital into reproducers of supernumeraries for which capital has no use. Female labor is further devalued, and women denigrated, as the function of the domestic (household) economy moves from rearing labor for incorporation into capitalist production to rearing supernumeraries. This is one important structural underpinning of the global "feminization of poverty" and is reciprocal to, and mutually reinforces, racial/ethnic dimensions of inequality. It helps explain the movement among Northern elites to dismantle Keynesians welfare benefits in a manner that disproportionately affects women and racially oppressed groups, and the impetuousness with which the neoliberal model calls for the elimination of even minimal social spending and safety nets that often mean, literally, the difference between life and death.

Eighth, deep contradictions in emergent world society make entirely uncertain the very survival of our species, much less the mid- to long-term stabilization and viability of global capitalism, and portend prolonged global social conflict.

The structure of global production, distribution, and consumption increasingly reflects the skewed income pattern. For instance, under the new global social apartheid, tourism is the fastest growing economic activity and even the mainstay of many Third World economies. This does not mean that more people are actually enjoying the fruits of leisure and international travel; it means that 20 percent of humanity has more and more disposable income simultaneous to the contraction of consumption by the remaining 80 percent. This 80 percent is forced to provide all sorts of ever more frivolous services to, and to orient its productive activity toward, meeting the needs and satisfying the sumptuous desires of that 20 percent.[24] By the turn of the century, private security forces and prisons had become the number one growth sector in the United States and the other Northern countries.[25] Social apartheid spawns decadence. Militarized fortress cities and spatial apartheid are necessary for social control under a situation in which an ever-smaller portion of humanity can actually consume the essentials of life, much less luxury goods.[26]

As national capitalism matured in the late nineteenth century in the North, the tendency inherent in capital accumulation toward a concentration of income and productive resources, and the social polarity and political conflict this generates, was offset by two factors. The first was the intervention of states to regulate the operation of the free market, to guide accumulation, and to capture and redistribute surpluses. This intervention was itself the outcome of mass working class struggles from below that forced reform on the system. The second was the emergence of modern imperialism to offset the polarizing tendencies inherent in the process of capital accumulation in the North, thereby transferring global social conflict to the South. Both these factors therefore fettered, in the core of the world system, the social polarity generated by capitalism. But by reducing or eliminating the ability of individual states to regulate capital accumulation and capture surpluses, globalization is now bringing (at a worldwide level) precisely the polarization between a rich minority and a poor majority that Karl Marx predicted. Yet this time there are no "new frontiers," no virgin lands for capitalist colonization that could offset the social and political consequences of global polarization.

Endemic to unfettered global capitalism, therefore, is intensified social conflict, which in turn engenders constant political crises and ongoing instability, both within countries and between countries. In the post-World War II period, the North was able to shift much social conflict to the South as a combined result of an imperialist transfer of wealth from South to North and the redistribution of this wealth in the North through Keynesian state intervention. No fewer than 160 wars were fought in the Third World from 1945 to 1990. However, globalization involves a distinct shift in global strife from interstate conflict (reflecting a certain correspondence between classes and nations in the stage of national capitalism) to global class conflict. The UNDP's 1994 report underscores a shift from "a pattern of wars between states to wars within states." Of the eighty-two armed conflicts between 1989 and 1992, only three were between states. "Although often cast in ethnic divisions, many have a political or economic character," states the report. Meanwhile, global military spending in 1992 was $815 billion ($725 billion of which corresponded to the rich Northern countries), a figure equal to the combined income of 49 percent of the world's people in that same year.[27] By 2015, military spending worldwide had more than doubled, to nearly $1.7 trillion.[28]

The period of worldwide political instability we face ranged from the late twentieth into the early twenty-first centuries from civil wars in the former Yugoslavia and in numerous African countries to simmering social conflict in Latin America and Asia; major transnational wars in the Middle East; endemic civil disturbances, sometimes low-key and sometimes high profile, in Los Angeles, Paris, Bonn, Athens, and most metropoles of the Northern countries. Uncertain survival and insecurities posed by global capitalism induces diverse forms of fundamentalisms, localisms, nationalisms, and racial and ethnic conflict. These themes will be discussed in detail in later chapters.

As the worldwide ruling class, the transnational bourgeoisie has thrust humanity into a crisis of civilization. Social life under global capitalism is increasingly dehumanizing and devoid of any ethical content. But our crisis is deeper: We face a *species crisis*. Well-known structural contradictions analyzed a century ago by Marx, such as overaccumulation, underconsumption, and the tendency toward stagnation, are exacerbated by globalization, as many analysts have pointed out. However, while these "classic" contradictions cause financial turmoil, social crisis and cultural decadence, new contradictions associated with twenty-first-century capitalism—namely, the incompatibility of the reproduction of both capital *and* of nature—is leading to an ecological holocaust that threatens the survival of our species and of life itself on our planet.[29] Yet "most analyses of the environmental problem today are concerned less with saving the planet or life or humanity than saving capitalism—the system at the root of our environmental problem," note Foster and his colleagues. "Not only has this generated inertia with respect to social change—indeed a tendency to fiddle while Rome burns—but it has also led to the belief that the crisis can be managed by essentially the same social institutions that brought it into being in the first place."[30]

Ninth, stated in highly simplified terms, much of the left worldwide is split between two camps.

One group is so overwhelmed by the power of global capitalism that it does not see any alternative to participation through trying to negotiate the best deal possible. This camp searches for some new variant of social democracy and redistributive justice that could become operant in the new world order. It therefore proposes diverse sorts of a global Keynesianism that do not challenge the logic of capitalism itself, and tends toward a political pragmatism. The other views global capitalism and its costs—including its very tendency toward the destruction of our species—as unacceptably high, so much so that it must be resisted and rejected. However, *it has not worked out a coherent socialist alternative* to the transnational phase of capitalism.

This dividing line is not new. It goes back to the early twentieth century split between socialism and social democracy, but it has taken on new characteristics in the novel context of capitalist globalization. We see this strategic dividing line in the Latin American, African, and Asian left, as well as in the North and among left and socialist groups attempting a renewal in the former Soviet-bloc countries. For instance, this was the fundamental underlying issue that ultimately led to formal splits in the 1990s and early twenty-first centuries in a number of Latin American leftist organizations, including the Sandinista National Liberation Front in Nicaragua and the Farabundo Martí National Liberation Front in El Salvador, to the fracturing of the Philippine left, the

Greek left, the African National Congress coalition in South Africa, leftist parties in the European Union, and so on (although care must be taken not to simplify complex issues or to draw broad generalizations from specific experiences).

My own view is that we should harbor no illusions that global capitalism can be tamed or democratized. This does not mean that we should not struggle for reform within capitalism, but we should recognize that all such struggle should be encapsulated in a broader strategy and program for revolution against capitalism. Globalization places enormous constraints on popular struggles and social change in any one country or region. The most urgent task is therefore to develop solutions to the plight of humanity under a savage capitalism liberated from the constraints that could earlier be imposed on it through the nation-state. An alternative to global capitalism must therefore be a *transnational* popular project. The transnational bourgeoisie is conscious of its transnationality, is organized transnationally, and operates globally. Many have argued that the nation-state is still the fulcrum of political activity for the foreseeable future. But it is *not* the fulcrum of the political activity of this global elite. The popular mass of humanity must develop a *transnational* class consciousness and a concomitant global political protagonism and strategies that link the local to the national and the national to the global.

A transnational counterhegemonic project requires the development of concrete and viable programmatic alternatives. The South African Communist Party, for instance, adopted in the postapartheid period, and popularized internationally, a strategy of seeking to "roll back" the market through the decommodification of key areas of South African society, not as an end in itself but as part of a broader struggle for socialism. Although it later abandoned this strategy, the World Social Forum, which brings together in its annual meetings representatives from thousands of popular social change organizations from around the world, has placed this struggle for reclaiming the global commons at the center of its agenda. The contradictions of global capitalism open up new possibilities as well as enormous challenges for a popular alternative. Without its own viable socioeconomic model, popular sectors run the risk of political stagnation under the hegemony of the transnational elite, or even worse, being reduced, if they come to occupy governments, to administering the crises of neoliberalism with a consequent loss of legitimacy. In many important respects, this is precisely what happened in several of the leftist governments that came to power in Latin America in the early twenty-first century, such as in Brazil under the Workers Party. Under such a scenario, the hegemonic view that there is no popular alternative to global capitalism becomes reinforced, leading to resignation and demobilization among popular sectors and betrayal of obligations among intellectuals and leaders.

The "race to the bottom"—the worldwide downward leveling of living conditions and the gradual equalization of life conditions in North and South—creates fertile objective conditions for the development of transnational social movements and political projects. The communications revolution has facilitated global elite communications, but it can also assist global coordination among popular classes, as demonstrated by the creative use that the Zapatistas in Mexico made of the Internet in the years following their 1994 uprising, during the Arab Spring that started in 2010 and with regard to the Occupy Wall Street Movement in the United States of 2011, among other examples. The formation of the World Social Forum in 2001 marked one turning point in the transnational coordination of national and regional struggles, despite all its shortcomings.

A transnational counterhegemonic project would not entail resisting globalization—alas, we cannot simply demand that historic processes be halted to conform to our wishes, and we would do better to understand how we may influence and redirect those processes—but rather converting it into a "globalization from below." Such a process from the bottom up would have to address the deep racial/ethnic dimensions of global inequality, parting from the premise that, although racism and ethnic and religious conflicts rest on real material fears among groups that survival is under threat, they take on cultural, ideological, and political dynamics of their own, which must be challenged and countered in the programs and the practice of counterhegemony. A counterhegemonic project will have to be thoroughly imbued with a gender equality approach, in practice and in content. It will also require alternative forms of democratic practice within popular organizations (trade unions, social movements, and so on), within political parties, and—wherever the formal state apparatus is captured, through elections or other means—within state institutions.

New egalitarian practices must eschew traditional hierarchical and authoritarian forms of social intercourse and bureaucratic authority relations, and they must overcome personality cults, centralized deci-

sion-making, and other such traditional practices. The flow of authority and decision-making in new social and political practices within any
counterhegemonic bloc must be from the bottom up, not from the top
down. Transnational political protagonism among popular classes means
developing a transnational protagonism at the mass, grassroots level—a
transnationalized participatory democracy—well beyond the old "inter-
nationalism" of political leaders and bureaucrats, and also beyond the
paternalistic forms of Northern "solidarity" with the South.

More than prolonged mass misery and social conflict is at stake: at
stake is the very survival of our species. A democratic socialism founded on a popular democracy may be humanity's "last best," and perhaps
only, hope.

TWO

CRITICAL GLOBALIZATION STUDIES

How can academics and intellectuals play a meaningful part in resolving the urgent issues that humanity faces in the twenty-first century—those of war and peace, social justice, democracy, cultural diversity, and ecological sustainability? If we are to do so, it is imperative that we gain an analytical understanding of capitalist globalization as the underlying structural dynamic that drives social, political, economic, and cultural processes around the world. The dual objective of understanding globalization and engaging in global social activism can best be expressed in the idea of a *Critical Globalization Studies*. As scholars it is incumbent upon us to explore the relevance of academic research to the burning political issues and social struggles of our epoch, to the many conflicts, hardships, and hopes bound up with globalization. More directly stated, we cannot be indifferent observers studying globalization as a sort of detached academic exercise. Rather, our intellectual production must be passionately concerned with the adverse impact of capitalist globalization on billions of people as well as our increasingly stressed planetary ecology. It is our obligation as scholars to place an understanding of the multifaceted processes of globalization in the service of those individuals and organizations that are dedicated to fighting its depredations.

In this chapter I call for a Critical Globalization Studies. But I am concerned as well with a related question: what is the role and responsibility of intellectual labor in global society? In what ways do we (or ought we) participate in the public life of the new global capitalist society taking shape? All intellectual labor is organic, in the sense that studying the world is itself a social act, committed by agents with a definite relationship to the social order. For academics this labor takes place within universities as capitalist institutions that serve to regenerate dominant ideologies and to organize knowledge production for capitalism. Moreover, the university as an institution has been subject to ever more extensive neoliberal restructuring and to commodification. This process has severely restricted the space in academia for critical teaching, research, and debate. More broadly, the role of intellectuals in society is admittedly a very old and recurrent theme. To talk of public sociologies today is to underscore both the social role and responsibility of intellectuals and academics. Scholars are indeed public intellectuals, whether or not we identify ourselves as such. By teaching, publishing, and participating in the administration of our universities and other social institutions, we engage in forms of social communication that influence the development of public consciousness, public understanding of social processes and political life, appraisals of the purpose and potential of social action, and imageries of alternative futures.

But there is more to say about the intellectual enterprise. Intellectual production is always a collective process. By collective I do not just mean collaborative projects among scholars or ongoing research programs. I want to foreground here the social and the historical character of intellectual labor. All those who engage in intellectual labor or make knowledge claims are *organic* intellectuals in the sense that all such labor is social labor, its practitioners are social actors, and the products of its labor are not neutral or disinterested.[1] We must ask ourselves, what is the relationship between our intellectual work and power? What is the relationship between our research into globalization and power in global society? To what end and whose interests does our intellectual production serve? In short, as academics and researchers examining globalization, we must ask ourselves, whose mandarins are we?

We are living in troubling times. The system of global capitalism that now engulfs the entire planet is in crisis. There is consensus among scientists that we are on the precipice of ecological holocaust, including the mass extinction of species; the impending collapse of agriculture in major producing areas; the meltdown of polar ice caps; global warming; and the contamination of the oceans, the food stock, water supply, and air. Social inequalities have spiraled out of control and the gap between the global rich and the global poor has never been as acute as it is in the early twenty-first century. While absolute levels of poverty and misery expand around the world under a new global social apartheid, the richest

20 percent of humanity received in 2015 nearly 95 percent of the world's wealth while the remaining 80 percent had to make do with less just 5 percent, according to the international development agency Oxfam.[2] Driven by the imperatives of overaccumulation and transnational social control, global elites have increasingly turned to authoritarianism, militarization, and war to sustain the system. Many political economists concur that a global economic collapse beyond the finance meltdown of 2008 is possible, even probable.[3]

In times such as these, intellectuals must choose between legitimating the prevailing social order and providing technical solutions to the problems that arise in its maintenance, or exposing contradictions in order to reveal how they may be resolved by transcending the existing order. How do we address the crisis of global capitalism, clearly a crisis of civilizational proportions? While I cannot provide the answer, my contention here is that solutions require a *critical* analytical and theoretical understanding of global capitalism that is the first task of a Critical Globalization Studies.

GLOBAL CAPITALISM

The task of a Critical Globalization Studies is certainly daunting, given such a vast and complex theoretical object as emergent global society and the character of the current situation as transitionary and not accomplished. Globalization in my analysis is a qualitatively new stage in the history of world capitalism. If earlier stages brought us colonial conquest, a world economy and an international division of labor, the partition of the world into North and South, and rising material prosperity amidst pauperization, this new era is bringing us into a singular global civilization, in which humanity is bound together as never before, yet divided into the haves and the have-nots across national and regional borders in a way unprecedented in human history. This new transnational order dates back to the world economic crisis of the 1970s and took shape in the following decades. It is marked by a number of fundamental shifts in the capitalist system. These shifts include, first, the rise of truly transnational capital and the integration of every country into a new global production and financial system. The era of the primitive accumulation of capital is coming to an end as commodification penetrates every nook and cranny of the globe and invades public and community spheres previously outside its reach. In this process, millions have been wrenched from the means of production, proletarianized, and thrown into a (gendered and racialized) global labor market that transnational capital has been able to shape.

Second is the appearance of a new *transnational capitalist class*, a class group grounded in new global markets and circuits of accumulation, rather than national markets and circuits. In every country of the world, a portion of the national elite has become integrated into this new transnationally oriented elite. Global class formation has also involved the rise of a new global working class—a labor force for the new global production system—yet stratified less along national than along social lines in a transnational environment. Third is the rise of a *transnational state*, a loose but increasingly coherent network comprised of supranational political and economic institutions, and of national state apparatuses that have been penetrated and transformed by the transnational capitalist class and allied transnationally oriented bureaucratic and other strata. Once captured by such forces, national states tend to become components of a larger transnational state that serves the interests of global over national or local accumulation processes. The transnational state has played a key role in imposing the neoliberal model on the global South. It has advanced the interests of transnational capitalists and their allies over nationally oriented groups among the elite, not to mention over workers and the poor. National states become wracked by internal conflicts that reflect the contradictions of the larger global system.

A fourth fundamental shift in the capitalist system is the appearance of novel relations of inequality in global society. As capitalism globalizes, the twenty-first century is witness to new forms of poverty and wealth and new configurations of power and domination. Global capitalism has generated new social dependencies around the world. Billions of people have been brought squarely into the system, whereas before they may have been at the margins or entirely outside of it. The system is very much a life and death matter for billions of people who, willing or otherwise, have developed a stake in its maintenance. Indeed, global capitalism is hegemonic not just because its ideology has become dominant but also, and perhaps primarily, because it has the ability to provide material rewards and to impose sanctions.

Globalization is anything but a neutral process. It has produced winners and losers, and therefore has its defenders and opponents. There is a new configuration of global power that becomes manifest in each nation and whose tentacles reach all the way down to the community level. Each individual, each nation, and each region is being drawn into transnational processes that have undermined the earlier autonomies and provincialisms. This makes it entirely impossible to address local issues removed from global context. At the same time, resistance has been spreading throughout global society. There are burgeoning social movements of workers and the poor, transnational feminism, indigenous struggles, demands for human rights and democratization, and so on.

Where do scholars and academics fit in to all of this? Where ought they fit in? Universities are centers for the production and reproduction of knowledge and culture. As all social institutions, they internalize the power relations of the larger society to which they belong. Over the past decades, and in tandem with the spread of capitalist globalization, we have witnessed relentless pressures worldwide to commodify higher education, the increasing privatization of universities, and their penetration by transnational corporate capital. If the university is to pull back from such a course it must fulfill a larger social function in the interests of broad publics and from the vantage point of a social logic that is inevitably at odds with the corporate logic of global capitalism. Such a change will only come about by linking campus-based struggles with larger social, labor, and political movements from below.

The university in capitalist society has always been a capitalist institution and the site of class and social struggles. But under the onslaught of capitalist globalization and neoliberalism, the university has been subject to relentless commodification and to the rollback of spaces previously opened up by mass struggle in the post-World War II period. Witness, for instance, the cutback and even the elimination of labor studies, radical sociology, Black and feminist studies, and so on. As the production of positivist scientific knowledge becomes increasingly important for global capitalism in this age of computer and information technology, the so-called STEM areas (science, technology, engineering, and mathematics) hoard university resources, with ample funding from corporations that appropriate the knowledge produced, and from the state, which applies the research to the military-industrial complex or turns it over to capital. This turn to STEM areas devoid of any critical social content seduces millions of young people with the promise of a viable niche in the capitalist labor market, and both dazzles and depoliticizes them with the allure of technological glitz. At the same time, disciplinary mechanisms such as the denial of jobs and of tenure and control over funding streams for research lead many would-be dissident intellectuals to self-censor. For those who do not conform, there are more severe forms of academic and political repression.[4]

A "PREFERENTIAL OPTION" FOR THE SUBORDINATE MAJORITY

In the 1960s and 1970s in Latin America and elsewhere, lay people and grassroots clerics from the Catholic Church questioned the precepts of the prevailing dogma and turned to constructing a church of the poor under the banner of liberation theology. These leaders of what became known as the popular church had begun working in social and self-help projects in the countryside and among impoverished urban neighborhoods. They soon realized, however, that a narrow self-improvement outlook was insufficient in the face of glaring injustices and entrenched power structures. Liberation theology called for Christians to exercise a "preferential option for the poor" in their social and evangelical work.

What leaders of the popular church recognized in the 1960s and 1970s for the Catholic Church as an institution to which they belonged—namely, that it is part of a larger society; that it reflects the divisions, struggles, and power relations of that society; and that members of the church are not neutral in the face of the battles that rage in society—holds true for the university. It is time for scholars and intellectuals in the twenty-first century to exercise a preferential option for subordinate majorities of emergent global society.

What does it mean to exercise a preferential option for the majority in global society? In my view, what is required in global society, seen from the needs and aspirations of the poor majority of humanity (for whom global capitalism is nothing short of alienation, savagery, and dehumanization) are organic intellectuals capable of theorizing the changes that have taken place in the system of capitalism, in this epoch of globalization, and of providing theoretical insights as inputs to the real-world struggles of popular majorities to develop alternative social relationships and an alternative social logic (the logic of majorities) to that of the market and of transnational capital. In other words, a Critical Globalization Studies has to be capable of inspiring emancipatory action, of bringing together multiple publics in developing programs that integrate theory and practice.

This does not mean that practicing a Critical Globalization Studies is reduced to running out and joining mass movements. It is, to be sure, a good idea to do so, although academics must be careful not to impose their "knowledge power" on these movements. Great scholars throughout the ages, those that have truly had an impact on history, have also been social activists and political agents. But the key thing here is to bring our intellectual labor—our theorizing and systematic research—to bear on the crisis of humanity. This involves *critical thinking*. The distinction between critical and noncritical ways of thinking is what Max Horkheimer first called "traditional" versus "critical" thinking, and what Robert Cox more recently has referred to as "problem solving" versus "critical" thinking.[5] The critical tradition in the social sciences, not to be confused with the related but distinct *critical theory* as first developed by the Frankfurt School in Western Marxist thought, refers in the broadest sense to those approaches that take a critical view of the prevailing status quo and explicitly seek to replace the predominant power structures and social hierarchies with what are seen as more just and equitable social arrangements. Critical thinking, therefore, cannot take place without linking theory to practice, without a theoretically informed practice. *Praxis* is at the core of a Critical Globalization Studies.

Does such a Critical Globalization Studies imply that "politicizing" scholarship and the academic profession in this way compromises it? There is no value-free research and there are no apolitical intellectuals. (This is not to say that our research should not adhere to the social science rules of logic and empirical verification; indeed it must be lest it be reduced to propaganda.) We know from the philosophy and the sociology of knowledge that knowledge is never neutral or divorced from the historic context of its production, including from competing social interests.[6] Intellectual production always parallels, and can be functionally associated with, movement and change in society. There is no such thing as an intellectual or an academic divorced from social aims that drive research, not in the hard sciences, and much less in the social sciences and humanities. The mainstream scholar may "well believe in an independent, 'suprasocial,' detached knowledge as in the social importance of his expertise," observes the German Marxist philosopher Horkheimer. "The dualism of thought and being, understanding and perception is second nature to the scientist ... [such mainstream scholars] believe they are acting according to personal determinations, whereas in fact even in their most complicated calculations they but exemplify the working of an incalculable social mechanism."[7]

Many "mainstream" academics, shielded by the assumptions of positivist epistemologies, would no doubt take issue with this characterization of intellectual labor as, by definition, a social act by organic social agents. There are those who would posit a free-floating academic, a neutral generator of knowledge and ideas. But few would disagree that scholars and intellectuals are knowledge producers and that "knowledge is power." Hence it is incumbent on us to ask: Power for whom? Power exercised by whom? Power to what ends? The theoretical and research trajectories of social scientists, policymakers, and others within the academic division of labor are influenced by their social position as shaped by class as well as by gender, race, culture, and nationality. But many academics are linked to the state, to other social institutions, and to dominant groups in a myriad of ways, from corporate and state funding of research, to status, prestige, job security, and social approval that comes from integration into the hegemonic order, in contrast to the well-known sanctions one risks in committing to a counterhegemonic project, as the Marxist dialectician Bertell Ollman observes.[8]

Academics who believe they can remain aloof in the face of the conflicts that are swirling about us and the ever-higher stakes involved are engaged in a self-deception that is itself a political act. The claim to nonpolitical intellectual labor, value neutrality, and so forth is part of the very mystification of knowledge production and the ideological legitimation by intellectual agents of the dominant social order. To quote Jean-Paul Sartre (who is here following the great Italian socialist thinker Antonio Gramsci), such intellectuals are "specialists in research and servitors of hegemony."[9] The prevailing global order has its share of intellectual defenders, academics, pundits, and ideologues. These "functionaries of the superstructure," as Sartre called them, serve to mystify the real inner workings of the emerging order and the social interests embedded therein. They become central cogs in the system of global capitalism, performing not only legitimating functions but also developing practical and particularist knowledge intended to provide technical solutions in response to the problems and contradictions of the system. In short, whether intended or not, they exercise a "preferential option" for a minority of the privileged and the powerful in global capitalist society.

The mood in academia, especially in the United States, generally trails behind and reflects that of the political and social climate. At times of rising popular and mass struggles, when counterhegemonic forces are coalescing, the academy can become radicalized. At times of conservative retrenchment, the academy retreats and those playing a major role in intellectual legitimation of the state of affairs (and the affairs of the state) move more on the offensive and academic repression can set in. If the 1960s and 1970s saw a radicalization of the university in the United States and elsewhere, then the 1980s and 1990s saw a conservative counteroffensive. Since the 1980s, we have witnessed, in tandem with the onslaught of neoliberalism and capitalist globalization, the privatization of higher education (and increasingly of secondary education), the rise of neoliberal private universities, the defunding of the public academy, the unprecedented penetration (often takeover) of universities by transnational corporate capital, and the ever-greater commodification of education. (I discuss these matters in more detail in Chapter 7.)

TENETS OF A CRITICAL GLOBALIZATION STUDIES

REFLEXIVITY AND HISTORY

Critical theory, in the view of one well-known nineteenth century social thinker, is *"the self-clarification of the struggles and wishes of the age."*[10] A Critical Globalization Studies must be concerned with reflexivity and with history, such that it does not take for granted the prevailing power structures, but rather problematizes and historicizes existing arrangements and established institutions. A critical studies can *only* mean that we do not accept the world as we find it as being in any sense natural. Hence the first step in any Critical Globalization Studies is to problematize the social reality that we study and in which we exist; to acknowledge that the society in which we live is not the only possible form of society and that as collective agents we make and remake the world even if, as Marx famously admonished, under conditions not of our own choosing. If we acknowledge the historical specificity of existing social arrangements, then we cannot engage in a critical studies without identifying and foregrounding the nature of the particular historical society in which we live, which for us is global capitalist society.

Once we ask, what is the beginning—and how may we imagine the end—of the existing order of things, then the next question a critical studies must ask is, what are the collective agents at work? What are the real and potential human agencies involved in social change? What is their relationship to the prevailing order and to one another? Among the myriad of multilayered social forces in struggle, in analytical abstraction and simplified terms, there are those who seek to reorganize and reconstruct on new bases these arrangements (that is to say, they seek to advance struggles for social emancipation) and those who seek to defend or sustain the existing arrangements. We want to acknowledge struggles from below and struggles from above and focus our analytical attention on the interplay between them.

A GLOBAL PERSPECTIVE

A Critical Globalization Studies must take a global perspective, in that social arrangements in the twenty-first century can only be understood in the context of global-level structures and processes, that is to say, in the context of globalization. This is the "think globally" part of the oft-cited aphorism "think globally, act locally." The perceived problematics of the local and of the nation-state must be located within a broader web of interconnected histories that in the current era are converging in new ways. Any critical studies in the twenty-first century must of necessity also be a globalization studies.

But global-level thinking is a necessary but not a sufficient condition for a critical understanding of the world. Transnational corporate and political elites certainly have a global perspective. Global thinking is not necessarily critical and is just as necessary for the maintenance of global capitalism as critical global-level thinking is for emancipatory change. If we can conceptualize a Critical Globalization Studies, then we should be able to conceive of a "noncritical globalization studies." If a Critical Globalization Studies is one that acknowledges the historical specificity of existing social arrangements, then a "noncritical globalization studies" is one that takes the existing world as it is. Such a noncritical globalization studies is thriving in the twenty-first-century academy. It is a studies that denies that the world we live in—twenty-first-century global capitalist society—is but one particular historical form, one that has a beginning and an end, as do all historical forms and institutions.

THE SUBVERSIVE NATURE OF A CRITICAL GLOBALIZATION STUDIES

In the tradition of critical studies, a Critical Globalization Studies is subversive insofar as it explicitly seeks to replace predominant power structures and social hierarchies with what are seen as more just and equitable social arrangements. A Critical Globalization Studies involves exposing the ideological content of theories and knowledge claims often put forward as social scientific discourse, the vested interests before the façade of neutral scholarship, and how powerful institutions really work. This means challenging the dominant mythologies of our age—for example, that ecologically sound development is possible under capitalism, that "democracy" exists where tiny minorities control wealth and power, or that we are moving toward an "ownership society" when in fact we live in a usurped society in which the lot of the majority is one of increasing dispossession. In this sense, a Critical Globalization Studies is a counterhegemonic practice that seeks to rebuild public discourse by "speaking truth to power."

It involves making visible and unmasking power relations in our institutions, professional associations, in our locales and in the larger—ultimately global—society. While the substantive agenda of a Critical Globalization Studies must be open, the underlying enterprise involves applying our training and experience to elucidating the real inner workings of the social order and the contradictions therein. This must include putting forward a cogent and systematic critique of global capitalism that exposes injustices, makes invisible problems visible, and reveals pressure points in the system. Rendering visible what Paul Farmer terms the "pathologies of power" means "bearing witness,"[11] but more than that it means showing how suffering is a consequence of the structural violence that is immanent to the prevailing system and that links together apparently disconnected aspects of that system. We should recall, in this regard, Sartre's admonition, in his *A Plea for Intellectuals*, that "the exploited classes do not need an *ideology* so much as the practical truth of society; they need knowledge of the world in order to change it."[12] As regards a Critical Globalization Studies, we would do well to follow Susan George's advice to study not so much the oppressed as the powerful:

> Those that genuinely want to help the movement should study the rich and powerful, not the poor and powerless. Although wealth and power are in a better position to hide their activities and are therefore more difficult to study, any knowledge about them will be valuable to the movement. The poor and powerless already know what is wrong with their lives and those who want to help them should analyze the forces that keep them poor and powerless. Better a sociology of the Pentagon or the Houston country club than of single mothers or L.A. gangs.[13]

In the end, a Critical Globalization Studies involves questioning everything, deconstructing everything, interrogating every claim to knowledge, and yet it also means reconstructing what we have deconstructed and contributing to the construction of an alternative future.

ENGAGEMENT WITH EVERYDAY CONCERNS

To engage in a Critical Globalization Studies means to maintain contact with everyday concerns, a connection with social forces from below, in its theoretical and empirical research concerns. Such engagement with everyday concerns is the "act locally" of the oft-cited aphorism. People experience global capitalism in their localities and everyday lives. For a Critical Globalization Studies, the local–global link means identifying how global processes have penetrated and restructured localities in new ways, organically linking local realities to global processes. Sociologist Michael Burawoy and his colleagues have shown in their diverse locally situated studies what they call a "global ethnography," how "ethnography's concern with concrete, lived experience can sharpen the abstractions of globalization theories into more precise and meaningful conceptual tools."[14]

It is at this local, experienced level of global capitalism that intellectuals engage in active participation in everyday life, acting as agents or organizers, or (in Gramsci's phrase) as "permanent persuaders" in the construction of hegemonic social orders.[15] The intellectual in this case contributes to the active construction of hegemony by particular social forces that construct and maintain a social order on an ongoing basis. But such intellectual labor can also entail a connection with opposing initiatives, with forces from below and their attempts to forge a counterhegemony by drawing out the connections, through theoretical reflection, that link the distinct lived realities, everyday spontaneous and organized forms of struggle. By propagating certain ideas, intellectuals play an essential mediating function in the struggle for hegemony, Gramsci reminds us, by acting as "deputies" or instruments of hegemony, or by performing a valuable supporting role to subordinate groups engaged in promoting social change.[16]

CRITICAL GLOBALIZATION STUDIES AS PRAXIS

As should be clear from all the above, a Critical Globalization Studies is a *praxis*. Indeed, the broader point is that *all* intellectual labor is praxis and for that reason organic. The question is, a theory-practice by whom, for whom, and to what end? A Critical Globalization Studies is grounded in the linkage of theory to practice, insofar as we cannot really know the world without participating in efforts to change it, which is the same as to say that it is only when we engage in collective efforts to change the world that we truly come to know the world. At the pedagogical level, the praxis of a Critical Globalization Studies is a pedagogy of the oppressed, a process of conscientization, understood as learning to perceive social, political, and economic contradictions and to take action against the oppressive elements of reality. A Critical Globalization Studies must not only link intellectual production and knowledge claims to emancipatory projects. It must also enjoin discursive with material struggles, lest the latter become reduced to irrelevant word games.

To reiterate, the *praxis* of a Critical Globalization Studies implies bringing the intellectual labor of social scientists—our theoretical work and systematic research—to bear on the crisis of humanity. Universities, think tanks, and NGOs must be bastions of critique of the twenty-first-century global order, an incubator for critical thinking, and a reservoir for debate, alternative ideas and counterhegemonies. A Critical Globalization Studies must be capable of contributing in this way to the development of programs that integrate theory with practice and the local with the global, of *inspiring emancipatory action*. A Critical Globalization Studies is not satisfied with "the art of the possible"; its labor aims to help us move beyond the limits of the possible.

EPISTEMOLOGICAL "GROUND RULES" OF A CRITICAL GLOBALIZATION STUDIES

There are certain "epistemological ground rules" for "doing a Critical Globalization Studies," including a transdisciplinary, holistic, and dialectical approach that focuses on systemic connections that underlie the various aspects of the social—in this case, global—reality it studies. A Critical Globalization Studies should be an open space, broad enough to house a diversity of approaches and epistemologies, from Marxist to radical variants of institutional, Weberian, feminist, poststructural, and other traditions in critical thought, and should as well emphasize including questions of contingency, culture, and subjectivity. But, to reiterate, what distinguishes (or *must* distinguish) a Critical Globalization Studies from a noncritical globalization studies is reflexivity, a critical global perspective, the subversive nature of its thought in relation to the status quo, and a praxis as theoretically informed practice.

A Critical Globalization Studies is, by definition, interdisciplinary—or more accurately, transdisciplinary. It is holistic in conception and epistemology, which is not to say, as a matter of course, that particular studies necessarily take the "whole" as the object of inquiry. As Palan has noted, "the broadly critical tradition in the social sciences is naturally attracted to holistic interpretations of social relations ... The assumption being that there are totalizing processes driven by a predominant logic which we call capitalism, and that such totalizing processes manifest themselves in all aspects of social life."[17] The critical tradition maintains therefore that there is no point in studying each facet of social life as an independent system of relationships—for the simple reason that they are not independent but interdependent, as internally related elements of a more encompassing totality. Consequently, the critical tradition does not accept the analytical legitimacy of formal academic divisions.

This does not mean that there is any single "right" way to engage in a critical globalization studies. I would insist, nonetheless, that it is not possible to understand global society in the absence of a political economy analysis. Political economy historically has concentrated on the analytical as well as prescriptive questions of how order and change come about. The history of the breakup in the nineteenth and twentieth centuries of political economy into artificial and compartmentalized "disciplines" is well known.[18] We need to recapture the critical essence of political economy, which takes as its basis the production and reproduction of our material existence, and on that basis seeks to ask how change can be brought about, by whom, and for whom.

Yet it is equally true that the manifold dimensions of the social totality cannot be reduced to epiphenomena of the material bases of global society. Such an approach would not be dialectical—that is, holistic—but mechanical and misleading. The opposition of political economy to cultural analysis, for instance, is a false dualism that obscures rather than elucidates the complex reality of global society, insofar as our material existence as humans is always, of necessity, only possible through the construction of a symbolic order and systems of meaning that are themselves the products of historically situated social forces and have an ongoing recursive effect on material reality. Indeed, as Raymond Williams (among others) has constantly reminded us, culture is itself a material force.

A Critical Globalization Studies, therefore, requires dialectical thought at the level of epistemology, as a way of knowing. In epistemological terms, dialectics means a dialogue seeking truth through exploration of contradictions and through identifying the *internal* relations that bind together diverse and multifaceted dimensions of social reality into an open totality. In the dialectical approach the different dimensions of our social reality do not have an "independent" status insofar as each aspect of reality is constituted by, and is constitutive of, a larger whole of which it is an internal element. An *internal relation* is one in which each part is constituted in its relation to the other, so that one cannot exist without the other and only has meaning when seen within the relation, whereas an *external relation* is one in which each part has an existence independent of its relation to the other.[19] Viewing things as externally related to one another inevitably leads to dualist constructs and false dichotomies (e.g., political economy versus culture, the local/national and the global). The distinct levels of social structure—in this case, global social structure—cannot be understood independent of one another, but neither are these levels reducible to any one category. They are internally related, meaning that they can only be understood in their relation to one another and to the larger social whole.

Critical thought, in this regard, means applying a dialectical as opposed to a formal logic, one that focuses not on things in themselves but on the interrelations among them. A dialectical logic involves identifying how distinct dimensions of social reality may be analytically distinct (such as the three most oft-cited salient axes of social inequality—race, class, and gender) yet are mutually constitutive of each other as internal elements of a more encompassing process. Our task is to uncover internal linkages among distinct sets of historical relationships and their grounding in an underlying (that is, more primary) historic process, which in my view are material relations of production and reproduction and the historical ordering principle those relations put forth. This is to argue that historical processes of production and reproduction are *causal* processes. To take the case of race and class, it is not that racialization processes occurring around the world in the twenty-first century can be explained in terms of class, but that class itself became racialized in the formative years of the world capitalist system because of the particular history of that system. I will not draw out the point further here. Suffice it to note that ultimately we are concerned here with the dialectical relationship between consciousness and being.

Twenty-first-century global capitalist society is characterized by a far greater complexity and much faster change and interaction than at any time in human history. It is only possible to grasp both the complexity of these structures and processes, and the dynamics of change, through a dialectical approach. For Ollman, the dialectic method involves six successive moments. The *ontological moment* has to do with the infinite number of mutually dependent processes that make up the totality, or structured whole, of social life. The *epistemological moment* deals with how to organize thinking in order to understand such a world, abstracting out the main patterns of change and interaction. The *moment of inquiry* appropriates the patterns of these internal relationships in order to further the project of investigation. The *moment of intellectual reconstruction* or *self-clarification* puts together the results of such an investigation for oneself. The *moment of exposition* entails describing to a particular audience the dialectical grasp of the facts by taking into account how others think. Finally, the *moment of praxis* uses the clarification of the facts of social life to act consciously in and on the world, changing it while simultaneously deepening one's understanding of it.[20] Applied to the matter before us, we could say that, through social engagement, active theorizing, and political work, a critical globalization studies becomes *self-knowledge of global society*.

CONCLUSION

With the apparent triumph of global capitalism in the 1990s after the collapse of the old Soviet bloc, the defeat of Third World nationalist and revolutionary projects, and the withdrawal of the Left into postmodern identity politics and other forms of accommodation with the prevailing social order, many intellectuals who previously identified with resistance movements and emancipatory projects seemed to cede a certain defeatism before global capitalism. Such defeatism has no place in a Critical Globalization Studies. The decline of the Left and socialist movements worldwide (a result of the chronic gap between theory and practice, thought, and action, among other factors) led to a degeneration of intellectual criticism as well. An embrace of the "end of history" thesis[21] is the end not of history but of critical thought.

The current epoch is a time of rapidly growing global social polarization between a shrinking majority of haves and an expanding minority of have-nots. It is a time of escalating political and military conflict as contending social forces face each other in innumerable yet interwoven struggles around the world. The global capitalist system faces a structural crisis of overaccumulation and also an expanding crisis of legitimacy, as I explore later in the book. There is certainly no dearth of mass mobilization and political protagonism from below, to which a Critical Globalization Studies can and must contribute.

THREE

THE NEW GLOBAL ECONOMY AND THE RISE OF A TRANSNATIONAL CAPITALIST CLASS

In 2016 I decided to conduct a small-scale experiment. By that year, I had been writing for over two decades on the idea of globalization as an epochal shift in the world capitalist system characterized above all by the rise of truly transnational capital. I also continued in that year to engage in debates with my critics who reject my conception of global capitalism as a qualitatively new stage in the evolution of the system based on the rise of a transnational capitalist class. I opened up an online brokerage account at Wells Fargo bank with a $1,000 deposit. The point was to see if I could move my "capital" around the world effortlessly through the digital circuits of the global economy.

In a book I had published two years prior to the experiment, in 2014, I had quoted William J. Amelio, the CEO of Lenovo, a "Chinese" global technology company headquartered in Beijing:

> I live the worldsourced life. As CEO of Lenovo, I am an American CEO based in Singapore. Our chairman, who is Chinese, works from North Carolina. Other top executives are based around the globe. A meeting of my company's senior managers looks like the United Nations General Assembly. My company is like some of the world's most popular consumer products. It may say 'Made in China' on the outside, but the key components are designed and manufactured by innovative people and companies spread across six continents. The products of companies that practice worldsourcing may be labeled "Made in Switzerland" or "Made in the USA" or "Made in China," but in the new

world in which we all now live, they should more truthfully be labeled "Made Globally." In today's world, assessing companies by their nation of origin misses the point.[1]

I used the $1,000 to buy shares in Lenovo. Did this make me a "US," a "Chinese," or a "global" investor? If a trade war were to break out between the United States and China, would my "class interests" as a Lenovo investor be with Beijing or with Washington? If the Chinese state gave any preferential treatment to Lenovo over, say, US-based competitor IBM, would this not benefit me as an investor in Lenovo, so that China would be furthering my interests over those of any Chinese investors in IBM?

The next day I turned my $1,000 back into cash (minus the commission that the bank took) in the account and then invested it in Alibaba, the China-based global e-commerce firm, but then turned around and transferred the investment to its US-based competitor, Amazon. Over the next couple of weeks I continued to shift my investment around, so that I had come to acquire and then to sell shares in the Indian-based steel conglomerate, ArcelorMittal; the Brazil-based global mining conglomerate Vale; the Russian telecommunications giant Mobile TeleSystems and the Russian financial group QIWI PLC; the Egyptian consumer goods group Ajwa; the Mexican mining conglomerate Grupo México; and other companies based in Indonesia, Canada, Nigeria, throughout Europe, and in the United States. To be sure, there were some global corporate behemoths, such as Saudi Arabia's Aramco (the most valuable company in the world by market capitalization), that were not publicly traded (although Aramco announced in 2017 that it would go public). And other companies had to be accessed circuitously, such as the South African diamond producer De Beers, a "stake" in which I acquired by buying shares in the Paris-based firm Moelis & Company, which owns 50 percent of De Beers.

This was all done through my computer and could well have been accomplished from anywhere in the world with my laptop and Wi-Fi access. By the end of my experiment, it was clearer to me than ever that the world had become an open field for my "capital." The nation-state had become close to irrelevant as an obstacle in terms of my "class interests" in investing and accumulating capital. Any rivalries I may have developed had I continued to invest—and at amounts that would actually make me a capitalist—could not possibly be explained in nation-state terms. Something entirely new in the history of world capitalism was clearly at play.

Before I proceed, a few caveats are in order. First, this does *not* mean the nation-state is irrelevant. (My critics incessantly claim that I dismiss the nation-state and I tire of reiterating this point.) Second, recall that a true capitalist is one who actually lives off the surplus value extracted from labor so that global investors who could actually live off their investments become exploiters of workers all around the world, thus involving complex new transnational class relations beyond the transnational capitalist class that I cannot take up here. Third, as I discuss in detail below, there are still local, national, and regional capitals that may well be in rivalry with transnational capitalist groups. There were, for instance, giant Indian conglomerates that were not publicly traded; part of a research agenda is to analyze political and international dynamics from the vantage point of competition in the nation-state among these distinct fractions of capital. (I have extensively undertaken such analysis elsewhere.) Fourth, I live in Los Angeles, and were I a real capitalist I would have an interest, beyond the worldwide accumulation of my capital, in specifically US state policies, such as low taxes, or infrastructure, and in social and political stability/security in my city and country, and so on. Thus, there is a complex relationship between the economic and the political at the intersection of which is the nation-state. Finally, I argue that globalization represents a qualitatively new stage in the evolution of world capitalism; however, this is not a consummated end-state but a process that is ongoing and open-ended, subject to moving in unforeseen directions in the face of the many contradictions and conflicts that the process involves.

FROM A WORLD ECONOMY TO A GLOBAL ECONOMY

Globalization marks an *epochal shift* in the world capitalist system. The term *epochal shift* captures the idea of changes in social structure that transform the very way that the system functions. Periodization of capitalism is an analytical tool that allows us to grasp changes in the system over time and thus to identify such shifts. In my periodization of world capitalism, the first epoch was ushered in with the birth of capitalism out of its feudal cocoon in Europe and initial outward expansion, the so-called Age of Discovery and Conquest, symbolized by Columbus's arrival in 1492 in the Americas. This was the epoch of mercantilism and primitive accumulation, what Marx referred to as the "rosy dawn of the era of capitalist production." The second, competitive, or classical capitalism was marked by the industrial revolution, the rise of the bourgeoisie, and the forging of the modern nation-state, keynoted by the French revolution of 1789 and the eighteenth century manufacturing revolution in England. The late nineteenth century saw the transition to the third epoch, the rise of corporate ("monopoly") capitalism, the consolidation of a single world market and the nation-state system into which world capitalism became organized. It saw the appearance of the industrial corporation, intensified wars among the imperial powers, and the emergence of a socialist alternative.[2] By the end of the twentieth century, we had moved to the threshold of a new epoch, that of global capitalism, characterized by the rise of a globally integrated production and financial system and a transnational capitalist class (TCC).

The essence of capitalism is production undertaken through a particular form of social interaction, what we will call the *capital–labor relation* (or capitalist production relations), in order to exchange what is produced, *commodities*, in a market for profit. For capitalist production to take place there needs to be a class of people that has no means of production of their own, such as land with which to farm or tools and workshops with which to produce for themselves. This is the working class. And there needs to be a class of people who have come into possession of these means of production and in turn require a supply of labor to work these means of production so that commodities can be produced and sold for a profit. This is the capitalist class. The *capital–labor relation* refers to the relationship between workers and capitalists as they come together in the process of producing goods that people need or want.

People have come together to produce the necessities of life long before capitalism appeared—such production, the collective labor process, is in the very nature of our species. What distinguishes capitalism from other social systems, or what we call *modes of production*, is that human beings engage in the production process in order to exchange what is produced for a profit, and this production takes place through the capital–labor relation. Human beings can engage in production in a cooperative and egalitarian manner, through for example collective ownership of the means of production (a communal system). Or they could come together through the enslavement of one group of people by another, a slave system. In a feudal system, as in a slave system, one group of people (landlords) comes to control the means of production in the form of land. But production does not take place as commodity production, which refers to the production of useful things that people want or need expressly in order to exchange them on the market for a profit. Workers under capitalism are "free." Unlike the slave or the serf, no one physically coerces them into working for a capitalist. But because workers have no means of production of their own, they are forced, on pain of starvation, to provide their labor to capitalists, in exchange for a wage with which to acquire the necessities of life on the market. The process by which people come to be separated from the means of production—such as through colonial conquest or the loss of land to creditors—is known as *primitive accumulation*. It creates the conditions for capitalist production to take place. Each epoch of capitalism has involved waves of outward expansion, primitive accumulation, and commodification; these in their combination constitute the system's master process.

Capitalism is by its very nature an expansionary system. It is expansionary in a double sense. First, commodification has constantly extended outward around the world to new areas that were previously outside the system of commodity production. New territories, peoples, and societies have been forcibly incorporated into world capitalism through this outward expansion. We can call this capitalism's *extensive* enlargement. The principal method through which it has achieved this expansion has been through colonial conquest and imperialism. Second, capitalism expands by constantly deepening commodification. This type of expansion means that human activities that previously remained outside of the logic of capitalist production, or the logic of profit-making, are brought into this logic. For example, when health care and educational systems are public, they are run according to the logic of a social need; to meet the health and educational needs of people. But when these systems are privatized—that is, turned over to private capitalist investors who now "own" them—the provision of health and education is undertaken to generate profits for these investors. If one can pay for them, then these things are provided; if not, they are not accessible. Thus, health care and education become commodities. When such commodity relations penetrate spheres of social life that were formally outside of the logic of profit-making, this represents capitalism's intensive enlargement.

At the very heart of the transition to the new epoch of global capitalism is the near-culmination of the centuries-long process of the spread of capitalist production around the world and its displacement of all precapitalist relations.[3] What I mean by this is that, by the early twenty-first century, the vast majority of peoples around the world had been integrated into the capitalist market and brought into capitalist production relations. There were no longer any countries or regions in the world that remained outside of world capitalism, and there were no longer any precapitalist or noncapitalist modes of production on a significant scale. The final stage of capitalism's *extensive* enlargement began with the wave of colonizations of the late nineteenth and early twentieth centuries and concluded with the (re)incorporation of the former Soviet-bloc and Third World revolutionary states in the early 1990s. Capitalism began a dramatic new *intensive* expansion in the late twentieth century. Nonmarket spheres of human activity—public spheres managed by states, cultural and social spaces, and private spheres linked to community and family—are being broken up, commodified, and transferred to capital. Because globalization does not involve the earlier geographic expansions, such as the colonial conquest of new territories, this type of intensive enlargement of capitalism is not as visible, yet it is no less relentless. Capitalist production relations are coming to replace what remains of all pre-capitalist relations around the globe. With the deepening rather than the enlarging of its domain, capital is in the process of invading and commodifying all those public and private spheres that previously remained outside of its reach.

As capitalism has globalized, it has increasingly eroded national boundaries, and made it structurally impossible for individual nations to sustain independent (or even autonomous) economies, polities, and social structures. Globalization is therefore creating a single, and increasingly undifferentiated, field for world capitalism, leading to the supersession of the nation-state as the organizing principle of capitalism, and with it, of the interstate system, as the framework of capitalist development.[4] Hence, if we are to understand the new epoch, we must adopt a transnational or global perspective. This means moving beyond a focus on the social world emphasizing country-level analysis or an international system comprised of discrete nation-states. As I illustrated in the opening section of this essay, globalization has posed serious difficulties for theories of all sorts, trapped as they are within the straightjacket of what I have termed a *nation-state framework of analysis*.[5]

The communications and information revolution, along with revolutions in transportation, marketing, management, automation, robotization, and so on, are "globalizing" technologies in the sense that they have allowed capital to "go global." Capitalists have come in a double sense to achieve this newfound global mobility in their quest to maximize profits and minimize interference in their profit-making activities, in that the material *and* the political obstacles to freely moving their capital around the world have dramatically come down in recent decades. This global mobility has allowed capitalists to search around the world for the most favorable conditions for different phases of globalized production, and, increasingly, services, including: the cheapest labor; the most favorable institutional environment, such as low taxes and government subsidies; the least regulatory conditions, such as lax environmental and labor laws; and a stable political environment, which often means state repression of independent worker and social movements.

As capital has become transnational it has brought about a transition from a *world economy* to a *global economy*. To put it in simplified terms, in earlier epochs each country developed a national economy, and the different national economies were linked to one another through trade and finances in an integrated international market. This type of a world socioeconomic structure is what I mean by a world economy. Each country developed national circuits of accumulation that were linked externally to other national circuits through commodity exchanges and capital flows in the world market. By circuit of accumulation I mean the process by which the production of a good or a service is first planned and financed (by capitalists), followed by attaining and then mixing together the component parts (labor, raw materials, buildings and machinery, and so on) in production sequences, and then by the marketing of the final product. At the end of this process the capitalist recovers his initial capital outlay as well as profit and has thus "accumulated" capital. This is what Karl Marx referred to as the "circuit of capital." In earlier epochs, much of the circuit was "self-contained" within a single country. But what we have seen in the current epoch is the increasing globalization of the production process itself. Global capital mobility has allowed capital to reorganize production worldwide in accordance with a whole range of considerations that allow for maximizing profit-making opportunities. In this process, national production systems have become fragmented and integrated externally into new globalized circuits of accumulation.

To take the example of the world auto industry, in the previous epoch, auto companies in the United States produced cars from beginning to end, with the exception of the procurement of raw materials, and then exported them to other countries. Japanese and European auto companies did the same in Japan and Europe, as did some Third World countries such as Brazil that set out to establish national industries after independence.[6] But by the late twentieth century, the process of producing a car had become decentralized and fragmented among numerous different phases of production that are dispersed around the world. Individual parts are often manufactured in many different countries, assembly may be stretched out over several countries, and management may be digitally coordinated from a central computer terminal unconnected to actual production sites. The production process has thus become fragmented and geographically dispersed. By the 1990s, the world auto industry had become, in the words of one researcher, a "transnational spider's web . . . stretch[ing] across the globe,"[7] in which auto production processes have become so transnationalized that the final products could no longer be considered "national" products in any meaningful way.

While this globalization of production has entailed the fragmentation and decentralization of complex production chains and the worldwide dispersal and functional integration of the different segments in these chains, it has taken place together with the *centralization* of management and control of the global economy in transnational capital. The distinction between a world economy and a global economy, or the rise of globalized circuits of production and accumulation, is shown in figures 1.1 and 1.2. This emphasis on a globally integrated production and financial system is what distinguishes my approach from what I term *Market Marxism* accounts of globalization, such as that put forward by British political economist Bob Jessop, which emphasize market (trade) integration and often fail to see the more significant underlying productive and capital integration.[8]

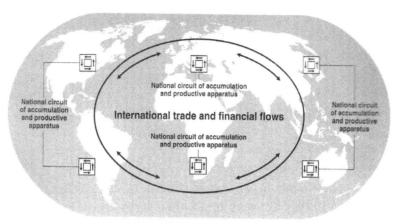

Figure 1.1 The world economy

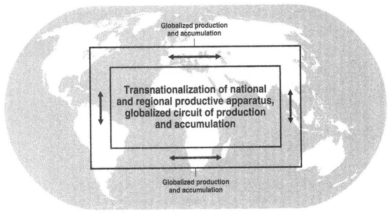

Figure 1.2 The global economy

Global capitalism, therefore, is not a collection of "national" economies but the supersession through transnational integration of "national"
economies understood as autonomous entities related through external
market exchanges to other such entities. Fundamentally, there has been
a progressive dismantling of autonomous national production systems
and their reactivation as constituent elements of an integral world production system. Economic geographer Peter Dicken had already noted
in the 1990s that "until recently, in terms of production, plan, firm and
industry were essentially national phenomena." In recent decades, however, "trade flows have become far more complex . . . transformed into
a highly complex, kaleidoscopic structure involving the *fragmentation*

of many production processes and their *geographic relocation* on a global scale in ways which slice through national boundaries."[9]

At the purely technical level, the reorganization of world production has been made possible by new technologies and organizational innovations that allow for different phases of production, and increasingly services, to be broken down into component phases that are detachable and can be dispersed around the world. As I noted above, new "globalizing" technologies are based on the revolution in information technology, or the convergence of computerization and telecommunications and the emergence of the Internet, and include new transportation technologies such as containerization, intermodal transport, and refrigeration; robotization and other forms of automation; computer aided design and computer aided manufacturing; and so on. In the second decade of the twenty-first century, analysts began to talk of a "fourth industrial revolution" based on yet a new wave of technological development, including three-dimensional printing, artificial intelligence and machine learning, the Internet of things, robotics, blockchain, nanotechnology and biotechnology, quantum computing, autonomous vehicles, and novel forms of energy storage. These technologies promise to bring about a more radical restructuring of the global economy and society in ways that will deepen the processes examined here.[10]

Novel organization forms include, among others, new management techniques, vertical disintegration, "just-in-time" and small-batch production, subcontracting and outsourcing, and formal and informal transnational business alliances. Subcontracting and outsourcing have become extremely widespread and have become a basic organizational feature of economic activity worldwide. In the earlier epochs of capitalism, firms tended to organize entire sequences of economic production, distribution, and service from within. To use again the example of the auto industry, Ford Motor Co. set up its own components, engine, transmission and body factories, other supply operations, engineering and design procedures, and so on. The process of producing a car was vertically integrated and housed within the firm. Under new "flexible" production models, many (in fact, most) of these activities are contracted out to other firms that specialize in one or another activity. The second firm becomes a supplier subcontracted by the first, and can also be subcontracted by other firms. In turn, the subcontracting firm often subcontracts yet another firm, or individual subcontractors, for specific jobs. In this way, the old vertical corporate hierarchy becomes a horizontal network. Moreover, accounting services, design, advertising, financing, marketing, individual production operations, and so forth, are now extensively subcontracted rather than organized inside the typical transnational corporation (TNC). These chains of subcontracting and outsourcing become spread in far-flung networks across the globe. The *maquiladoras*, or offshore sweatshop factories that are the epitome of the "global assembly line," are based on this type of worldwide subcontracting network.

If production was the first economic branch to globalize, followed by finance, we are now moving toward a service-based global economy. Services are increasingly decentralized and subcontracted around the world. The growth of trade in services worldwide has been outstripping that of goods since the 1990s and by 2017 represented some 70 percent of the total gross world product.[11] Let us now look at some of the mechanisms through which capital has been transnationalized.

THE MECHANISMS OF THE TRANSNATIONALIZATION OF CAPITAL

Social scientists have researched the varied mechanisms involved in the transnational interpenetration of national capitals. There is now a considerable and rapidly growing body of empirical evidence that the giant corporate conglomerates that drive the global economy ceased to be corporations of a particular country in the latter part of the twentieth century and increasingly represented transnational capital.[12] Some of these mechanisms are the spread of TNCs and their affiliates; the increase in world trade and the expansion of foreign direct investment; the phenomenal increase in cross-border mergers and acquisitions (M&As); increasing transnational interlocking of boards of directors; increasingly cross- and mutual investment among companies from two or more countries and transnational ownership of capital shares; the spread of cross-border strategic alliances of all sorts; vast global outsourcing and subcontracting networks; the proliferation of free trade zones; and the increasing salience of transnational peak business associations, among others. These patterns of capital transnationalization simply did not exist in earlier decades and centuries. They contribute to the development of worldwide networks that link local capitalists to one another and generate an identity of objective interests and of subjective outlook among these capitalists around a process of global (as opposed to local or national) accumulation.

There has been a sharp increase in the flow of foreign direct investment (FDI) among the nations of the world since the 1960s. FDI refers to the relocation of capital as productive investments by investors in one country into one or more other countries; by definition it transnationalizes production and the capitalists and workers involved. Annual worldwide inflows of FDI went from $54 billion in 1980 to $1.8 trillion in 2015.[13] Perhaps the single most comprehensive indicator of the growth of transnational production is the global stock of FDI, which shot up from $701 billion in 1980 to $25 trillion in 2015.[14] This growth of direct and equity investment flows is part of the integration of world capital markets through the commodification of financial instruments. The global economy is closely associated with the rise of a new globally integrated financial system and with frenzied speculative financial investments, which has earned the new global capitalism the dubious title of "casino capitalism."[15] The rise of a new globally integrated financial system since the 1980s has been truly phenomenal. National financial markets are a thing of the past. National stock markets have ceased to exist in all but name. Financial globalization dates to the 1970s and took off in the following two decades with financial deregulation and the introduction of information technologies that allowed for 24-hour financial transactions in real time around the world.

World trade has experienced a similar phenomenal growth. The total value of world merchandise trade went from $2 trillion in 1980 to $16.6 trillion in 2015. This trade, moreover, far outstripped the growth in world production, meaning that an ever-greater percentage of what the world produces is traded across national borders rather than consumed within these borders. Global exports as a share of world output, in fact, increased from 10 percent in 1960 to 30 percent in 2014.[16] These figures do not include trade in services—the fastest growing sector of the global economy—which went from $2.7 trillion in 2005 to $4.8 trillion in 2015.

A key indicator of the rise of the TCC and its agents is the spread of TNCs. *Transnational corporations* are defined as firms with headquarters in more than three countries, which makes them distinct from multinational corporations. The ability of TNCs to plan, organize, coordinate, and control activities across countries makes them central agents of globalization. The number of TNCs increased from 7,000 in 1970 to 104,000 by 2010.[17] These TNCs accounted for some two-thirds of world trade, and their sales climbed from $2.5 trillion in 1982 to $36.7 trillion in 2015.[18] As of 2013, nearly 900,000 affiliates of TNCs produced goods and services estimated at $34 trillion,[19] which represented 45 percent of the entire world economic output. "Corporate nationality, and with it the nationality of investors in and owners of foreign affiliates, is becoming increasingly blurred," noted the United Nations Conference on Trade and Development in a 2016 report. "The result is ever 'deeper' corporate structures (with affiliates ever further removed from corporate headquarters in chains of ownership), dispersed shareholdings of affiliates (with individual affiliates being owned indirectly through multiple shareholders), cross shareholdings (with affiliates owning shares in each other), and shared ownerships (e.g. in joint ventures)."[20]

The concentration and centralization of capital is a fundamental tendency of accumulation under capitalism. It is part of the very process of capitalist development and was an integral aspect in an earlier period of national class formation and the rise of national bourgeoisies. The great merger wave of the early twentieth century swept through every advanced capitalist country and was viewed at that time as representing a qualitatively new capitalist reality, resulting in the concentration and centralization of *national* capitals, evermore centralized national conglomerates of capital competing against foreign rivals. Out of that earlier merger wave, competitive capitalism gave way to the age of corporate or monopoly capitalism, characterized by the consolidation of national corporations and markets and the rise of powerful national capitalist classes.[21]

Since the 1980s, global M&As have had a similar importance for the rise of a transnational bourgeoisie. M&As occur when an enterprise acquires control over the whole or a part of the business of another enterprise. In the case of mergers, *cross-border* means the integration of capitals from at least two distinct countries. In an acquisition, it means that a given firm incorporates a foreign company with its employees, managers, and "national" interests. Some cross-border acquisitions involve the merger of TNCs, but much of them entail the acquisition of national companies by TNCs, which draws local class groups and social forces into the transnationalization process.

The value of cross-border M&As, a mere $6 billion in 1980, surpassed $1 trillion in 1999 before leveling off in 2015 at $720 billion.[22] The number of cross-border M&As jumped from a mere fourteen in 1980 to 9,655 in the peak year 1999.[23] Cross-border M&As have involved not just the most globalized sectors of the world economy, such as telecommunications, finances, and autos, but also mega-retailers, companies trading in primary commodities, petroleum, farming and foods, chemicals, steel, pharmaceuticals, and numerous services (entertainment, media and television, legal firms, insurance, management, and utilities).

The rise of national bourgeoisies in the nineteenth and twentieth centuries involved the spread of national-level interlocking directorates that congealed the objective links and the subjective identity of national capitalist classes. In his study on the growth of transnational corporate board interlocks, sociologist William Carroll finds that "transnational interlocking became less the preserve of a few internationally well-connected companies, and more a practice in which nearly half of the world's largest firms participate." He shows how "transnational corporate networks" have emerged that bring together corporate executives with policy planning bodies and other civil society forums.[24]

The astonishing spread since the late 1970s of diverse new economic arrangements that I noted above—outsourcing, subcontracting, transnational intercorporate alliances, licensing agreements, joint ventures, equity swaps, long-term sourcing agreements, and so on—have resulted in vast transnational production chains and complex webs of vertical and horizontal integration across the globe. According to Dicken:

> TNCs are also locked into *external* networks of relationships with a myriad of other firms: transnational and domestic, large and small, public and private. It is through such interconnections, for example, that a very small firm in one country may be directly linked into a global production network, whereas most small firms serve only a very restricted geographic area. Such inter-relationships between firms of different sizes and types increasingly span national boundaries to create a set of *geographically nested relationships from local to global scales* .... There is, in fact, a bewildering variety of interorganizational *collaborative* relationships. These are frequently multilateral rather than bilateral, polygamous rather than monogamous.[25]

There are other less researched mechanisms that facilitate transnational capitalist integration, such as the spread of stock exchanges in most countries of the world linked to the global financial system. The spread of these stock markets from the principal centers of the world economy to most capital cities around the world, combined with twenty-four hour trading, facilitates an ever greater global trading and hence transnational ownership of shares. There are now stock exchanges in some 120 countries, from Afghanistan and Vietnam to Bangalore in India, from Botswana and Nigeria to the capitals of all five Central American republics. While many of these stock exchanges are limited in their offerings these exchanges are integrated with one another either directly or indirectly. An Argentine can channel investment through the Buenos Aires stock exchange into companies from around the world, while investors from around the world can channel their investment into Argentina through the Buenos Aires stock exchange.

Beyond stock exchanges, investors anywhere in the world need no more than Internet access to invest their money through globalized financial circuits into mutual and hedge funds, bonds markets, currency swaps, and so on. The global integration of national financial systems and new forms of money capital, including secondary derivative markets, has also made it easier for capital ownership to transnationalize. The network of stock exchanges, the computerized nature of global trading, and the integration of national financial systems into a single global system allow capital in its money form to move with almost no friction at all through the arteries of the global economy and society.

FROM FORDISM TO FLEXIBLE ACCUMULATION AND CAPITAL'S LIBERATION FROM THE NATION-STATE

Despite the importance of technology and organizational innovation, globalization is not driven by a technological determinism, as technology is not causal to social change but a dependent variable. What has caused the dynamic of economic globalization is the drive, built into capitalism itself by competition and class struggle, to outcompete and to maximize profits by reducing labor and other costs of production. A study of globalization is fundamentally *historical*, in that social processes or conditions (such as globalization) can be conceived in terms of previous social processes and conditions that gave rise to them. The world capitalist crisis that began in the 1970s followed a lengthy period of worldwide class struggle, including anti-colonial and socialist movements, from the 1890s into the 1970s. Those struggles led in the wake of the Great Depression and World War II to a particular model of capitalism known as *Fordism-Keynesianism*.

Fordism refers to a way of organizing the economy that was associated with a large number of easily organizable workers in centralized production locations; mass production through fixed, standardized processes; and mass consumption. It was known as *Fordism* because it became generalized following the lead of the automobile tycoon Henry Ford. Ford argued that capitalists and governments should stabilize the national industrial capitalist systems that had emerged in the previous century by incorporating workers into the new society through higher salaries, benefits, and secure (tenured) employment coupled with tight control and regimentation of the workforce (although Ford himself was a bitterly anti-union industrial tyrant). Ford's initial shop-floor changes grew into Fordism as a "class compromise" between workers and capitalists mediated by the state, involving government measures to regulate capitalist competition and the class struggle.

Fordism combined with Keynesianism in the post-World War II social order. The British economist John Keynes had broken with the assumption of classical economic theory that the natural state of the capitalist economy was an equilibrium brought about by market forces allowed to operate unimpeded. Keynes observed that the market on its own could not generate sufficient aggregate demand and argued that such demand had to be fomented in order to avoid more crises like the 1930s depression. His demand-side economic strategy emphasized state intervention through credit and employment creation, progressive taxation, and government spending on public works and social programs to generate demand and other mechanisms for regulating (and therefore stabilizing) accumulation. In this way, governments could overcome crises, assure long-term growth and employment, and stabilize capitalist society.

The Keynesian revolution swept through the industrialized capitalist world and formed the basis for economic policy for much of the twentieth century. Fordism-Keynesianism took a wide range of forms around the world in the twentieth century, referred to in its diverse manifestations and in popular parlance as "New Deal capitalism," "welfare capitalism," "social capitalism," "social democracy," "Third World developmentalism," and so on. The key points here is that Fordism-Keynesianism involved a *logic of redistribution*, for instance, through minimum wage laws and labor protections, public spending on social services, progressive taxation, unemployment and welfare benefits, and public sector enterprises and services. This logic of redistribution fundamentally conditioned the process of capitalist production, or the accumulation of capital in the twentieth century. In the first place, this redistribution came about not because of the generosity of capitalists but because of fierce social and class struggles as well as anti-colonial and national liberation struggles around the world that "forced" capital into this "class compromise," putting a check on the unbridled power of capital over labor and the popular classes as mass popular struggles heated up around the world in the 1960s and 1970s.

In the wake of the 1970s crisis of the Fordist–Keynesian model, capital went global as a strategy of the emergent TCC and its political representatives to reconstitute its class power by breaking free of nation-state constraints to accumulation. This liberation of capital from the nation-state helped free the TCC from the compromises and commitments placed on it by the working classes and popular social forces in the nation-state phase of capitalism. Transnational capital was able to take advantage of newfound mobility and new forms of globalized spatial organization of social processes discussed above to break the power of territorial-bound organized labor—to roll back wages, break trade unions, disorganize the working class, impose austerity, privatize public sectors, and on. Globalization shifted the worldwide correlation of class and social forces in the late twentieth century in favor of the TCC. It dramatically altered (at least momentarily) the balance of forces among classes and social groups in each nation of the world and at a global level toward the emergent TCC.

The attack on the working and popular classes involved a new capital–labor relation based on the fragmentation and flexibilization of labor. The Fordist–Keynesian model has been replaced by what is known as *flexible accumulation*. This new model involves the organizational changes I have already discussed, such as global decentralization, "just in time" production, subcontracting and outsourcing both within and across countries. However, at the heart of flexible accumulation is a new capital–labor relation based on making workers flexible, casualized, or precarious. Workers in the global economy are themselves under these flexible arrangements, increasingly treated as a subcontracted component rather than a fixture internal to employer organizations. In this new capital–labor relation, labor is increasingly only a naked commodity, no longer embedded in relations of reciprocity rooted in social and political communities that have historically been institutionalized in nation-states. Each laborer is expected to negotiate himself or herself as a commodity, to become a seller "freed" from political or social constraints, an "entrepreneur" of himself or herself as the owner of a commodity.

The new systems of labor control span subcontracting and contract labor, labor outsourcing, part-time and temporary work, informal work, home-work, and the revival of patriarchal, "sweatshop," and other oppressive production relations. Well-known trends associated with the restructuring of the capital–labor relation include "downward leveling," deunionization, "ad hoc" and "just-in-time" labor supply, the superexploitation of immigrant communities as a counterpart to capital export, the lengthening of the working day, the rise of a new global "underclass" of supernumeraries or "redundants"—what I call *surplus humanity*—subject to new forms of social control and even to genocide, and new gendered and racialized hierarchies among labor. Millions of people around the world have been wrenched from their communities and their means of production, proletarianized, and thrown into a global labor market that transnational capital has been able to shape. Global class formation has involved the accelerated division of the world into a global bourgeoisie and a global proletariat. The global working class is increasingly a *precariat*—a proletariat that labors in precarious conditions.[26] According to the International Labor Organization, more than half of all workers in the world labor under precarious, or "vulnerable," employment arrangements.[27] Most workers around the world have always worked in precarious conditions. What has changed from the twentieth to the twenty-first century is that precariousness is again become the "normal" (normative) form of the capital–labor relation.

The rise of a new global proletariat is potentially a tremendously positive development, seen from the perspective of workers and the poor, as Hardt and Negri point out in their provocative study, *Empire*, because it opens up new potentialities of resistance and emancipation. But the challenge is how to achieve this potential.[28] The exclusionary processes of globalization, especially post-Fordist restructuring and the new capital–labor relation, forces workers within and across countries to compete with one another and fragments large sectors of the global working class. A transnational working class is increasingly a reality, a *class-in-itself*, meaning that it objectively exists within the structure of the global economy. But this emerging global proletariat it is not yet *for-itself*, meaning that it has not necessarily developed a consciousness of itself as a transnational class, constructed an identity or organized itself as such because of the continued existence of the nation-state. In sum, global class formation involves the increasing division of the world into a global bourgeoisie and a global proletariat, even though global labor remains highly stratified along old and new social hierarchies that cut across national boundaries and has brought changes in the relationship between dominant and subordinate classes around the world, with consequent implications as well for world politics, working class, and social justice struggles.

THE GLOBAL RULING CLASS

Marx and Engels spoke in the prescient passages of *The Communist Manifesto* of the essential global nature of the capitalist system and of the drive of the bourgeoisie to expand its transformative reach around the world. "The need of a constantly expanding market for its products chases the bourgeoisie over the whole surface of the globe," they argued, in perhaps one of the most oft-quoted passage in world literature. "It must nestle everywhere, settle everywhere, establish connexions everywhere."[29] But for Marx, and for many Marxists after him, the bourgeoisie is a global agent who is *organically national* in the sense that its development takes place within the bounds of specific nation-states and is by fiat a nation-state-based class. Early twentieth century theories of imperialism, such as those advanced by V.I. Lenin and his fellow Bolsheviks, established the Marxist analytical framework of rival national capitals, a framework carried by subsequent political economists into the latter twentieth century through theories of dependency and the world system, radical international relations theory, and studies of US intervention.

According to this perspective, the capitalist class is organized through the distinct political boundaries of nation-states. The competition among capitals that is inherent to the system therefore takes the form of competition (as well as cooperation, depending on the circumstances of the moment) among capitalist groups of different nation-states, and is expressed as interstate competition, rivalry, and even war. As I discuss in Chapter 5, these earlier theories of imperialism were not "wrong." They were developed to explain actual world historic events, such as the two twentieth-century world wars, and to orient practice, such as national revolutions in the Third World seen as directed against particular imperialist countries. The problem was not that these theories stepped outside of history—to the contrary, they were theoretical abstractions from actual historical reality. In fact, much of the dynamics of international relations and world development over the past five centuries can be explained by these dynamics of interstate rivalries and national capitalist competition.

Rather, the problem is when we extrapolate a transhistoric conclusion regarding the dynamics of international relations and world class formation from a certain historic period in the development of capitalism. What I mean by this is that there is no reason to assume that the nation-state is the only possible political form for organizing social life in the capitalist system and in the modern era. And neither is there any reason to assume that social classes—and specifically the capitalist class—are necessarily organized along national lines. That they have been until recently is something which must be problematized, that is, explained with reference to how the course of history actually unfolded and not by reference to some abstract law or principle of the capitalist system and the modern world.

The leading capitalist strata worldwide are crystallizing into a TCC. The new transnational bourgeoisie or capitalist class comprises the owners of transnational capital, that is, the group that owns the leading worldwide means of production as embodied principally in the TNCs and private financial institutions. This class is *trans*national because it is tied to globalized circuits of production, marketing, and finances unbound from particular national territories and identities, and because its interests lie in global over local or national accumulation. The TCC therefore can be located in the global class structure by its ownership and/ or control of transnational capital. What distinguishes the TCC from national or local capitalists is that it is involved in globalized production and manages globalized circuits of accumulation that give it an objective class existence and identity spatially and politically in the global system above any local territories and polities. Transnational capital constitutes the "commanding heights" of the global economy. The members of the TCC are the owners of the major productive resources of the world. As the agent of the global economy, transnational capital has become the hegemonic fraction of capital on a world scale. The *hegemonic fraction of capital* is that fraction which imposes the general direction and character on production worldwide and conditions the social, political, and cultural character of capitalist society worldwide.

The TCC is represented by a class-conscious transnational elite, made up of an inner circle of transnational capitalists, along with transnational managers, bureaucrats, technicians, and leading ideologues and intellectuals in the service of the TCC. This inner circle has become increasingly organized in transnational political, corporate, policy planning, and cultural forums. Particularly notable in this regard is the World Economic Forum, an exclusive transnational policy planning institution made up of TNC executives, leading transnationally oriented politicians, media moguls, and cultural elites that holds its famed annual meetings in Davos, Switzerland. At the level of agency, the TCC, as represented by its inner circles, leading representatives, and politicized elements, has become conscious of its transnationality. The TCC is in this regard a *class-in-itself* and *for-itself.* Since the 1980s, it has pursued a class project of capitalist globalization, as reflected in its global decision-making and the rise of a transnational state apparatus under the auspices of this fraction, as I discuss in the next chapter. The TCC is the new global ruling class.

To summarize: The logic of global accumulation, rather than national accumulation, guides the political and economic behavior of the TCC. The politicized leadership of the TCC has attempted to forge a global ruling bloc, or globalist bloc. The bloc brings the TCC together with major forces in the dominant political parties, media conglomerates, and technocratic elites and state managers in both North and South, along with select organic intellectuals and charismatic figures who provide ideological legitimacy and technical solutions. Below this transnational elite are a small and shrinking layer of middle classes that exercise very little real power but that—pacified with mass consumption—form a fragile buffer between the transnational elite and the world's poor majority.

All this is *not* to say that there is a single TCC and that all capitalists belong to it. There are still local, national, and regional capitalists, and there will be for a long time to come. But they must "de-localize" and link to transnational capital if they are to survive. Territorially restricted capital cannot compete with its transnationally mobile counterpart. To paraphrase the academic slogan "publish or perish," in the case of global capitalism, capitalists in any part of the world beyond the smallest of scale find that they must "globalize or perish." The existence of multiple, overlapping, and competing forms of capital around the world generates complex relationships among them that may be contradictory and conflictive and that may also express themselves as *inter*-national tensions to the extent that national governments are subject to pressure from competing groups. Competing TCC groups can and do turn to states to gain advantage in this competitive struggle, and states are indeed overwhelmed by the pressures placed on them by transnational capital. This new situation, in which states are subject to multiple pressures from competing capitalist groups that are now transnational as well as from national and regional capitals, and from electorates and other constituencies, can lead to bewildering political dynamics and contributes to crises of state legitimacy, as I discuss in later chapters.

The transnational bourgeoisie is not a unified group. "The same conditions, the same contradiction, the same interests necessarily called forth on the whole similar customs everywhere," noted Marx and Engels in discussing the formation of new class groups. "But separate individuals form a class only insofar as they have to carry on a common battle against another class; otherwise they are on hostile terms with each other as competitors."[30] Fierce competition among oligopolist clusters, conflicting pressures, and differences over the tactics and strategy of maintaining class domination and addressing the crises and contradictions of global capitalism make any real internal unity in the global ruling class impossible. In fact, at every which way, the TCC is wracked by conflicts that swirl around at every level. By the second decade of the twenty-first century, the crisis of TCC rule reached explosive proportions, a theme we will return to in several chapters to come.

THE TRANSNATIONAL ELITE AGENDA

The contradictory logics of national and global accumulation are expressed in distinct political projects in countries around the world. The interests of national fractions of dominant groups lie in national accumulation, including the whole set of traditional national regulatory and protectionist mechanisms, while transnational fractions find that their interests are advanced through an expanding global economy based on worldwide market liberalization. These two fractions have vied for control of local state apparatuses since the 1970s, and local states have become battlegrounds for completing nationally and transnationally oriented dominant groups. Transnational fractions of local elites and capitalist classes swept to power in countries around the world in the 1980s and 1990s. They clashed in their bid for hegemony with nationally based class fractions. They won control over the "commanding heights" of state policymaking—key ministries and bureaucracies in the policymaking apparatus, especially central banks and finance and foreign ministries, as key government branches which link countries to the global economy.

Transnational blocs became hegemonic in the 1980s and 1990s in the vast majority of countries in the world and set out to transform their countries, using national state apparatuses to advance globalization and to restructure and integrate into the global economy. In this process, they established formal and informal liaison mechanisms between the national state structures and transnational state apparatuses. As the transnational ruling bloc emerged in the 1980s and 1990s, it carried out a "revolution from above" aimed at promoting the most propitious conditions around the world for the unfettered operation of the new global capitalist production system. They set about to dismantle the old nation-state-based Keynesian welfare and developmentalist projects and sought worldwide market liberalization, projects of economic integration such as the North American Free Trade Agreement (NAFTA), the Asia-Pacific Economic Cooperation forum, and the European Union; and they promoted a supranational infrastructure of the global economy, such as the World Trade Organization. The number of free trade agreements worldwide jumped from some seventy in 1980 to 659 in 2017.[31]

This global restructuring came to be know as *neoliberalism*, a doctrine of laissez-faire capitalism legitimated by the assumptions of neoclassical economics and modernization theory, by the doctrine of comparative advantage, and by the globalist rhetoric of free trade, growth, efficiency, and prosperity. Global neoliberalism has involved twin dimensions, rigorously pursued by global elites with the backing of a powerful and well-organized lobby of transnational corporations. One is worldwide market liberalization and the construction of a new legal and regulatory superstructure for the global economy. The other is the internal restructuring and global integration of each national economy. The combination of the two—policies such as deregulation, privatization, trade liberalization ("free trade"), regressive taxation, integration agreements, and social austerity—was intended to break down all national barriers to the free movement of transnational capital *between* borders and the free operation of capital *within* borders. The neoliberal model thus facilitated the subordination and integration of each national economy into the global economy. Greased by neoliberalism, global capitalism tears down all nonmarket structures that have in the past placed limits on, or acted as a protective layer against, the accumulation of capital. By prying open and making accessible to transnational capital every layer of the social fabric, neoliberalism has disembedded the global economy from global society, and the state cedes to the market as the sole organizing power in the economic and social sphere.

However, cracks in the neoliberal consensus had become apparent by the close of the century in the face of the deep social contradictions generated by the model, including unprecedented inequalities, escalating social conflicts, political crises, and warfare. If one set of conflicts was between fractions of dominant groups, a second was among subordinate groups and classes as globalization altered their traditional patterns of social mobilization, political identity, and livelihood. Popular class organizations and grassroots social movements became sites of intense struggle between fractions as globalization created new cleavages and eroded earlier loyalties and identities, particularly those constructed on corporatist models of subordinate class incorporation characteristic of national capitalism in Latin America and other Third World zones. Global elites have pursued their transnational agenda amidst sharp social struggles and multiple forms of resistance from subordinate groups and also from dominant groups not brought into the emerging global capitalist bloc. But the principal social contradiction in global capitalism is still between dominant and subordinate classes. The financial collapse of 2008 revealed the fragile and crisis-ridden nature of the new global capitalism as the hegemony of ruling groups appeared to collapse.

The hope of humanity now lies with a measure of transnational social governance over the process of global production and reproduction, the first step in effecting a radical redistribution of wealth and power to poor majorities. This means, ultimately, that the logic of capital accumulation, the organization of global society in order to generate endless profit for transnational capital, must be replaced by the logic of meeting human needs—the logic of the poor, laboring majority of humanity. This *democratization of global society* can only be accomplished by wresting from transnational capital and its agents their control over the material and cultural resources of humanity and the enormous power that control brings. If we are to face the crisis of global capitalism and the perils that

it represents for humanity, from never-ending wars to mass immiseration and ecological holocaust, the new global proletariat must lead the
global counterhegemonic struggle *against* transnational capital that has
been breaking out everywhere and develop it into a global struggle *for* a
democratic socialist alternative.

FOUR

THE NATION-STATE AND THE TRANSNATIONAL STATE

In recent decades, it has become fashionable for writers on globalization to produce quotes from top-level global capitalists on their views regarding the "end of the nation-state" and the stateless corporation. The following remarks by Carl A. Gerstacker, CEO of Dow Chemical, are typical of such sentiments: "I have long dreamed of buying an island owned by no nation and of establishing the World Headquarters of the Dow Company on the truly neutral ground of such an island, beholden to no nation or society."[1] If the transnational capitalist class is increasingly detached from particular territories and from the old political and social projects of nation-states, does this not imply that this new global ruling class is stateless? Are transnational corporations really *state*less? Or are they *nation*less? Indeed, are *state* and *nation* the same thing?

The emergence of the global economy and the rise of a politically active transnational capitalist class cannot be understood apart from transnational state apparatuses. In pursuing its project of an integrated global economy and society, the transnational capitalist class has articulated its economic interests with political aims. This is what I referred to in the previous chapter as *the transnational elite agenda*, aimed at creating the most favorable conditions for global capitalism to function. To advance that agenda, it has had to rely on political instruments that I refer to here as *transnational state apparatuses*. In this essay, I present an historical materialist analysis of the transnationalization of the state. Some of what Marx had to say about the world in his day no longer applies. But the historical materialist method that he developed based on knowledge grounded in praxis (the unity of theory and practice) is not restricted to particular historical circumstances of his day. Indeed, historical materialism is emancipatory precisely because it allows us to cut though the reification that results from naturalizing historical arrangements and to reveal the historical specificity of existing social forms.

The debate on globalization and the state has been misframed. Either the state is seen as no longer important, as in diverse "end of the nation-state" theses, or it is seen as retaining its primacy as the axis of international relations and world development. But it is not either-or. To suggest so is to fall in a dualist construct that posits separate logics for a globalizing economy and a nation-state-based political system. By *dualism*, I mean the division of something conceptually into two opposed or contrasted aspects, or the state of being so divided. For instance, humans and nature are often discussed in dualist terms, as if they are separate or independent of each other. And the global and the national (or the local) are similarly too often discussed in this dualist manner. Dualism is always suspicious (and anti-dialectic) because it negates the interconnections among things that give them an essential internal unity. The global economy and the political system are not separate and independent of one another. They form part of a larger unity and must be understood in relation to one another.

In critiquing and moving beyond the global–national dualism, I put forward three interrelated propositions:

1. Economic globalization has its counterpart in transnational class formation and in the emergence of a transnational state that has been brought into existence to function as the collective authority for a global ruling class.
2. The nation-state neither retains its primacy nor disappears; rather, it becomes transformed and absorbed into this larger structure of a transnational state.
3. This emergent transnational state institutionalizes a new class relation between labor and capital worldwide.

Exploring these issues is important for popular struggles and socialist politics today. Globalization is anything but a peaceful process. It has involved protracted and bloody social conflict. As an open-ended process, it is highly contested from below and subject to alterations in its course. By the second decade of the twenty-first century, global capitalism was in deep crisis. But strategies for an alternative "globalization from below" must involve a critique that identifies how capitalist globalization has unfolded, the contradictions it confronts, and new sites of political contestation, such as the transnational state.

GLOBALIZATION: THE LATEST STAGE OF CAPITALISM

Globalization represents an epochal shift in world capitalism. The new global order is characterized by the rise of a globally integrated production and financial system, the rise of a transnational capitalist class, emergent transnational state apparatuses, and new forms of inequality and domination worldwide. Economic globalization has been well researched. Capital has achieved a newfound global mobility and is reorganizing production worldwide in search of maximizing profit-making opportunities. Production has been decentralized worldwide even as command and control of the global economy has been centralized in the hands of the transnational capitalist class. In this process, national economies become fragmented and integrated into new globalized circuits of accumulation. The increasing dissolution of space barriers in the new global economy and subordination of the logic of geography to that of production compel us to reconsider the geography and the politics of the nation-state.

The political reorganization of world capitalism has lagged behind its economic reorganization. There is a disjuncture between economic globalization and the political institutionalization of new social relations unfolding under globalization. Nevertheless, as the material basis of human society changes, so too does its institutional organization. From the seventeenth century treaties of Westphalia that originally established the nation-state/interstate system into the 1960s, capitalism unfolded through a system of nation-states that generated national structures, institutions, and agents and also led much of humanity to develop a national consciousness as people came to identify themselves and to experience the world emotionally and cognitively as members of a particular nation-state. Globalization has increasingly eroded these national boundaries and made it structurally impossible for individual nations to sustain independent, or even autonomous, economies, polities, and social structures even as national consciousness has tenaciously persisted. A key feature of the current epoch is the supersession of the nation-state as the organizing principle of capitalism, and with it, of the interstate system as the institutional framework of capitalist development.[2] What I mean by the supersession of the nation-state as the organizing principle of capitalism is that as the commanding heights of capital have become integrated transnationally, capital no longer organizes itself into competing national capitals and nation-states that drive capitalist development. In turn, this capitalist development takes place in emergent transnational space and through "rescaling" so that the most significant "spaces of capital" are no longer organized as a nation-state/interstate system. Moreover, there are no longer any countries or regions that remain outside of world capitalism, any pre-capitalist zones of significance that can still be colonized, or autonomous accumulation outside of the sphere of global capital.

It is a sociological law that a set of social relations must become institutionalized in order to be sustained. So how are the social relations of global capitalism institutionalized and reproduced? To answer this question we must make a theoretical excursion. The nation-state centrism of many established paradigms impedes our understanding of the dynamics of change under globalization. The literature on globalization is full of discussion on the increasing significance of supranational or transnational institutions. However, what these diverse accounts share is a nation-state centrism that entraps them in a global-national dualism. This dualism stems from the conception of the state put forward by the early twentieth century sociologist Max Weber. The way out of the dualist approach to globalization and the state is to move beyond Weber and to return to an historical materialist conception of the state. I ask the reader to follow a certain level of abstraction in the next few pages. This is followed by an historical and empirical discussion on how the transnational state has operated that demonstrates the importance of the theoretical excursion.

THEORIZING THE TRANSNATIONAL STATE: FROM WEBER TO MARX

Weber defined the state as a set of cadre and institutions that exercise authority, a "legitimate monopoly of coercion," over a given territory. Markets for Weber were where economic agents interacted outside of the state. In his explicitly dualist approach, the political (states) and the economic (markets) are externally related, separate and even oppositional, spheres, each with its own independent logic.[3] This state-market dualism has become the dominant framework for analysis of globalization and the state. State officials confront the implications of economic globalization and footloose transnational capital as an external logic.[4] In this dualism, economic globalization is analyzed as if it is independent of the institutions that structure the social relations of the global economy—in particular, states and the nation-state. In other words, separate logics are posited for a globalizing economy and a nation-state-based political system.[5]

The way out of this dualism is to move beyond Weber and return to a historical materialist conception of the state. In the Marxist conception, the state is the institutionalization of class relations around a particular configuration of social production. The separation of the economic from the political for the first time under capitalism accords each an autonomy—and implies a complex relationship that must be problematized—but also generates the illusion of independent externally related spheres. In the historical materialist conception, the economic and the political are distinct moments (or dimensions) of the same totality. The political arena is shaped by its relationship to the economy, and the economy is constituted in relation to the political sphere of the larger totality of the social whole. Under capitalism, the relation between the economy, or social production relations, and states as sets of institutionalized class relations that adhere to those production relations, is an *internal* one.

In this dialectical approach, an *internal relation* is one in which each part is constituted in its relation to the other, so that one cannot exist without the other and only has meaning when seen within the relation, whereas an *external relation* is one in which each part has an existence independent of its relation to the other.[6] (Viewing something as externally related is often related to viewing something in a dualist manner, as discussed above.) For example, antagonistic social classes are internally related, in that "slave" only has meaning in relation to "slave owner," or "worker" only has meaning in relation to "capitalist."

This is to say that the state is internally related to society, to the social forces and structures that make up society. The task of analysis is to uncover the complex of social processes and relations that embed states in the configuration of civil society and political economy. Civil society refers to the diverse sets of nonstate institutions that make up society, ranging from the church, to news media, social clubs, professional associations, and private businesses (everything between the state and the family). The analytical task at hand is to uncover how states are deeply nested in civil society. Relatedly, there is nothing in the historical materialist conception of the state that necessarily ties it to territory or to nation-states. That capitalism has historically assumed a geographic expression and a particular nation-state form is something that must be problematized.

So how, in the Marxist conception, is the state nested in civil society? A fundamental aspect of civil society is its class relations: the division of the population into distinct classes that are internally related. These class relations shape the state. States as coercive systems of authority are class relations and social practices congealed and operationalized through institutions. In Marx's view, the state gives a political form to economic institutions and production relations. "Since the state is the form in which the individuals of a ruling class assert their common interests, and in which the whole civil society of an epoch is epitomized," argued Marx and Engels in *The German Ideology*. "It follows that the state mediates in the formation of all common institutions and that the institutions receive a political form."[7] Marx's discussion of so-called primitive accumulation in his work *Capital* (Book VIII) highlights the role of the state in facilitating the conditions for new economic and social relations. Here I want to highlight the role of the transnational state in facilitating the conditions for the new types of economic and social relations developing under globalization.

Markets are the sites of material life; states spring from economic (production) relations and represent the institutionalization of social relations of domination. Consequently, the economic globalization of capital cannot be a phenomenon isolated from the transformation of class relations and of states. In the Weberian conception, states are by definition territorially bound institutions and therefore a transnational state cannot be conceived as long as the nation-state system persists. Weberian state theory reduces the state to the states apparatus and its cadre and thereby reifies the state. Yet states are not actors as such. Social classes and groups are historical actors. States do not "do" anything per se. Social classes and groups acting in and out of states (and other institutions) "do" things as collective historical agents. State apparatuses are those instruments that enforce and reproduce the class relations and practices embedded in states.

The institutional structures of nation-states may persist in the epoch of globalization—in fact, they remain highly visible and salient—but globalization requires that we modify our conception of these structures. A transnational state apparatus is emerging under globalization from within the system of nation-states. What is required is a return to an historical materialist theoretical conceptualization of the state, not as a "thing" but as a specific social relation inserted into larger social structures that may take different, and historically determined, institutional forms, only one of which is the nation-state.

To summarize and recapitulate: A state is the congealment of a particular and historically determined constellation of class forces and relations, and states are always embodied in sets of political institutions. Hence, the state is (a) a moment of class power relations and (b) a set of political institutions (an "apparatus"). The state is not one or the other; it is *both* in their unity. The separation of these two dimensions is purely methodological. (Weber's mistake is to reduce the state to an apparatus.) National states arose as particular embodiments of the constellations of social groups and classes that developed within the system of nation-states in the earlier epochs of capitalism and became grounded in particular geographies.[8]

What then is a transnational state? Concretely, what is (a) the moment of class power relations and (b) the set of political institutions, or the apparatus of a transnational state? The transnational state is not a global government and not a single institution. It is an analytical abstraction. The transnational state is a particular constellation of class forces and relations bound up with capitalist globalization and the rise of a transnational capitalist class, embodied in a diverse set of political institutions. These institutions are transformed national states plus diverse supranational institutions that serve to institutionalize the domination of this class as the hegemonic fraction of capital worldwide. Hence, the state as a class relation is becoming transnationalized. The class practices of a new global ruling class are becoming "condensed" (to use the term of Greek political sociologist Nicos Poulantzas) in an emergent transnational state. According to Poulantzas, the state is "the *specific material condensation* of a relationship of forces among classes and class fractions."[9]

The transnational state comprises those institutions and practices in global society that maintain, defend, and advance the emergent hegemony of a global bourgeoisie and its project of constructing a new globalist bloc. This transnational state apparatus is an emerging network that comprises transformed and externally integrated national states, together with the supranational economic and political forums and that has not yet acquired—and may never acquire—any centralized institutional form. The rise of a transnational state entails the reorganization of the state in each nation—I henceforth refer to these states of each country as *national states*—and it involves simultaneously the rise of truly supranational economic and political institutions. These two processes— the transformation of nation-states and the rise of supranational institutions—are not separate or mutually exclusive. In fact, they are twin dimensions of the process of the transnationalization of the state. Under globalization the national state does *not* "wither away" but becomes transformed with respect to its functions and becomes a functional component of a larger transnational state.

The transnational state apparatus is multilayered and multicentered, linking together functionally institutions that exhibit distinct gradations of "state-ness" and which have different histories and trajectories. The supranational organizations are economic and political, formal and informal. The economic forums include the International Monetary Fund, the World Bank, the Bank for International Settlements, the World Trade Organization (WTO), regional banks such as the Inter-American Development Bank and the Asian Development Bank,[10] and so on. Supranational political forums include the Group of 7 (G7) and the more recently formed Group of 20, among others, as well as more formal forums such as the distinct agencies of the United Nations system, the Organization of Economic Cooperation and Development, the European Union, the Conference on Security and Cooperation in Europe, and so on. They also include regional groupings such as the Association of South East Asian Nations and the supranational juridical, administrative, and regulatory structures established through regional agreements such as the North American Free Trade Agreement (NAFTA) and the Asia-Pacific Economic Cooperation forum.

Since the 1980s, these supranational institutions have appeared to play an ever greater role in policy development and global management and administration of the global economy. The function of the nation-state has been shifting from the formulation of national policies to the administration of policies formulated through supranational institutions. However, it is essential is to avoid the national–global duality: national states are *not* external to the transnational state but are becoming incorporated into it as component parts. The supranational organizations function in consonance with transformed national states. The transnational functionaries who staff supranational organizations have as counterparts the transnational functionaries who staff transformed national states. These transnational state cadre act as midwives of capitalist globalization.

The transnational state is attempting to fulfill the functions for world capitalism that in earlier periods were fulfilled by what world-system and international relations scholars refer to as a *hegemon*, or a dominant capitalist power that has the resources and the structural position that allows it to organize world capitalism as a whole and impose the rules, regulatory environment, and so on that allows the system to function. The global ruling class and its political and technocratic agents have attempted to create a transnational hegemony through supranational structures that have not proved to be capable of providing the economic regulation and political conditions for the reproduction of global capitalism nor to resolve its explosive contradictions, as I discuss later.

Just as the national state played this role in the earlier period, the transnational state has sought to create and maintain the preconditions for the valorization and accumulation of capital in the global economy—that is, for global profit-making. Recall that the global economy is not simply the sum of national economies and national class structures. The reproduction of this global economy requires a centralized authority to represent the whole of competing capitals, the major combinations of which are no longer "national" capitals. The nature of state practices in the emergent global system resides in the exercise of transnational economic and political authority through the transnational state apparatus to reproduce the class relations embedded in the global valorization and accumulation of capital. However, as I discuss later, the transnational state has not been able to play this role, and there has been a deepening crisis of transnational state rule.

THE POWER OF NATIONAL STATES
AND THE POWER OF TRANSNATIONAL CAPITAL

By the latter decades of the twentieth century, the nation-state had begun to constrain capitalist groups that wanted to break free of its controls. Beginning in the late nineteenth century through the 1970s, repeated waves of mass popular and working class struggles around the world forced capitalist classes in many countries into arrangements—labor laws, market regulations, progressive tax structures, and so on—that restricted their ability to freely accumulate their capital. It was these restraints on capitalists' abilities to accumulate that drove capital to transnationalization in the first place. In more theoretical terms, the nation-state went from being a particular historical form that made possible the development of capitalism to one that fettered its further development. Let me elaborate on this crucial point.

Many analysts of globalization have noted the apparent declining ability of the national state to intervene in the process of capital accumulation and to determine economic policies in each country. This declining ability reflects the newfound power that transnational capital acquired over nation-states and popular classes. Diverse classes and groups fight in each nation-state over state policies, but real power in the global system is shifting to a transnational space that is not subject to "national" control. The transnational capitalist class has used this structural power of transnational capital over the direct power of national states to instill discipline on working classes, to dismantle welfare states, and to lift the array of regulations on capital that had been imposed by popular class struggles in the decades prior to globalization. In addition, the transnational capitalist class has been able to use this newfound structural power to undermine the ability of popular classes or of nationally oriented capitalists and elites to develop state policies in their interests. Popular forces that won state power beginning in the 1970s through the twenty-first century in various countries—such as Nicaragua, Haiti, South Africa, and Venezuela—ran up against this structural power.[11]

This situation *appeared* as an institutional contradiction between the structural power of transnational capital and the direct power of states. Some critics of globalization saw this as a contradiction between nation-states and global agents—or as states confronting globalized markets. But to put in in technical terms: this is a structural contradiction internal to an evolving capitalist system. It appears outwardly as an institutional contradiction. But its inner essence is a class relation, a class contradiction between transnational capital and nationally organized popular classes. One set of social relations, "states against markets," reflects a more fundamental set of social relations, global capital against global labor. On the surface, the structural power of capital over the direct power of states is enhanced many times over by globalization. In its essence, the relative power of exploiting classes over the exploited classes has been enhanced many times over, at least in this momentary historic juncture of the late twentieth and early twenty-first centuries. The newfound relative power of global capital over global labor is becoming fixed in the new global capital–labor relation discussed earlier, that is, global casualization, or precariatization of work associated with the new model of flexible accumulation.

State practices and policies are the outcome of struggles among competing and antagonistic social forces. These practices and policies are not fixed; they are constantly negotiated and renegotiated in specific historic period through changes in the balance of social forces as capitalism develops and classes struggle. By "going global" since the 1970s, capital has been able to break free of nation-state constraints that had been imposed earlier to its control and its unbridled profit-making. The new capital–labor relation is facilitated by globalization in a dual sense: first, capital has exercised its power over labor through new patterns of flexible accumulation made possible by enabling "third wave" technologies, the elimination of spatial barriers to accumulation, and the control over space these changes bring; second, globalization itself involves a vast acceleration of the primitive accumulation of capital worldwide, a process in which millions have been wrenched from the means of production, proletarianized, and thrown into a global labor market that transnational capital has been able to shape.

As the globalization process restructures classes, there is a rapid proletarianization among formerly precapitalist classes, particularly national peasant classes and urban artisans, and also of sectors of small and medium manufacturers and other middle classes that were tied to the domestic market and the demand it generated. New urban and rural working classes linked to transnational production processes appear. Another aspect of global class formation is the rise of newly "superfluous" masses in most if not all countries of the world. One of the many consequences of globalizing processes is a reduced demand for labor as new technologies raise productivity and as these technologies replace human labor. Vast pools of surplus humanity have become dispossessed from the means of production but not incorporated as wage labor into the capitalist production process and are of no *direct* use to capital. But indirectly they hold down wages; they fragment and disperse collectives of people who may otherwise organize to politically challenge the status quo.

The continued existence of the nation-state helps the transnational capitalist class exercise its power over a global working class that is objectively transnational but whose power is constrained and whose subjective consciousness is distorted by its compartmentalization into individual nation-states. Central to capitalism is securing a politically and economically suitable labor supply. National labor pools are merging into a single global labor pool that services global capitalism. The global labor supply is, in the main, no longer coerced (subject to extraeconomic compulsion, such as in outright slavery), but its movement is legally controlled. Nation-states become "population containment zones."[12] But this containment function applies to labor and not to capital. Globally mobile capital is not restricted to national borders, but labor is. The interstate system thus acts as a condition for the structural power of globally mobile transnational capital over labor, which is transnational in its actual content and character but is subjected to different institutional arrangements and to the direct control of national states. National boundaries are *not*, in fact, barriers to transnational migration but are mechanisms functional for the supply of labor on a global scale and for the reproduction of the system. The nation-state system boxes in and controls populations within fixed physical (territorial) boundaries so that their labor can be more efficiently exploited and their resistance contained.

How then is the newfound relative power of global capital over global labor related to our analysis of the transnationalization of the state? *Out of the emerging transnational institutionality, the new class relations of global capitalism and the social practices specific to it are becoming congealed and institutionalized.* For instance, when the International Monetary Fund, the World Bank, or the Central Bank of the European Union condition financing on enactment of new labor codes to make workers more "flexible" or on the rollback of state social spending through austerity programs, they are producing this new class relation. Similarly, these class relations of global capitalism are produced by deregulation, fiscal conservatism, monetarism, regressive tax, austerity, dismantling of welfare provisions, and so on.

But now we need to specify further the relationship of national states to the transnational state. Capital acquires its newfound power vis-à-vis (*as expressed within*) national states. The transnational bourgeoisie attempts to exercise its class power through the dense network of supranational institutions and relationships that increasingly bypass formal states, and in conjunction, through the utilization of national governments as territorially bound juridical units (the interstate system). National states may be transformed into "transmission belts" and into filtering devices for the transnational agenda of the transnational capitalist class. But they are also *proactive instruments* for advancing the agenda of global capitalism. This assertion—that transnational social forces impose their structural power over nations and the simultaneous assertion that national states, as they come under the control of transnational fractions of local elites, are proactive agents of the globalization process—only appears to be contradictory if one abandons dialectics for the Weberian dualist construct of states and markets and the national–global dualism.

Governments undertake restructuring and serve the needs of transnational capital not because they are "powerless" in the face of globalization as something external, but because a particular historical constellation of social forces came into existence in the late twentieth century that presented an organic social base for this global restructuring of capitalism. Hence, it is not that nation-states become irrelevant or powerless vis-à-vis transnational capital and its global institutions. Rather, power as the ability to issue commands and have them obeyed, or more precisely, the ability to shape social structures, shifts from social groups and classes with interests in national accumulation, or development, to those whose interests lie in new global circuits of accumulation. These latter groups realize their power and institutionalize it in emerging transnational state apparatuses that include supranational organizations and also existing states of nation-states that are captured and reorganized by transnationally oriented groups and become, conceptually, part of an emergent transnational state apparatus.

The contradictory logics of national and global accumulation are at work in this process. Class fractionation—that is, the division of classes into distinct subgroups—is occurring along a new national/transnational axis with the rise of transnational corporate and political elites. The interests of nationally oriented elites lie in national accumulation, including the whole set of traditional national regulatory and protectionist mechanisms. The interests of transnationally oriented elites lie in an expanding global economy based on worldwide market liberalization. The struggle between descendant national fractions of dominant groups and ascendant transnational fractions has often been the backdrop to surface political dynamics and ideological processes in recent decades. These two fractions have vied for control of local state apparatuses since the 1970s. Transnational fractions of local elites have ascended political-ly in countries around the world, clashing in their bid for hegemony with nationally based class fractions.[13]

Transnational blocs gradually became hegemonic in the 1980s and 1990s within nation-states. Transnational fractions in the North utilized the superior structural and direct power that core national states exercise in the global system *not* to advance "national interests" in rivalry with other nation-states, but to mold transnational structures. Hence, national states do not disappear or even diminish in importance and may still be powerful entities. But these states tend to be influenced, and often cap-tured, by transnational social forces that internalize the authority struc-tures of global capitalism. Far from the "global" and "national" as mutual-ly exclusive fields, the global becomes incarnated in local social structures and processes. The disciplinary power of global capitalism—and especial-ly global financial markets—shifts actual policy-making power within national states to the global capitalist bloc, which is represented by local social forces tied to the global economy. In sum, the capturing of local states by agents of global capitalism resolves the institutional contradic-tion between transnational capital and national states, that is, local state practices are increasingly harmonized with global capitalism. But this only intensifies underlying class and social contradictions.

Now we are in a position to reconstruct the emergence of a trans-national state in the latter decades of the twentieth century and into the twenty-first, tracing how transnational capitalists sought to institution-alize their interests through a transnational state.

THE EMERGENCE OF A TRANSNATIONAL STATE: 1960S AND BEYOND

In the post-World War II period, national capitalist groups began a new period of internationalization and external integration under the polit-ical-military canopy of US global supremacy. Yet this escalating inter-national economic activity unfolded within the institutional framework of the nation-state system and the cross-border regulation of what were known as "international regimes," in particular, the Bretton Woods system that had been set up in 1944 and that comprised the International Monetary Fund, the World Bank, and the General Agreement on Tariffs and Trade (which later became the WTO). The Bretton Woods system established fixed currency rates for national currencies and rules for the tight regulation by nation-states of the cross-border movement of money, known as capital controls. This system of international economic regulation was designed for the international economy of the post-World War II period and worked well in its first few decades.

But as multinational corporations extended their reach around the world, they sought to evade the central bank controls associated with the Bretton Woods system of national regulation by depositing their capital in foreign currency markets. These corporations, in other words, did not send the dollars back home but rather deposited them in third country banks. Economic internationalization thus brought the massive spread of dollars and other core country currencies around the world. What became known as eurodollar deposits, or dollar-denominated bank deposits outside the United States, ballooned from just $3 billion in 1960 to $75 billion in 1970—prompting the Nixon administration to abandon the gold standard in 1971—and then climbed to more than $1 trillion in 1984.[14] This collapse of the Bretton Woods system of fixed currency exchange and national economic regulation via capital controls was the first step in the liberation of embryonic transnational capital from the institutional constraints of the nation-state system.[15]

Liquid capital became accumulated in offshore capital markets established by nascent transnational banks seeking to evade the regulatory powers of national states. In the 1970s, the transnational banks began to recycle this liquid capital through massive loans to Third World governments. International bank lending jumped from $2 billion in 1972 to $90 billion in 1981, before falling to $50 billion in 1985.[16] These newly liberated global financial markets began to determine currency values and exchange rates, to destabilize national finances, and to undermine the national macroeconomic management of the earlier post-World War II Keynesian regime of capitalism. By the early 1990s, some $1 trillion in various currencies was being traded daily, all beyond the control of national governments.[17]

The dramatic loss of currency control by governments meant that state managers could no longer regulate the value of their national currency. The power to influence state economic policymaking passed from these state managers to currency traders, portfolio investors, and transnational bankers—the representatives of transnational finance capital—by virtue of their ability to move funds around the world. The former chair of Citicorp, writing in an op-ed article in *The New York Times* in 1992, noted that currency traders sit at 200,000 trading room monitors around the world and conduct "a kind of global plebiscite on the monetary and fiscal policies of the governments issuing currency," in which "there is no way for a nation to opt out."[18] Offshore capital markets grew from $315 billion in 1973 to over $2 trillion in 1982, and by the end of the 1970s, trade in currencies was more than eleven times greater than the value of world commodity trade. (As I discuss later in the book, this shift in power from state managers to transnational finance capital intensified many times over in the twenty-first century, and trade in currencies escalated phenomenally into the hundreds of trillions of dollars annually.)

Because this global movement of liquidity created unpredictable conditions of profitability, transnational corporations reduced their risks by diversifying their operations around the world, thus accelerating the entire globalization process and the political pressures for a transnational state apparatus. Transnational capitalists were quite aware of their role in pushing for a transnational state apparatus. For example, transnational bankers worked collectively to transform the Bretton Woods agencies into their collective supranational instrument in the face of the 1980s Third World debt crisis. The banks had loaned so much money to Third World countries that they stood to lose everything should the Third World go into default, so they turned to the Bretton Woods organizations, to the US state, and to other nascent transnational state institutions to force a payback and to begin to restructure the whole world economy in the direction of deregulation, liberalization, and globalization. "The banks want to be assured that the [debtor] country is going to be pursuing the necessary adjustment program to take it out of its external debt situation to monitor what it is doing," noted William H. Rhodes, the Citibank official in charge of Latin American debt negotiations. "The banks have found that this is a very difficult role to play as a group and felt that a multilateral agency like the International Monetary Fund is better equipped to do so."[19]

As these transnational corporate and political elites emerged on the world scene in the 1980s, they made explicit claims to building and managing the global economy through restructured multilateral and national institutions. They pressured for the dismantling of Keynesian welfare and developmentalist states and the lifting of national controls over the free movement of globally mobile capital. They pushed for public sectors and nonmarket community spheres to be opened up to profit making and privatized, and set about to impose new production relations of flexible accumulation.

The transnational bourgeoisie also became politically organized. The formation in the mid-1970s of the Trilateral Commission, which brought together transnationalized fractions of the business, political, and intellectual elite in North America, Europe, and Japan, was one marker in its politicization. Others were the creation of the Group of 7 (G7; the United States, Great Britain, France, Germany, Japan, Italy, and Canada; later on Russia was added), a forum at the governmental level that has met each year since it first began in 1975 to institutionalize collective management of the global economy by corporate and political elites from core nation-states; the transformation of the Organisation of Economic Co-operation and Development, formed in the 1950s as a supranational institution by the twenty-four largest industrialized countries to observe their national economies, into a forum for economic policy coordination and restructuring; and the creation of the World Economic Forum, which brought together the top representatives of transnational corporations and global political elites. Studies on building a global economy and transnational management structures flowed out of think tanks, university centers, and policy planning institutes in core countries.[20]

The diverse activities, strategies, and power positions of global elites as they sought practical solutions to the problems of accumulation around the world gradually converged around a program of global economic and political restructuring centered on market liberalization. This became known as the "Washington consensus."[21] This program was pieced together in the 1980s. The global elite set out to convert the world into a single unified field for global capitalism, amidst sharp social struggles and multiple forms of resistance from subordinate groups and also from dominant groups not brought into this emerging global capitalist bloc. It pushed for greater uniformity and standardization in the codes and rules of the global market—a process similar to the construction of national markets in the nineteenth century but now replicated in the new global space. In 1982, the G7 designated the International Monetary Fund and the World Bank as the central authorities for exercising the collective power of the capitalist national states over international financial negotiations.[22] At the Cancun Summit in Mexico in 1982, the core capitalist states, led by the United States, launched the era of global neoliberalism as part of this process and began imposing structural adjustment programs on the Third World and the then-Second World. Transnational elites promoted international economic integration processes, including NAFTA, the European Union, and Asia-Pacific Economic Cooperation, among others. They created new sets of institutions and forums, such as the WTO and the Multilateral Agreement on Investment.

In this process, the existing supranational institutions, such as the Bretton Woods and the UN institutions, were not bypassed but rather instrumentalized and transformed. The reformed Bretton Woods institutions took the reigns in organizing global economic restructuring, especially through neoliberal programs. Similarly, the UN conference system helped achieve consensus on reshaping the world political and economic order, while UN agencies such as the United Nations Development Program and the UN Conference on Trade and Development began to promote the transnational elite agenda of economic liberalization. Speaking before the World Economic Forum in 1998, UN Secretary General Kofi Annan explained how the UN sought to establish the international security and regulatory environment, and the social, political and ideological conditions, for global markets to flourish:

> [The UN agencies] help countries to join the international trading system and enact business-friendly legislation. Markets do not function in a vacuum. Rather, they arise from a framework of rules and laws, and they respond to signals set by Governments and other institutions. Without rules governing property, rights and contracts; without confidence based on the rule of law; without an overall sense of direction and a fair degree of equity and transparency, there could be no well-functioning markets, domestic or global. The UN system provides such a global framework—an agreed set of standards and objectives that enjoy worldwide acceptance. A strong United Nations is good for business.[23]

This type of public–private fusion between institutions of emerging transnational state apparatuses and the lead transnational corporations had by the early twenty-first century spread throughout the United Nations system. The UN and its agencies had signed hundreds of agreements with transnational corporations for joint projects and for UN sponsorship of corporate initiatives.[24] The United Nations Development Program described itself as an agency helping

> to build the emerging markets of tomorrow, within which the private sector can grow and prosper. [The] UNDP is building linkages with the global business community to facilitate private investments and innovations that can build a global market economy in the new millennium. . . . UNDP supports entrepreneurial cultures in countries in which the private sector has historically been largely absent or underdeveloped.[25]

Even such UN agencies as the World Health Organization and the United Nations Educational, Scientific and Cultural Organization came to operate within the logic of global capital accumulation, taking an approach to health, education, refugees, and so on that paralleled the commodification of these spheres at the nation-state level.[26]

The Uruguay Round of world trade negotiations that began in 1986 established a sweeping new set of world trade rules to regulate the new global economy based on (a) freedom of investment and capital movements; (b) the liberalization of services, including banks; (c) intellectual property rights; and (d) a free movement of goods. On the conclusion of the Uruguay Round the General Agreement on Tariffs and Trade created the WTO, in 1995, to supervise this new "free trade" regime. Although its powers are far from absolute, the WTO is perhaps the archetypical transnational institution of the new era. The WTO assumed unprecedented powers to enforce the General Agreement on Tariffs and Trade "free trade" provisions. It has independent jurisdiction; its rules and rulings are binding on all members; and it has the power to sanction, to overrule state and local powers, and to override national regulatory powers. The theoretical import here is that the WTO is the first supranational institution with a coercive capacity not embedded in any particular nation-state but rather directly in transnational functionaries and the transnational corporate elite.

By the early twenty-first century, the transnational state as an institution attempting to impose its authority on a fluid and spatially open process of capital accumulation was assuming some powers and historic functions that the nation-states had lost in organizing collective action to facilitate and reproduce this process in the global economy. The creation of a capitalist superstructure that carries out at the transnational level functions indispensable for the reproduction of capital, especially those that national states are unable to perform, is not to say that a transnational state has fully become consolidated as a fully functioning political, administrative, and regulatory structure. There is no clear chain of command and division of labor within the transnational state apparatus, or anything resembling, at this time, the type of internal coherence of national states, given the embryonic stage of this process. Instead of a coherent transnational state, there seem to be multiple centers and partial regulatory mechanisms. Moreover, diverse institutions that comprise a transnational state have distinct histories and trajectories, are internally differentiated, and present numerous entry points as sites of contestation.

Nonetheless, the transnational state has developed mechanisms to assume a growing number of functions traditionally associated with the national state, such as compensation for market failure (e.g., International Monetary Fund bailouts), money creation (e.g., European Union currency), legal guarantees of property rights and market contracts (the powers of the WTO), and the provision of public goods (social and physical infrastructure). Despite this expanded transnational state activity, there are numerous functions that the transnational state has not been able to assume, such as reigning in speculation and excesses that so characterize the frenzied "casino capitalism" of the global economy. The confidence exuded by transnational elites in the late twentieth century gave way by the turn of the century to fear of looming crisis. The series of economic crises in the late 1990s exposed the fragility of the world monetary system and caused rising alarm and growing fissures in the inner circle of the global ruling class. The G7 and the G20 countries scrambled in the wake of the 2008 global financial collapse to develop collective crisis management, while the World Economic Forum launched programs to create a new transnational governing architecture, as I discuss in later chapters.

It is out of the process summarized here that a transnational state apparatus began to emerge, not as something planned as such, but as the political consequences of the social practice and class action of the transnational capitalist class in this historic juncture, and as an apparatus that is not replacing but emerging out of the preglobalization infrastructure of world capitalism. But the transnational elite has also operated through an array of *private* transnational business associations and political planning groups that have proliferated since the 1970s and point to the expansion of a *transnational civil society* as part of the globalization process and parallel to the rise of a transnational state. They include such well-known bodies as the Trilateral Commission, the International Chamber of Commerce, and the World Economic Forum. The matter of transnational civil society is of great significance since the transnational state exists as part of a larger totality and because the practices of an emerging global ruling class take place at both levels.

We have witnessed not the "end of the nation-state" but rather its transformation into "neoliberal national states." As component elements of a transnational state, they perform three essential services: (a) adopt fiscal and monetary policies that assure macro-economic stability; (b) provide the basic infrastructure necessary for global economic activity (air and sea ports, communications networks, educational systems, and so on); and (c) provide social order, that is, stability, which requires sustaining instruments of direct coercion and ideological apparatuses. When the transnational elite speaks of "governance," it is referring to these functions and the capacity to fulfill them. This was made explicit in the World Bank's World Development Report for 1997, *The State in a Changing World*, which pointed out that the aegis of the national state is central to globalization. In the World Bank's words, "globalization begins at home."[27] But the functions of the neoliberal state are contradictory. As globalization proceeds, internal social cohesion declines along with national economic integration. The neoliberal state retains essential powers to facilitate globalization, but it loses the ability to harmonize conflicting social interests within a country, to realize the historic function of sustaining the internal unity of nationally conceived social formation, and to achieve legitimacy. The result is a dramatic intensification of legitimacy crises and explosive social conflicts and political crises.

TRANSNATIONAL MOBILIZATION FROM BELOW TO COUNTER TRANSNATIONAL MOBILIZATION FROM ABOVE

So what is to be done? Smash the transnational state and attempt a return to nation-state projects of popular social change? The problem with such propositions is that globalization, although it involves agency as much as structure, is not a project conceived, planned, and implemented at the level of intentional human conduct. We need to look forward rather than backward. Such historic processes cannot be reverted as such, but they can be influenced, redirected, and transcended. This returns us to my opening affirmation that historical materialism is emancipatory precisely because it reveals the historical specificity of existing forms of social life. Emancipatory projects operate *in* history. As Marx would have us recall, we do make our own history, but we do not make it just as we please, "but under circumstances directly found, given and transmitted from the past."[28]

Capitalism has always been a violent and unstable system fraught with contradictions. In the early twenty-first century, global capitalism faced an expanding crisis, one that, beyond short-term and cyclical, was long-term and structural and perhaps systemic. All of the contradictions germane to the capitalist system have been rising to the surface in the new epoch of globalization, and in particular *overaccumulation*, which refers to accumulated capital that cannot find outlets for profitable reinvestment, and *social polarization*, in which wealth accumulates at one end of the pole and misery and impoverishment at the other. Data for 2010 showed, for instance, that companies from the United States were sitting on $1.8 trillion in uninvested cash. Corporate profits were at near record highs at the same time that corporate investment had declined.[29]

In the past, these contradictions led to periodic crises that tended to result each time in a reorganization of the system. Imperialism, for instance, allowed core countries to displace to the colonial world, momentarily, some of the sharpest social antagonisms that capitalism generated, while Keynesian mechanisms to create demand such as credit creation and "military Keynesianism" (i.e., military spending to offset stagnation) helped postpone overaccumulation crises. But many if not all of capitalism's recurrent crises have been mediated by the nation-state. Under globalization the national-state is less able to address these manifold crises, yet the emergent transnational state is similarly ill equipped to resolve them, especially those of overaccumulation and social polarization.

The globalist bloc has run up against one setback after another in its effort to secure its leadership and reproduce hegemony. There are twin dimensions to the bloc's ongoing crises of authority. The first dimension is objective; the inability to attenuate polarization tendencies inherent in capitalism and aggravated by new global modes of accumulation. The ability of transnational capital to reorganize production and profit-making worldwide and to undercut popular and working class constraints to this unbridled profit-making at the national level has unleashed unprecedented inequalities and immiseration. Hegemony requires a material base and it has become increasingly doubtful that this base is broad enough to sustain a transnational hegemonic project. The second dimension is subjective and has to do with the challenge to global capitalist hegemony posed by diverse oppositional forces, not all of them progressive.

The system will not be defeated by challenges from outside its logic such as those of the former Soviet bloc countries and Third World liberation movements. Rather, defeat will be from within the global system itself. The contradictions between capitalist and precapitalist classes, for instance, are increasingly irrelevant. Resistance to capitalist colonization from without is giving way to resistance to capitalism from within. The universal penetration of capitalism through globalization draws all peoples not only into webs of market relations but also into webs of resistance. Everywhere there has been organized resistance movements in recent decades, ranging from the Zapatistas in Mexico to the Assembly of the Poor in Thailand, South Africa's Shack Dwellers Movement, Brazil's Landless Workers Movement, India's National Alliance of People's Movements, Vía Campesina (with chapters all over the world), the Occupy Wall Street movement, the Arab Spring, Black Lives Matter, the Bolivarian revolution in Venezuela, the Shack Dwellers Movement in South Africa, and the mass worker struggles breaking out in China, among countless others.

Fundamental change in a social order becomes possible when an organic crisis occurs. An organic crisis is one in which the system faces a structural (objective) crisis and also a crisis of legitimacy or hegemony (subjective). An organic crisis is not enough to bring about fundamental, progressive change in a social order (and indeed, it has in the past led to social breakdown, authoritarianism, and fascism). A popular or revolutionary outcome to an organic crisis also requires that there be a viable alternative that is in hegemonic ascendance, that is, an alternative to the existing order that is viable and that is seen as viable and preferable by a majority of society. Global capitalism entered into an organic crisis in the wake of the 2008 financial collapse from which the prospects for the system to recover appear dim. But a viable alternative and the transnational political instruments to struggle to impose that alternative still seemed to be missing.

To defend the relevance of Marx and the continuing vitality of historical materialism is not to say that everything Marx had to say is still applicable to the conditions humanity faces in the new millennium. Marx's and Engel's argument that "the proletariat of each country must, of course, first of all settle matters with its own bourgeoisie," is now outdated.[30] "Its own bourgeoisie" is now transnational; each "national" bourgeoisie is as well the bourgeoisie of the proletariat of numerous countries. In the age of globalization, popular classes may still need to organize in the first instance locally and nationally, but such organization must be linked to an expansive organic transnationalization of struggles. The mobilization of the transnational bourgeoisie from above can only be countered by a transnational mobilization from below. Working and popular classes whose fulcrum has been the nation-state must transpose to transnational space their mobilization and their capacity to place demands on the system. This means developing the mechanisms—alliances, networks, direct actions, and organizations—that will allow for a transnational resistance. It also means developing a transnational socialist ideology and politics, and targeting the transnational state as contested terrain.

We stand at a crossroad as the twenty-first century advances. Given the prospects of a global police state, why are the abstract theoretical debates (such as those I have taken up in this chapter) important? At times of great social transformation, established social theories are called into question and new ones proliferate to give explanation. And at times of great social crisis such as the one that we face in twenty-first-century global society, sound theoretical understandings are crucial if we hope to intervene effectively in reality and assure our survival in these dangerous times. An accurate reading of the nature of global capitalism is essential for the struggle to resist its depredations and is as much, or more so, a political as an intellectual undertaking.

FIVE

BEYOND THE THEORY OF IMPERIALISM

T heories of a "new imperialism" proliferated in the years following the September 2001 attack on the World Trade Towers and the Pentagon and the subsequent US invasions of Afghanistan and Iraq. These theories argued that the United States has set about in the twenty-first century to renew a US empire and offset the decline in its hegemony amidst heightened inter-imperialist rivalry.[1] So popular were new imperialism theories that they came to be seen as common sense; critics were seen as heretics or nutcases, and alternative explanations nearly disappeared from the intellectual and political radar. "It is now a universal belief on the left that the world has entered a new imperialist phase," insisted John Bellamy Foster, Marxist sociologist and editor the New York-based socialist magazine *Monthly Review*.[2] Yet these theories rested on a crustaceous bed of assumptions that must be peeled back if we are to get at the root of twenty-first-century global social and political dynamics. The dramatic escalation of US interventionism in the first two decades of the new century is not a departure from capitalist globalization but a response to its crisis.

"New imperialism" theories are grounded in the classical statements on imperialism by early twentieth century Marxists V.I. Lenin, Nikolai Bukharin, and Rudolf Hilferding and are based on this assumption of a world of rival national capitals and economies, conflict among core capitalist powers, the exploitation by these powers of peripheral regions, and a nation-state-centered framework for analyzing global dynamics. In his classic study on imperialism, *Finance Capital*, Hilferding argued that national capitalist monopolies turn to the state for assistance in acquiring international markets and that this state intervention inevitably leads to intense political-economy rivalries among nation-states. There is a struggle among core national states for control over peripheral regions in order to open these regions to capital export from the particular imperialist country and to exclude capital from other countries. "Export capital feels most comfortable ... when its own state is in complete control of the new territory, for capital exports from other countries are then excluded, it enjoys a privileged position," observed Hilferding.[3] In his 1917 pamphlet *Imperialism: The Latest Stage of Capitalism*, Lenin stressed the rise of *national* financial–industrial combines that struggle to divide and redivide the world among themselves through their respective nation-states. The rivalry among these competing national capitals led to interstate competition, military conflict, and war among the main capitalist countries.

Hilferding, Lenin, and others analyzing the world of the early twentieth century established this Marxist analytical framework of rival national capitals that was carried by subsequent political economists into the late twentieth and early twenty-first centuries via theories of dependency and the world system, radical international relations theory, studies of US intervention, and so on. This outdated framework of competing national capitals continued to inform observers of world dynamics in the early twenty-first century. The following 2003 assertion by Klare was typical:

> By geopolitics or geopolitical competition, I mean the contention between great powers and aspiring great powers for control over territory, resources, and important geographical positions, such as ports and harbors, canals, river systems, oases, and other sources of wealth and influence. Today we are seeing a resurgence of unabashed geopolitical ideology among the leadership cadres of the major powers ... the best way to see what's happening today in Iraq and elsewhere is through a geopolitical prism.[4]

Such thinking provided the scaffolding for the torrent of "new imperialism" literature. Some argued that unilateral US interventionism belied earlier claims that we are moving toward a globalized world order and refuted "misguided" theories of globalization.[5] According to Walden Bello:

> What was seen, by many people on both the left and the right, as the wave of the future—that is, a functionally integrated global economy marked by massive flows of commodities, capital and labor across the borders of weakened nation states and presided over by a "transnation-

al capitalist class"—has retreated in a chain reaction of economic crises, growing inter-capitalist rivalries and wars. Only by a stretch of the
imagination can the USA under the George W. Bush administration
be said to be promoting a "globalist agenda."[6]

The actual empirical data, however, made clear that only by a stretch
of the imagination could one ignore the profound intensification of economic globalization—especially the escalating flows of commodities,
capital, and labor across the borders of nation-states—that took place in
the first two decades of the twenty-first century. And both the Bush and
Obama administrations did indeed promote the globalist agenda of intensified globalization. What evidence has there been of "growing inter-capitalist rivalries" among nation-states? There were no trade wars or military
tensions among the major capitalist powers during those two US administrations but rather attempts, desperate at times, on the part of their governments to collectively manage the system and its crisis tendencies. "New
imperialism" theories fail to make the distinction between conjunctural
analysis and structural causation and mistake surface appearance, such as
public statements by policymakers, for underlying essence.

The linchpin of "new imperialism" theories is the assumption that
world capitalism in the twenty-first century is made up of national capitals and distinct national economies that interact with one another and
a concomitant analysis of world politics as driven by the pursuit by governments of their "national interest." But what does "national interests"
mean? Marxists have historically rejected notions of "national interests"
as an ideological subterfuge for class and social group interests. What
is a "national economy"? Is it a country with a closed market? Protected territorially based production circuits? The predominance of national
capitals? An insulated national financial system? No capitalist country in
the world fits this description.

The "new imperialism" literature stubbornly refuses to address the
reality of transnational capital. US imperialism is seen as a bid to secure
the advantage of "US capital" over rival national capitals in the face of
political and military rivalry among core nation-states. In *Empire of Capital*, political scientist Ellen Meiksins Wood insists that "the national organization of capitalist economies has remained stubbornly persistent."
The United States, she says, aims to shore up "US" capital over other
competing national capitals, to "compel other economies to serve the
interests of the imperial hegemon in response to the fluctuating needs

of *its own domestic capital.*"[7] Wood and others *assume* without a shred of empirical evidence that capital remains organized (as it was in earlier moments of the world capitalist system) along national lines and that the development of capital has been frozen in its nation-state form. Once we belie the notion of a world of national economies and national capitals, then the logical sequence in "new imperialism" argumentation collapses like a house of cards since the whole edifice is constructed on this notion. By coming to grips with the reality of transnational capital, we can grasp US foreign policy in relation to the global capitalist system.

THE DUALISM OF NEW IMPERIALISM THEORIES

Most "new imperialism" theorists acknowledge to varying degrees that changes have taken place, and particularly, that capital has become more global. Yet capital in these accounts has not transnationalized; it is still national and national capital has "internationalized." Once in the world arena, these national capitals confront other national capitals that have internationalized. These accounts are concerned with explaining the *inter*national order, which by definition places the focus on interstate dynamics exclusive of the *trans*national. This need to accommodate the reality of transnationalizing capital within a nation-state-centric framework for analyzing world political dynamics leads "new imperialism" theories to a dualism of the economic and the political. By dualism, I mean the division of something conceptually into two opposed or contrasted aspects, or the state of being so divided. For instance, humans and nature are often discussed in dualist terms, as if they are separate or independent of each other. Dualism is always suspicious (and anti-dialectic) as it negates the interconnections among things that give them an essential internal unity.

Before I get back to discussing the resurgence of US interventionism and the case of Iraq, let us undertake a theoretical excursion through an examination of perhaps the landmark treatise in this literature, *The New Imperialism*, by renowned Marxist political economist David Harvey. In it, he argues that capital is economic and globalizes but states are political and pursue a self-interested territorial logic. Harvey's theory starts with the notion that

> the fundamental point is to see the territorial and the capitalist logic of power as distinct from each other.... The relation between these two

logics should be seen, therefore, as problematic and often contradictory ... rather than as functional or one-sided. This dialectical relation sets the stage for an analysis of capitalist imperialism in terms of the intersection of these two distinctive but intertwined logics of power.[8]

Harvey's approach here, however, is distinctly not dialectical but mechanical. Dualist approaches such as Harvey's view the parts under analysis as externally related, whereas the hallmark of a dialectical approach is recognition that relations between different parts—processes, phenomena—are internal relationships. An *internal relation* is one in which each part is constituted in its relation to the other, so that one cannot exist without the other and only has meaning when seen within the relation, whereas an *external relation* is one in which each part has an existence independent of its relation to the other.[9] The different dimensions of social reality in the dialectical approach do not have an "independent" status insofar as each aspect of reality is constituted by, and is constitutive of, a larger whole of which it is an internal element. Distinct dimensions of social reality may be analytically distinct yet are internally interpenetrated and mutually constitutive of each other as internal elements of a more encompassing process, so that, for example, the economic/capital and the political/state are a dynamic unity that is internal to capitalist relations.

It is remarkable that Harvey proposes such a dualist separation, since the history of modern critical thought has demonstrated both the *formal* (apparent) separation of the economic and the political under the capitalist mode of production and the illusion that such a separation is organic or real.[10] This separation has its genealogy in the rise of the market and its apparently "pure" economic compulsion. This means that under capitalism, the dominant groups do not need to rely on state coercion to force the exploited classes to work for capital since the market compels them to do so; they can survive only by working for capital. This separation appears in the history of social theory with the breakup of political economy, the rise of classical economics and bourgeois social science, and disciplinary fragmentation.[11]

Dualist accounts share a notion of the state first advanced by the early twentieth century German sociologist Max Weber, as an independent institution staffed by functionaries that interacts externally with capital in pursuit of its own territorial/institutional interests. It is to this dualism that Harvey now turns to explain the "new imperialism." Yet dual logics of state and capital ignore the real-world policymaking process in which the state extends backward, is grounded in the forces of civil society, and is fused in a myriad of ways with capital itself. The analysis of the state cannot remain frozen at a nation-state level to the extent that capital and diverse social forces in civil society are transnationalizing. Instead of remaining frozen in twentieth century theories of world order, our attempt to make sense of resurgent US interventionism should focus on the changing nature of the political management (rule) of global capitalism. We want to understand how the political and the economic become articulated in new ways in the current era of capitalist globalization. This requires a conception of the relationship between agency and institutions. The agency of historically situated social forces is exercised through institutions that they themselves have created and constantly recreate. We need to focus not on states as fictitious macroagents but on historically changing constellations of social forces operating through multiple institutions, including state apparatuses that are themselves in a process of transformation as a consequence of collective agencies.

The dualism I am critiquing here rests on reification of the state and of territory. *To reify* means to understand something that social agency has produced as though it exists and operates quite independently of this agency, according to its own laws. It is to perceive a social practice that we engage in as some external "thing" that exists on its own. To reify something is to attribute a thinglike status to what should be more properly seen as a complex and changing set of social relations that our practices have created. The problem is that the social world is so complex and multidimensional that we must create numerous concepts to try to describe, codify, and understand the varied dimensions that we have created. Thus, "society," "race," "culture," "identity," "state," and "nation-state" are concepts we have created to help us understand reality. They have no ontological status (i.e., existence) independent of human agency. But when we forget that the reality to which these concepts refer is our own sets of social relations and instead attribute some independent existence to them, then we are reifying them. For instance, a "nation-state" is not a tangible "thing" insofar as borders are imaginary lines we draw through real space. A "state" is not the physical buildings which house government officials or a capital city but a set of social relations and practices we have created and institutionalized. To see the state as some thing-in-itself is to reify the state.

Instead of offering an explanation of how social agents operate through historically constituted institutions, much of the "new imperialism" literature ends up reifying these institutions. Institutions are nothing more than institutionalized (i.e., codified) patterns of interaction among people that structure different aspects of their social relations. When we explain global dynamics in terms of institutions that have an existence or an agency independent of the social forces that create these institutions, we are reifying them. To critique a nation-state framework of analysis as I do is not to dismiss the nation-state but to dereify it. In the reified approach of "new imperialism" theories, nation-states are discrete units that interact with one another through the interstate system in pursuit of their state/national interests. But if we want to explain resurgent US interventionism consistent with the actual empirical evidence, we must look beneath an interstate/nation-state framework, that is, at historical social forces, the evolving structures they create and the changing institutional configurations through which they operate. And we must look beyond an interstate/nation-state framework to capture what is taking place in the world today.

The state, says Harvey, "struggles to assert its interests and achieve its goals in the world at large."[12] But Harvey does not stop with this blatant reification of the state, as if it were a conscious macroagent. He then introduces an additional territorial reification, so that territorial relations become inherent to social relations. "The wealth and well-being of particular territories are augmented at the expense of others," writes Harvey.[13] This is a remarkably reified image—"territories" rather than people or social groups have "wealth," enjoy "well being," and interact with one another. In this way, Harvey gives space an independent existence as a social/political force in the form of territory in order to advance his thesis of the "new imperialism." For Harvey, territory acquires a social existence of its own, an agentic logic. We are told that "territorial entities" engage in practices of production, commerce, and so on.

But do "territorial entities" really do these things? Or should we not focus on how social forces are organized both in space and through institutions, and how, in the real world, individuals and social groups, not territories, engage in production, commerce, and so on? And these social groups do so through institutions through which they organize, systematize, and demarcate their activities as agents. I am arguing here that social groups became aggregated and organized in the modern era through the particular institutional form of the territorially based na-tion-state. But this particular institutional form does not acquire a life of its own; neither is it immutable. Nation-states continue to exist, but their nature and meaning evolve as social relations and structures be-come transformed, particularly as they transnationalize.

It is true that the social does not exist outside of the spatial and that human beings experience the world in time and in space (and that, more-over, space is distance measured in time). It is equally true that space is relative and experienced subjectively, as the French philosopher and socialist Henri Lefebvre observed.[14] Drawing on insights from Lefeb-vre, Marx, Rosa Luxemburg, and others, Harvey earlier introduced the highly fertile notion of "spatial fixes" to understand how capital momen-tarily resolves contradictions (particularly crises of overaccumulation) in one place by displacing them to other places through geographic expan-sion and spatial reorganization. For instance, rich countries displace to poor countries (through imperialism) the effects of crises of capitalism. Following Marx's famous observation that the expanded accumulation of capital involves the progressive "annihilation of space through time," Harvey also coined the term "time–space compression" in reference to globalization as a process involving a new burst of time–space compres-sion in the world capitalist system.[15]

But "places" have no existence or meaning in and of themselves. It is people living in particular spaces that do this displacing (literally), these spatial fixes. The asymmetric exchange relations between rich and poor (or core and peripheral) countries that are at the heart of Harvey's emphasis on the territorial basis of the "new imperialism" must be for Harvey territorial exchange relations. But not only that: they must be nation-state territorial exchanges. But exchange relations are social re-lations, exchanges among particular social groups. There is nothing in the concept of asymmetric exchanges that by fiat gives them a territo-rial expression; there is no reason to assume that uneven exchanges are necessarily exchanges that take place between distinct territories, much less specifically between distinct nation-states. That they do or do not acquire such an expression is one of historical, empirical, and conjunc-tural analysis. Certainly spatial relations among social forces have his-torically been mediated in large part by territory; spatial relations have been territorially defined relations. But this territorialization is in no way immanent to social relations.

If most of the people in one place that we can call a territory or nation-state achieve "wealth" and "well-being" by having displaced contradictions to most of the people in another place, then we may be able to justify the view that this set of social relations acquires a territorial expression—hence the territorial (nation-state) basis to classical theories of colonialism and imperialism and later world-system and related theories of geographically defined core and periphery. But we know that under globalization, masses of people in core regions such as Los Angeles or New York may suffer the displacement of contradictions offloaded on them from people physically contiguous to them in the very same city, whereas rising middle class and affluent sectors in India, Brazil, Mexico, or South Africa may benefit as much from spatial fixes that offload crisis to the global poor through neoliberal mechanisms as their counterparts in First World global cities.

Any theory of globalization must address the matter of place and space, including changing spatial relations among social forces and how social relations are spatialized. This has not been satisfactorily tackled, despite a spate of recent theories, ranging from sociologist Manuel Castells's notion of the *network society* (in which a "space of flows" replaces the "space of place") to sociologist Anthony Giddens's idea of "time-space distanciation" as the "lifting" of social relations from territorial place and their stretching around the globe in ways that overcome territorial friction.[16] This notion of ongoing and novel reconfigurations of time and of social space is central to a number of globalization theories. It in turn points to the larger theoretical issue of the relationship of social structure to space, the notion of space as the material basis for social practices, and the changing relationship under globalization between territoriality/geography, institutions, and social structures. The crucial question here is the ways in which globalization may be transforming the spatial dynamics of capital accumulation and the institutional as well as political arrangements through which it takes place. The subject—literally, that is, the agents/makers of the social world—is not global space but people in those spaces. What is central, therefore, is to theorize a spatial reconfiguration of social relations in the epoch of capitalist globalization that allows us to see beyond a nation-state/interstate framework.

Nation-states are in essence sets of social relations that have historically been territorialized, but those relations are not by definition territorial. To the extent that officials from the United States and other national states promote deterritorializing social and economic processes, they are not territorial actors. The US state can hardly be considered as acting territorially, as Harvey claims, when it promotes the relocation abroad of production that was previously concentrated in US territory. Harvey's approach is hard-pressed to explain such behavior, since by his definition the US state must promote its own territorial aggrandizement. Harvey observes that as local banking was supplanted by national banking in the development of capitalism, "the free flow of money capital across the national space altered regional dynamics."[17] In the same vein, what we now see is that the free flow of capital across global space alters these dynamics on a worldwide scale.

THE CRISIS OF GLOBAL CAPITALISM, THE US STATE, AND THE TRANSNATIONAL STATE

Here we arrive at the pitfall of what I call *theoreticism*, or the effort to make the real world fit our theoretical conceptions rather than having our theoretical conceptions develop and change on the basis of the changing nature of the real world. Theory needs to illuminate reality; it is useless as a tool for social action. Since nation-state theories establish a frame of an interstate system made up of competing national states, economies, and capitals, then twenty-first-century reality must be interpreted so that it fits this frame one way or another. Once we turn to the real world of capitalist globalization, we can see the general contradiction in the "new imperialism" literature: the dualism of the economic and political, of capital and the state is negated by the claim that the state functions to serve (national) capital.

How does Harvey view US foreign policy? "If, for example, the US forces open capital markets around the world through the operations of the IMF and the WTO," he says, "it is because specific advantages are thought to accrue to US financial institutions."[18] Hence foreign policy is a function of financial interests. (What a "US" financial institution in the twenty-first century actually refers to is not specified.) More generally, "new imperialism" theories analyze US foreign policy in relation to the assumption of competition among national capitals and consequent political and military rivalry among core nation-states. "Intercapitalist rivalry remains the hub of the imperialist wheel," claims Foster. "In the present period of global hegemonic imperialism the United States is geared above all to expanding its imperial power to whatever extent possible and subordinating the rest of the capitalist world to its interests."[19] Henwood insists that US foreign policy in recent years has been singularly aimed at the restoration of the relative strength of "American" capitalists.[20] US policy, says Wood, aims to subordinate the EU, which "is potentially a stronger economic power than the U.S.,"[21] to the interests of US "domestic capital."

Yet empirical study of the global economy reveals that *trans*national corporations operate both inside as well as outside of the territorial bounds of the EU, that transnational investors from all countries hold and trade in trillions of euros and dollars each day, that share ownership has significantly transnationalized, that European investors are as deeply integrated into transnational circuits of accumulation that inextricably pass through the "US" economy as are US investors into such circuits that pass through the "EU" economy. These transnational capitalists operate across US–EU frontiers and have a material and political interest in stabilizing the "US" and the "EU" economy and "their" financial institutions.

During a 2004 visit to Chile, I came across a report that Chilean capitalists had invested the previous year some $40 billion around the world in diverse pension funds, securities, and other financial outlets. An IMF report that same month explained that Malaysian, German, Russian, Japanese, Argentine, and US investors were among those thousands of holders of Argentine bonds that had demanded from the IMF and the Group of 8 (G8) that the Argentine government reverse default it had declared two years earlier and honor these bonds. Hence, when the US state, the IMF, or the G8 pressure the Argentine government to honor its debt to private capitalists from around the world, including from Chile and from Argentina itself, is this a case (as new imperialism theory would have it) of the US state serving the interests of "its own domestic capital" or the even more amorphous "interests of the imperial hegemon"? Or is it that the US state, together with the IMF and the G8, are serving the interests of transnational capital and the interests of global capitalist circuits over those of specifically local or national circuits?

More recently, my critics point to China–US relations as a case of "hegemonic rivalry" and rising interimperialist competition. But geopolitical competition must be explained within the logic of, and the contradictions internal to, global capitalism. The US and Chinese economies became inextricably interwoven in the early twenty-first century. They were less autonomous national economies than two key constituent parts of an integrated global economy, and the transnational capitalist class in both China and the United States were dependent on their expanding economic ties. Foreign direct investment between the United States and China have surged since the 1990s. In 2015, more than 1,300 US-based companies had investments of $228 billion in China, while Chinese companies invested $64 billion in the United States, up from close to zero just ten years earlier, and held $153 billion in assets.[22] Chinese exports to the United States were transnational capitalist exports. And an overvalued Chinese currency actually benefitted transnational corporations that exported from China to US and global markets.

As US President Donald Trump himself indicated after taking office in 2017, his anti-China rhetoric and threats of a "trade war" were aimed at creating an environment in which the US government could twist the Chinese state into making greater concessions to global capital. (The same can be said for Trump's trade negotiations with Mexico.)[23] The largest foreign holder of US debt was China, which owned in 2016 more than $1.24 trillion in bills, notes, and bonds or about 30 percent of the over $4 trillion in Treasury bills, notes, and bonds held by foreign countries.[24] In turn, deficit spending and debt-driven consumption has made the United States in recent decades the "market of last resort," helping to stave off greater stagnation and even collapse of the global economy by absorbing Chinese and world economic output.

The disjuncture between a globalizing economy and a nation-state-based system of political authority, along with the problems of legitimation that this creates for national states, provides a more satisfactory framework than national capitalist and inter-imperialist rivalry for analyzing United States-China geopolitical competition and evident international antagonisms. In the particular case of China, the state-party elite is interlocked with, but distinct from, the Chinese transnationally integrated capitalist class. To the extent that the former extracts value from the latter—and from the transnational capitalist class more broadly—through the state-party apparatus, it is dependent on the international extension of Chinese state power in ways that may generate geopolitical conflict. The same can be said (though in a very different context) for the Russian state elite.

Yet these antagonisms are not national capitalist rivalries. It is crucial that explanations of geopolitical and international conflict be grounded in the determination exercised by the configuration of class and social forces as they congeal in distinct ways in different national states and become articulated in distinct ways to global capitalism.[25] There are, in fact, no contradictions between states as reified fictitious macroagents; the contradictions are between or among class and social groups that operate through institutions, the principal one being the national state. What about the claim of new imperialism theories that the United States and other major capitalist powers are locked in interimperialist competition for control over Third World markets and resources? The July 2004 *Le Monde Diplomatique* reported that Thailand's largest corporate conglomerate, the Charoen Pokphand Group (CPG), employed 100,000 people in twenty countries in operations ranging from poultry and other food production to seeds, telecoms, feed, and franchises on 7-Eleven retail shops.[26] Clearly, whenever US or IMF pressures open up any of those twenty countries to the global economy, CPG and its investors are just as much the beneficiaries as are transnational investors from the United States, the EU, Chile, or elsewhere. And surely the CPG was pleased that it was able that year to start selling cut chicken pieces (for which it is best known) in a new Iraqi market opened up by the 2003 US invasion.

To take another example: As I write, a scramble has begun among global mining conglomerates for the global market in lithium, the key ingredient in rechargeable batteries that are the cutting edge of new transportation, communications, and energy technologies. A major portion of known lithium reserves is located in Chile. *The Economist* reports that a Chinese firm CITIC Group was bidding for part of the controlling shares currently held by the Chilean-based company SQM (Sociedad Química y Minera de Chile). Meanwhile, a competing Chinese firm, Tianqi Lithium, has partnered with a US-based company, Albermarle, to produce lithium in Australia. A year earlier, in 2015, Albemarle, the world's biggest lithium producer, bought Rockwood, owner of Chile's second biggest lithium deposit. Next door to Chile, a big lithium-brine project in Argentina is run by a joint venture bringing together an Australian-based mining group, Orocobre, and Toyota. The lithium is sent on by these transnational networks of mining conglomerates to China for the production of communications equipment, car batteries, and so forth, by such global corporate behemoths as FoxComm, which assembles Apple, Sony, Samsung, Panasonic, and LG products.[27] The nation-state paradigm would sort out capital into particular national boxes and then link these "national" capitals to their respective national states in order to explain the dynamics of international relations. The transnational class relations and political dynamics behind the entanglement that makes up the global lithium trade are obscured behind the effort to frame them within international relations and interimperialist rivalry. In fact, transnational capitalist class groups in both North and South, regardless of their country of origin, are able to take advantage of differential rates and intensities of exploitation to exploit workers and other subordinate classes throughout the global economy. In India, where there are now more than 100 billionaires, the Tata Group has grown into a global behemoth, operating in more than 100 countries in six continents involved in everything from automobiles and finance to medical equipment, construction, food and beverage, retail, steel, telecommunications, chemicals, energy, airlines, engineering, and much more. In the first decade of the twenty-first century, the group acquired several corporate icons of its former British colonial master, among them Land Rover, Jaguar, Tetley, British Steel, and Tesco supermarkets.[28] Remarkably, Tata is now the largest employer *inside* the United Kingdom. Indian capitalists exploit British workers together with others from the global web of investors brought together by the Tata conglomerate.

Does this mean that India is now the imperial country that has subordinated its former colonial overlord, the United Kingdom? To the contrary, we cannot understand these developments in the context of such statecentric and nation-state-centric paradigms. First, countries do not dominate one another; social groups and classes do. Second, it is not that Indian capitalists now subordinate British capitalists to themselves. Rather, the leading capitalist groups from around the world have increasingly transcended their historical bases in particular nation-states. In doing so they have cross-penetrated with capitalist groups from around the world. These are *transnational class relations* among the dominant groups and between them and subordinate groups. These transnational class relations have been cultivated, in part, by US policy over the past few decades of globalization.

Many "new imperialism" theorists dismiss the concepts of a transnational capitalist class and a transnational state, because in their view these concepts are based on the idea that the territorial state is increasingly "obsolete." This is a strawman; I have never suggested that the nation-state is disappearing, or that capital can now, or ever has been able to exist without a state. There are vital functions that the national state performs for transnational capital, among them the creation of sets of local economic policies aimed at achieving macroeconomic equilibrium, the provision of property laws, infrastructure, and of course, social control and ideological reproduction. However, there are other conditions that transnational capitalists require for the functioning and reproduction of global capitalism. National states are ill-equipped to organize a supranational unification of macroeconomic policies, create a unified field for transnational capital to operate, impose transnational trade regimes and supranational "transparency," and so forth. The construction of a supranational legal and regulator system for the global economy in recent years has been the task of sets of transnational institutions whose policy prescriptions and actions have been synchronized with those of neoliberal national states that have been captured by local transnationally oriented forces.

We cannot simply shrug off the increasingly salient role of a transnational institutional structure in coordinating global capitalism and imposing capitalist domination beyond national borders. "New imperialism" dogma reduces IMF practices to instruments of "US" imperialism. Yet I know of no single IMF structural adjustment program that creates conditions in the intervened country that favored "US" capital in any special way, rather than opening up the intervened country, its labor and resources, to capitalists from any corner of the world. This outcome is in sharp distinction to earlier imperialism, in which a particular core country sealed off the colonized country or sphere of influence as its own exclusive preserve for exploitation. Therefore, it is more accurate to characterize the IMF (or for that matter, the World Bank, other regional banks, the World Trade Organization, and others) as an instrument not of "US" imperialism but of transnational capitalist exploitation.

The continued existence of the national state is a central condition not for "US hegemony" or a "new US empire" but for the class power of transnational capital. The transnational capitalist class has been able to use local core states to mold transnational structures and to impose these on distinct nations and regions. The real issue is not the continued existence of national states and of powerful national states in a globalized system—a fact that does not contradict the thesis of a transnational capitalist class and a transnational state—but their function. We must analyze US foreign policy in relation to the structural role of US state power in advancing neoliberalism and global capitalism. US policies such as the imposition of neoliberal structural adjustment programs and the sponsorship of free trade agreements by and large served to further pry open regions and sectors around the world to global capitalism. US policies in the main have advanced transnational capitalist interests. And an analysis of transnational state apparatuses suggests that they act not to enforce "US" policies but to force nationally oriented policies in general into transnational alignment.

One of the fundamental contradictions of capitalist globalization is that economic globalization unfolds within the framework of a nation-state/interstate political system and its fragmented formal authority structures. The transnational state can politically wield the structural power of transnational capital by imposing conditionality in lending, issuing credit ratings, and imposing financial embargoes. But it does not have a coercive apparatus that is truly supranational. The US state wields the only significant instruments of coercion on a world scale. This coercive apparatus is wielded in the interests of transnational accumulation. Nonetheless, such an institutional configuration presents significant contradictions because global elites as a whole do not have access to that apparatus in the way the US contingent of that elite does. Even when there is ever greater transnational consultation among global elites and transnational state managers, the transnational elite is unable, when it comes to the US (or any national) state, to undertake the types of internal strategic debate, the consensus-building processes, consensual mechanisms and also conspiratorial dimensions of policymaking that take place at the level of the national state. Moreover, the US and other national states are subject to the pressures of internal (national) legitimacy and to particularist interests.

There is little disagreement among global elites, regardless of their formal nationality, that US power should be rigorously applied when it comes to advancing the interests of transnational capital, such as imposing IMF programs, bailing out the global banking system, sending "peacekeeping " and "humanitarian" missions to Haiti or the Horn of Africa, or bombing the former Yugoslavia, in order to sustain and defend global capitalism. The US state is a key point of condensation for pressures from dominant groups around the world to resolve problems of global capitalism and to secure the legitimacy of the system overall. In this regard, "US" imperialism refers to the use by transnational elites of the US state apparatus to continue to attempt to expand, defend, and stabilize the global capitalist system. We are witnessing not so much "US" imperialism per se but rather a global capitalist imperialism. We face an empire of global capital, headquartered, for evident historical reasons, in Washington. The questions for global elites are as follows: In what ways, under what particular conditions, arrangements, and strategies should US state power be wielded? How can particular sets of US state managers be responsive and held accountable to global elites who are fractious in their actions, dispersed around the world, and operating through numerous supranational institutional settings, each with distinct histories and particular trajectories?

The structural changes that have led to the transnationalization of national capitals, finances, and markets, and the actual outcomes of recent US-led political and military campaigns, suggest new forms of global capitalist domination, whereby interventions in Iraq, East Africa, Honduras, Haiti, and the former Yugoslavia aim to create conditions favorable to the penetration of transnational capital and the renewed integration of the intervened region into the global system. US intervention facilitates a shift in power from locally and regionally oriented elites to new groups more favorable to the transnational project. The result of US military conquest is not the creation of exclusive zones for "US" exploitation, as was the result of the Spanish conquest of Latin America, the British of East Africa and India, the Dutch of Indonesia, and so forth, in earlier moments of the world capitalist system. The enhanced class power of capital brought about by these changes is felt around the world. We see, not a reenactment of this old imperialism, but rather the colonization and recolonization of the vanquished for the new global capitalism and its agents. The underlying class relation between the transnational capitalist class and the US national state should be understood in these terms. The US state houses the ministry of war in a much-divided global elite cabinet.

MILITARIZED ACCUMULATION AND THE CASE OF IRAQ

Most observers saw the US invasion and occupation of Iraq as the premier example of the "new imperialism" —a US attempt to control Iraqi oil in the face of rivals and to shore up its declining hegemony. In criticizing my theory of the transnational state, Kees Van der Pijl stated that "the U.S. and the UK have used (in Iraq for instance) their military 'comparative advantage' to trump the Russian and French willingness to strike oil deals with the Saddam Hussein regime when it appeared that UN sanctions were unraveling."[29] Yet the very first transnational oil company to be assisted by the US state department in the wake of Washington's invasion and occupation was the "French" oil company Total, followed by Chinese oil companies that were able to enter the Iraqi oil market thanks to the US occupation.

The opposition of France, Germany, and other countries to the Iraq invasion indicated not national capital rivalry but sharp tactical and strategic differences over how to respond to crisis, shore up the system, and keep it expanding. Baker has shown how the invasion of Iraq violently opened up the country to transnational capital and integrated it into new global circuits. It resulted in a shift from the old nationally oriented to transnationally oriented elites cultivated and placed in power by the occupation force, the imposition of radical neoliberal restructuring, and a change in the regional balance of forces in favor of the global capitalist power bloc.[30] As Klein has observed, "the architects of the invasion … unleashed ferocious violence because they could not crack open the closed economies of the Middle East by peaceful means."[31] In addition, the invasions of Iraq and of Afghanistan opened up vast profit-making opportunities for the transnational capitalist class at a time when the global economy showed serious signs of stagnation, a process I refer to as *militarized accumulation*.

If the US state has attempted to play a leadership role on behalf of transnational capitalist interests, it has been increasingly unable to do so, not because of heightened national rivalry, but rather because of the impossibility of the task at hand given a spiraling crisis of global capitalism. This crisis has generated intense discrepancies and disarray within the globalist power bloc, which at best has been held together by fragile threads and appeared as we moved further into the twenty-first century to be tearing apart from the seams under the pressure of conflicts internal to it and from forces opposed to its logic. The political coherence of ruling groups always frays when faced with structural and/or legitimacy crises as different groups push distinct strategies and tactics or turn to the more immediate pursuit of sectoral interests.

Faced with the increasingly dim prospects of constructing a viable transnational hegemony (in the sense of a stable system of consensual domination as articulated by Antonio Gramsci), the transnational bour-geoisie has not collapsed back into the nation-state. Global elites have, instead, mustered up fragmented and at times incoherent responses in-volving heightened military coercion, the search for a post-Washing-ton consensus, and acrimonious internal disputes. The more politically astute among global elites have clamored in recent years to promote a "post-Washington consensus" project of reform—a so-called "globaliza-tion with a human face"—in the interests of saving the system itself.[32] But there were others from within and outside of the bloc that called for more radical responses, included a turn to right-wing authoritarianism and even neofascism, as symbolized by Trumpism in the United States.

Neoliberalism "peacefully" forced open new areas for global capital in the 1980s and the 1990s. This was often accomplished through economic coercion alone, made possible by the structural power of the global econo-my over individual countries. But this structural power became less effec-tive in the face of the escalating crisis of global capitalism. Opportunities for both intensive and extensive expansion dried up as privatizations ran their course, as the "socialist" countries became integrated, as the con-sumption of high-income sectors worldwide reached ceilings when spend-ing through private credit expansion could not be sustained. As the space for "peaceful" expansion, both intensive and extensive, became ever more restricted, military aggression became an instrument for prying open new sectors and regions, for the forcible restructuring of space in order to fur-ther accumulation. The train of neoliberalism became latched on to mil-itary intervention and the threat of coercive sanctions as a locomotive for pulling the moribund Washington consensus forward. The "war on terror-ism" provided a seemingly endless military outlet for surplus capital, gen-erated a colossal deficit that justified deeper dismantling of the Keynesian welfare state and locking neoliberal austerity in place, and legitimated the creation of a police state to repress political dissent in the name of security.

In the period that began with the September 11, 2001, attacks in the United States, the military dimension appeared to exercise an overde-termining influence in the reconfiguration of global politics.[33] The Bush White House militarized social and economic contradictions generat-ed by crisis tendencies in global capitalism, launching a permanent war mobilization to try to stabilize the system through direct coercion. The Obama White House followed suit, as did the Trump White House, despite distinct rhetorical discourses. Was this evidence for a new US bid for empire? Interventionism and militarized globalization have been less a campaign for US hegemony than a contradictory political response to the crisis of global capitalism—to economic stagnation, legitimation problems, and the rise of counterhegemonic forces. In fact, the US state has undertaken an almost unprecedented role in creating profit-making opportunities for transnational capital and pushing forward an accumulation process that, left to its own devices (the "free market"), would likely have ground to a halt well before the 2008 Great Recession.

Some saw the billions of dollars invested by the US state in the invasion and occupation of Iraq as evidence that the US intervention benefits "US capital" to the detriment of other national capitals. However, Bechtel, the Carlyle Group, and Halliburton—giant US-based financial, engineering, and construction conglomerates that were prime recipients of US military contracts—are themselves transnational capital conglomerates. Carlyle, for example, is one of the largest private equity (holding) companies in the world, with investors from seventy-five countries and hundreds of companies from around the world. Among its officials are former British prime minister John Major, former UN Secretary General Javier Perez de Cuéllar, former president of the Deutsche Bundesbank Karl Otto Pöhl, former South Korean prime minister Park Tae-joon; the Saudi royal family (including members of the bin Laden family); Montenegro President Milo Djukanović; global financier George Soros; numerous officers from European-based businesses; and representatives from Nigeria, Dubai, China, India, Brazil, South Africa, and Singapore.[34] Rothkopf observes that defense firms around the world are becoming more and more integrated into a global network through strategic alliances, joint ventures, and cross-border mergers.[35]

The "creative destruction" of war (and natural and humanitarian disasters) generates new cycles of accumulation through "reconstruction." And the military-energy-engineering-construction-financial complex constitutes one of those sectors of global capital that most benefits from the "creative destruction" of crises, wars, and natural and humanitarian disasters (i.e., militarized accumulation). Transnational capitalists are themselves aware of the role of the US state in opening up new possibilities for unloading of surplus and creating new investment opportunities. "We're looking for places to invest around the world," explained one former executive of a Dutch-based oil exploration and engineering company, and then, "you know, along comes Iraq."[36]

The billions invested by the US state in war and "reconstruction" in Iraq went to a vast array of investors and sub-contractors that spanned the globe. First Kuwaiti General Trading & Contracting Company, Alargan International Real Estate Company of Kuwait, Gulf Catering Company, and Saudi Arabian Trading and Construction Company were just some of the Middle East-based companies that shared in the bonanza, along with companies and investor groups as far away as South Africa, Bosnia, the Philippines, and India.[37] The picture was one in which the US state mobilized the resources to feed a vast transnational network of profit-making that passed through countless layers of outsourcing, subcontracting, alliances, and collaborative relations, benefiting transnationally oriented capitalists from many parts of the globe. The US state was the pivotal gear in a transnational state machinery dedicated to reproducing global capitalism.

IMPERIALISM AND THE EXTENSIVE AND INTENSIVE ENLARGEMENT OF CAPITALISM

If the world is not divided into rival national economies and national capitals, do we still need a theory of imperialism? Is there any contemporary relevance to the concept? In the post-World War II period, and drawing on the tradition established by Rosa Luxemburg, Marxists and other critical political economists shifted the main focus in the study of imperialism to the mechanisms of core capitalist penetration of Third World countries and the appropriation of their surpluses. Imperialism in this sense referred to this exploitation and also to the use of state apparatuses by capitalist groups emanating from the centers of the world capitalist system to facilitate this economic relation through military, political, and cultural mechanisms. If we mean by imperialism the relentless pressures for outward expansion of capitalism and the distinct political, military, and cultural mechanisms that facilitate that expansion and the appropriation of surpluses it generates, then it is a structural imperative built into capitalism. It is not a policy of particular core state managers but a practice immanent to the system itself. The imperialism practiced by successive US administrations without interruption is nothing particular to a group of politicians and government administrators in the United States.

We need tools to conceptualize, analyze, and theorize how this expansionary pressure built into the capitalist system manifests itself in the age of globalization. We need these tools politically so as to help make effective our confrontation with the system. We do indeed need a theory of imperialism to understand the "brave new world" of global capitalism as well as the place of the South and uneven development in that order.[38] Yet even with the correct tools, capitalist imperialism is considerably more complex under globalization than the facile North–South, the First World–Third World, the developed–underdeveloped, or the core–periphery framework through which it is typically viewed. To reiterate: The class relations of global capitalism are now so deeply internalized within every nation-state that the classical image of imperialism as a relation of external domination is outdated. Failure to comprehend this leads to superficial and misleading conclusions—for instance, that the failure of popular projects to materialize under the rule of the Workers' Party in Brazil or the African National Congress in South Africa is a result of a "sell out" by the leaders of those parties or simply because "imperialism" undercut their programs.

Imperialism is not about nations but about groups exercising their social power—through institutions—to control the worldwide production of wealth (value), to appropriate surpluses, and to reproduce these arrangements. The theoretical challenge is to ask is this: how and by whom in the world capitalist system are wealth or values produced (organized through what institutions), how are they appropriated (through what institutions), and how are these processes changing through capitalist globalization? During the more than 500 years since the genesis of the world capitalist system, colonialism and imperialism coercively incorporated zones and peoples into its fold. This historical process of "primitive accumulation" is coming to a close.

The end of the extensive enlargement of capitalism is the end of the imperialist era of world capitalism. The system still conquers space, nature, and human beings. It is dehumanizing, genocidal, suicidal, and maniacal. But with the exception of a few remaining spaces—Iraq until recently, North Korea, others—the world has been brought into the system over the past half millennium. The implacable logic of accumulation is now largely internal to worldwide social relations and to the complex of fractious political institutions through which ruling groups attempt to manage those relations. The effort by the US state to design repressive immigration legislation to assure a cheap, repressed, and tightly controlled Latino workforce within US territory is no different than the efforts of the transnational state to impose intellectual property rights in Latin America, privatization in Southern Africa, or deregulated and flexible labor in the EU—all this, and more, is the ugly face of global capitalism. But it is not imperialism in the old sense either of rival national capitals or conquest by core states of precapitalist regions. We need a *theory of capitalist expansion*—of the political processes and the institutions through which such expansion takes place and the class relations and spatial dynamics it involves.

SIX

GLOBAL CAPITALISM, MIGRANT LABOR, AND THE STRUGGLE FOR SOCIAL JUSTICE

I n recent years, the international media has been full of stories on the rising tide of immigrant workers in the global system—their struggles, trials, and tribulations and the widespread repression and hostility they face everywhere from authoritarian states and racist publics. Some of the stories from around the world have made headlines: the crisis, largely contrived, of Central American child migration and the fiasco of "comprehensive immigrant reform" in the United States, along with the openly racist tirades by US President Donald Trump against Mexican immigrants as "rapists and criminals"; the rising tide of racist violence against immigrant workers in North America, Europe, Israel, and elsewhere; the tragedy of thousands of Africans drowning in the Mediterranean as they attempt to reach Europe; pogroms against southern African immigrant workers in South African cities; and the suicide of dozens of internal immigrant workers in China's coastal sweatshops, among others. Everywhere, borders are militarized, states are stepping up repressive anti-immigrant controls, and native publics are turning immigrants into scapegoats for the spiraling crisis of global capitalism. Yet everywhere, immigrant justice movements are forming and workers are fighting back (and immigrant workers are playing a pivotal and often leading role in that struggle).

The massive displacement and primitive accumulation unleashed by free trade agreements and neoliberal policies, as well as state and "private" violence, has resulted in a virtually inexhaustible immigrant labor reserve for the global economy. In turn, repressive state controls over immigration and migrant labor have several functions for the system. First, state repression and criminalization of undocumented immigration makes these immigrants vulnerable and deportable, and therefore subject to conditions of superexploitation, supercontrol, and hypersurveillance. Second, anti-immigrant repressive apparatuses and social control systems are themselves ever more important sources of accumulation, ranging from private, for-profit immigrant detention centers to the militarization of borders and the purchase by states of military hardware and systems of surveillance. Third, the anti-immigrant policies associated with repressive state apparatuses help turn attention away from the crisis of global capitalism among more privileged sectors of the working class, such as middle layers in the global South or white workers in the North, and convert immigrant workers into scapegoats for the crisis, thus deflecting attention from the root causes of the crisis and undermining working class unity.

The story of immigrant labor in the twenty-first century is therefore absolutely central to that of the new global capitalism and also to that of the struggles of the global working class for justice and emancipation. This essay will reflect on a portion of this story with a particular focus on structural and historical underpinnings of the phenomenon of immigrant labor in the new global capitalist system and on the United States as an illustration of the larger worldwide situation with regard to migration and immigrant justice.

CAPITALISM, THE WORLD LABOR MARKET, AND MIGRATION/IMMIGRATION

Perhaps the most pressing problem the capitalist system faces is how to secure a politically and economically suitable supply of labor. But what does securing "suitable" labor mean? In the first place, it means uprooting people from their land and other means of livelihood, or what is known as *primitive accumulation*, so that they have no other choice but to work for capital if they want to survive. Second, it means generating a large enough pool of labor so that this pool can be dipped into as needed and later these same workers can be disposed of when not needed. Third, it means generating the means and conditions to deploy that labor wherever it is needed around the world. Finally, it means developing systems of repression and ideological hegemony to assure that workers are tightly controlled, disorganized, disciplined, and obedient.

Central to the formation of the world capitalist system was the creation of a world market in labor. Securing this politically and economically suitable labor supply has historically been a key function of colonialism and imperialism. Dominant groups have created and constantly recreated this market over the past five centuries of world capitalism through the most violent and destructive processes imaginable. The formation of a world market in labor has involved such mechanisms as the kidnapping and forced removal of some 20 million Africans to the New World; the internal transfer in this New World of tens of millions of indigenous populations; the displacement from their lands of millions of European peasants by the forces of capitalist expansion and their migration around the world as laborers; and the so-called second slavery from the 1870s into the 1930s of millions of "coolie" labor from India and China who, under the weight of colonialism, found themselves displaced, dispossessed, and swept up by international labor recruiters by hook or by crook to build railroads or work plantations in Africa, Asia, and the Western hemisphere.[1]

This creation of a world labor market is simultaneously the history of migration, and it is the history of the racialization of global class relations through the creation by dominant groups of racial and ethnic hierarchies within the labor pools that the system has brought into being and sustained over the 500 years of its existence. If migration/immigration has thus been central to the creation of the world capitalist system, today it is just as crucial to the reproduction of the new global capitalism. However, under capitalist globalization a new global immigrant labor supply system has come to replace earlier direct colonial and racial caste controls over labor worldwide. There is a new global working class that labors in the factories, farms, commercial establishments, and offices of the global economy—a working class that faces conditions of precariousness, is heavily female, and (for the purposes of this article) is increasingly based on immigrant labor.

The rise of new systems of transnational labor mobility and recruitment have made it possible for dominant groups around the world to reorganize labor markets and recruit transient labor forces that are disenfranchised and easy to control. Toward the latter decades of the twentieth century, massive new migrations worldwide began to take place. In 1960 there were some 75 million immigrant workers worldwide and 100 million in 1980. The International Labor Organization put the figure for 2014 at 232 million.[2] The United Nations reported that the number of migrant workers worldwide more than doubled from 1980 to 2005, reaching 200 million, and then increased by 2017 to 285 million.[3] Moreover, these figures do not take into account the tens of millions of Chinese who have migrated from the interior of that country to the coastal cities to work in the industrial sweatshops that now serve as the leading workshop of the world, and who constitute in the practice an immigrant workforce as a result of Chinese internal pass and residency laws, known as the *hukou system*.[4]

Immigrant labor historically has flowed from the colonized regions to the metropolitan countries. Still today, major transnational migrant flows are from Latin America and Asia into North America; from Africa, the Middle East, and South Asia into Europe, and so on—that is, from the traditional peripheries to the traditional cores of the world capitalist system. However, that pattern is rapidly changing. Now we see that major axes of accumulation in the global economy attract immigrant labor from neighboring regions. Intense transnational corporate activity, wherever it takes place in the new global economy—from the factories along China's southern coastal belt, to the South African mines and farms, the Middle East oil meccas, and Costa Rica's service industry— become magnets drawing in immigrant workers. And wherever these workers end up, they face the same conditions: relegation to low-paid, low-status jobs; the denial of labor rights; political disenfranchisement; state repression; racism; bigotry; and nativism.

Nicaraguans migrate to Costa Rica; Bolivians to Argentina; Peruvians to Chile; Southern and Central Africans to South Africa; Indians, Pakistanis, and Sri Lankans to the Middle East oil producers; Indonesians to Malaysia and Myanmar to Thailand. Israel has recently become a major importer of transnational immigrant labor from Asia and North Africa. (This is a particularly attractive option for Israel because it does away with the need for politically troublesome Palestinian labor.) Over 300,000 immigrant workers from Thailand, China, Nepal, and Sri Lanka now form the predominant labor force in Israeli agribusiness in the same way as Mexican and Central American immigrant labor does in US agribusiness, and under the same precarious conditions of superexploitation and discrimination. The Philippines presents an extreme case: the Philippine government and private recruitment firms organize the export of Philippine workers to some 200 countries around the world.[5] These labor migrations are not voluntary in the sense that the structural violence of the system is what forces people to migrate. It is important to see transnational immigrant labor therefore as a form of *coerced* labor.

Once they arrive at their destinations, undocumented immigrants join the ranks of a superexploitable labor force available for transnational corporations, local employers, and native middle classes. It is often said that capital has torn down national barriers to its global mobility and that it is now free to cross borders at will, and this is quite true. It is also true, however, that labor is globally mobile, not in the sense that it can freely cross borders but in the sense that, in practice, the structural conditions of capitalist globalization not only make possible but actually facilitate the worldwide deployment of immigrant labor as needed by capital worldwide. Immigrant workers are globally mobile, but under conditions of extreme repressive control over the movement and over their very existence. Borders and the international state system are essential for capitalist domination over workers and the creation and reproduction of a global reserve army of immigrant workers.

GLOBALIZATION AND THE CREATION OF "IMMIGRANT LABOR"

Global capitalism is characterized by a number of fundamental changes in the capitalist system that have implications for how we understand the role of labor and the struggle for social justice. Among these changes is the rise of truly transnational capital and the integration of every country into the new system of globalized production, finances, and services and the rise of a transnational capitalist class. The transnational capitalist class is a new class group grounded in global over local or national circuits of accumulation and which, together with transnationally oriented state bureaucrats and politicians, is the manifest agent of capitalist globalization.[6]

Capital responded to the worldwide structural crisis of the 1970s by "going global" in an attempt to break through the constraints that the nation-state (i.e., the working and popular classes operating at the nation-state level) placed on accumulation. These working and popular classes were unwilling to shoulder the burden of the crisis; as long as they could pressure states to place constraints on capital, they could sustain a standoff with capital that generated "stagflation," a decline in profits, and a growing political and ideological crisis of hegemony. In response, dominant groups called for a vast restructuring of world capitalism. With the election of Ronald Reagan in the United States and Margaret Thatcher in Britain, they launched the "neoliberal counterrevolution" as an offensive against working and popular classes everywhere, involving the dismantling of developmentalist, socialist, and redistributive projects.[7]

The global mobility of capital associated with globalization allowed the transnational capitalist class to break free of nation-state constraints to accumulation as it restructured the world economy, fragmented production and the labor process, and altered the correlation of class and social forces in its favor, at least in the momentary historic conjuncture of the late twentieth and early twenty-first centuries. Free trade agreements and neoliberal policies have displaced hundreds of millions of people around the world and generated a vast pool of under- and unemployed labor thrown into the global labor market. The North American Free Trade Agreement that went into effect in 1994, for instance, resulted in the displacement of up to 5 million families from the Mexican countryside, many of whom then became transnational migrants. Similarly, neoliberal policies imposed on Central America following the wars of revolution and counterrevolution in the 1980s displaced millions and turned them into transnational migrants.[8]

As a result, the transnational capitalist class has been able to forge a new capital–labor relation based on the "flexibilization" or "Walmartization" of labor. Under this new modality of flexible labor, workers no longer enjoy the protection of state regulation of the capital–labor relation. They face conditions of deunionization, are informalized, casualized, part-time, contract, and temporary. Crucial to the new labor relations of global capitalism is the elimination of any reciprocity between capital and labor; capital bears no responsibility for the social reproduction of labor, on the one hand, and on the other, the state abandons redistributive policies that recirculates value back to labor in the form of the social wages and instead subsidizes capital. Workers have increasingly become a "naked" commodity, an input into production just as any other raw material. They can be hired and fired at will and enjoy no stability, what many are now referring to the new "precariat" or the proletariat that labors under conditions of permanent insecurity and precariousness.[9]

These new class relations of global capitalism have been made possible in part by capital's newfound mobility and in part by the dramatic expansion of the global superfluous population—that portion marginalized and locked out of productive participation in the capitalist economy and constituting some one-third of humanity.[10] This mass of "supernumeraries" is of no direct use to capital. However, in the larger picture such surplus labor is crucial to global capitalism insofar as it places downward pressure on wages everywhere—especially to the extent that global labor markets can be tapped and labor can be mobilized throughout the global economy—and allows transnational capital to impose discipline over those who remain active in the labor market.

There is a broad social and political base, therefore, for the maintenance of flexible, supercontrolled, and superexploited immigrant labor pools. The system cannot function without it. But if global capital needs the labor power of transnational migrants, this labor power belongs to human beings who must be tightly controlled, given the special oppression and dehumanization involved in extracting their labor power as noncitizen immigrant labor. The state must play a balancing act by finding a formula for a stable supply of cheap labor for employers and at the same time for greater state control over immigrants. The dilemma (and the contradiction) for capital, dominant groups, and affluent and privileged strata becomes how to assure a steady supply of immigrant labor while at the same time promoting anti-immigrant practices and ideologies. The instruments for achieving the dual goals of superexploitability and supercontrollability are (a) the division of the working class into immigrant and citizen, and (b) racialization and criminalization of the former. In this way race and class converge. Racialization is an instrument in the politics of domination, and racism is critical to the rule of capital.

Criminalization and militarization increasingly drive undocumented immigrants around the world underground, where they become vulnerable to intermediaries in the quest for survival, such as gangs, drug traffickers, sexual exploitation, shady temporary labor agencies, and unscrupulous employers. The array of state and other institutional controls over immigrants further drive down black and informal market wages and working and living conditions, and they give employers an ever freer hand.[11] At the same time, borders must be militarized if they are to be effective instruments for regulating and controlling the supply of im-

migrant labor. By the end of the twentieth century, the United States–
Mexico border was one of the most militarized stretches of land in the
world, with ten guards for every mile for the length of the 2,000-mile
border. Many stretches along the frontier are akin to a war zone.[12] US
President Donald Trump's fanatical campaign to "build the wall" was
distinct only in rhetoric from the border militarization pursued by his
predecessors, Democratic and Republican alike.

A key point here is that the globalization of production, finances,
and services has increased transnational capital's ability to fragment labor markets in each locale and to create and reproduce new forms of
labor market segmentation at the transborder level. There are particular
institutional arrangements through which this worldwide deployment
of immigrant labor occurs: "immigrant labor" is created by states as a
distinct juridical category of labor. The global working class thus becomes divided between "citizen" and "immigrant" labor. This is a major
new axis of inequality worldwide. The superexploitation of an immigrant
workforce would not be possible if that workforce had the same civil,
political, and labor rights as citizens, if it did not face the insecurities and
vulnerabilities of being undocumented or "illegal." State controls over
immigrant labor are intended not to prevent but to control the transnational movement of labor and to lock that labor into a situation of
permanent insecurity and vulnerability. The creation of these distinct
categories ("immigrant labor") replaces earlier direct colonial and racial
caste controls over labor worldwide.

In this age of globalization, this creation of two distinct categories
of labor around the world ("immigrant" and "citizen") constitutes a new,
rigid caste system that has become central to the global economy and
worldwide capital accumulation. Reproducing the division of workers
into immigrants and citizens requires contradictory practices on the part
of states. The state must provide capital with immigrant labor but must
also in its ideological activities generate a nationalist hysteria by propagating such images as "out of control borders" and "invasions of illegal immigrants" in order to legitimate the mechanisms of control and
surveillance and to turn native against immigrant labor. Granting full
citizenship rights to the hundreds of millions of immigrants and their
families would undermine the division of the global working class into
immigrants and citizens and would weaken capital's ability to divide and
exploit the global working class. The struggle of immigrant workers is

therefore at the cutting edge of popular movements worldwide against the depredations of global capitalism and is central to the struggle of the global working class.

States practice a "revolving door" function in the era of globalization—opening and shutting the flow of immigration in accordance with the needs of capital accumulation during distinct periods and the flux of national politics. Immigrants are sucked up when their labor is needed and then spit out when they become superfluous or potentially destabilizing to the system.[13] The condition of *deportable* must be created and then reproduced—periodically refreshed with new waves of "illegal" immigrants—since that condition assures the ability to superexploit with impunity and to dispose of without consequences should this labor become unruly or unnecessary. Driving immigrant labor deeper underground and absolving the state and employers of any commitment to the social reproduction of this labor allows for its maximum exploitation together with its disposal when necessary.

Labor supply through transnational migration constitutes the export of commodified human beings. This commodification goes beyond the more limited concept first developed by Marx, in which the worker's labor power is sold to capital as a commodity. To Marx we must add Foucaultian insights, in particular, recognition that control reaches beyond the productive structure, beyond consumption and social relations, to encompass the body itself (hence "biopolitics"). In the classical Marxist construct, workers face alienation and exploitation during the time they sell this commodity to capital, that is, during the work shift. In between this regularized sale of labor power, they are not commodities but rather alienated human beings, "free" to rest and replenish in the sphere of social reproduction.

In its archetypical form, the new immigrant worker as a mobile input for globalized circuits of accumulation is not just selling commodified labor during the work period; the whole body becomes a commodity, mobilized and supplied in the same way as are raw materials, money, intermediate goods, and other inputs. It is, after all, the whole body that must migrate and insert itself into the global accumulation circuits as immigrant labor. Hence, even when each regular sale of labor power concludes (i.e., after each work period), the worker is not "free" to rest and replenish as in the traditional Marxist analysis of labor and capital because he or she remains immigrant/undocumented labor twenty-four hours a day, unable to engage in the "normal" channels of rest and social reproduction because of the whole set of institutional exclusions, state controls, racialized discrimination, xenophobia, and oppression experienced by the undocumented immigrant worker in the larger social milieu. The worldwide immigrant labor regime becomes the very epitome of transnational capital's naked domination in the age of globalization.

In the United States and Europe and in a number of countries in Latin America and Asia, immigrants have been denied access to basic social services and benefits (the social wage). The immigrant labor force in these countries becomes responsible for its own maintenance and reproduction and also (through remittances) for their family members in their home countries. This makes immigrant labor low-cost and flexible for capital and also costless for the state compared to native-born labor. Immigrant workers become the archetype of the new global class relations, the quintessential workforce of global capitalism. They are yanked out of relations of reciprocity rooted in social and political communities that have historically been institutionalized in nation-states. As well, immigrant workers send billions of dollars home to their families and communities. These monies make possible social reproduction in home countries, and this alleviates pressures that may otherwise generate political crises and allows receiving families to consume goods made in the Global Factory and distributed in the Global Mall. These transnationally recycled wages also enter the financial system and help balance state budgets and achieve macroeconomic stability.[14]

ANTI-IMMIGRANT POLITICS
AND THE IMMIGRANT JUSTICE MOVEMENT:

THE CASE OF THE UNITED STATES

As the United States has led the way in globalization, it has also led the way in the construction of a new transient labor system. Eight million Latin American emigrants arrived in the United States during the 1980s as globalization, neoliberalism, and global labor market restructuring induced a wave of outmigration from Latin America. This was nearly equal to the total figure of European immigrants who arrived on US shores during the first decades of the twentieth century and made Latin

America the principal origin of migration into the United States. Some 36 million immigrant workers were in the United States in 2010, at least 20 million of them from Latin America.

Right-wing politicians, law-enforcement agents, and neofascist anti-immigrant movements may intentionally generate racist hostility toward Latinos and other immigrants. The US Southern Command has gone so far as to frame migration as a national security threat, calling it (in the words of General John Kelly) a "crime-terror convergence."[15] (Kelly, who said this while serving as commander of US military forces operating throughout Latin America, was appointed by the Trump administration in 2017 to head the Department of Homeland Security and then moved on to become the chief of staff.) Yet this anti-immigrant hostility may also be the effect of the structural and legal-institutional subordination of immigrant workers and their communities, or simply an unintended (although not necessarily unwelcomed) byproduct of the state's coercive policies. Embodied in this structural condition is the rise and the ongoing recomposition of an internally stratified global working class controlled by political borders, state repression, criminalization, and militarization. The state's war on immigrants in the United States, including an escalation of workplace and community raids, detentions and deportations, racial profiling, new surveillance systems (such as E-Verify), police abuse, and so forth has fed hate crimes against immigrants and hostility toward Latino/a communities. Donald Trump's openly racist and rabidly anti-immigrant discourse further fueled an escalation of such hate crimes.

The activities of the American Legislative Exchange Council (ALEC) expose the inner connections between corporate interests, the state, militarization and policing, and anti-immigrant and other neofascist tendencies in civil society.[16] ALEC brings together state and federal elected officials and law enforcement and criminal justice system representatives with some 200 of the most powerful transnational corporations, among them ATT, Coca Cola, Exxon Mobile, Pfizer, Kraft Foods, Walmart, Bank of America, Microsoft, Nestlé, AstraZeneca, Dow Chemical, Sony, and Koch Industries; the latter is one of the biggest ALEC funders. ALEC develops legislative initiatives that advance the transnational corporate agenda, hammering out in its gatherings draft criminal justice, anti-union, tax reform, financial and environmental deregulation, and related bills that are then tabled by state and local elected officials associated with ALEC. These bills have included the notorious "three strikes law" that mandates twenty-five years to life sentences for those committing a third offense (even for minor drug possession) and "truth in sentencing," which requires people to serve all of their time with no chance of parole.

State assemblyman Russell Pearce, an ALEC board member, first introduced the notorious anti-immigrant law SB1070, passed in Arizona in 2010, into the state legislature. In 2009, ALEC members, including Pearce and representatives from the Corrections Corporation of America (CCA, the largest private prison operator in the United States), drafted a model anti-immigrant law. Pearce then introduced the bill into the Arizona legislature with the support of thirty-six co-sponsors, thirty of whom received campaign contributions from CCA lobbyists as well as from lobbyists for two other private prison companies, Geo Group and Management and Training Corporation. The bill was then signed by Arizona Governor Jan Brewer, who herself has close ties to CCA and to ALEC. The CAA (which rebranded itself as CoreCivic) has received lucrative contracts to run immigrant detention centers in Arizona.[17] SB1070 legalized racial profiling by instructing state law enforcement agents to detain and question anyone who appeared to be undocumented and authorizing anyone to sue police who failed to do so, requiring in effect everyone to carry proof of citizenship or legal residence at all times. Among other stipulations, it also required teachers to compile lists of suspected immigrant children and directed emergency rooms and social service agencies to deny care to those who cannot prove citizenship or legal residence.

Although some of the most draconian provisions were struck down later by federal courts, the Arizona law became a model for "copycat" legislation passed in five other states and introduced in several dozen more. The magazine *Mother Jones* built a database of hundreds of repressive local and state level anti-immigrant laws introduced around the United States in the wake of SB1070, including 164 such laws passed by state legislatures in 2010 and 2011 alone.[18] The database also uncovered the extensive interlocking of far-right organizations comprising the anti-immigrant movement, other neofascist organizations in civil society, government agencies and elected officials (local and federal), politicians, and corporate and foundation funders, lobbies, and activists.

Immigrant labor is extremely profitable for the transnational corporate economy in a double sense. First, it is labor that is highly vulnerable, forced to exist semi-underground, and deportable, and therefore superexploitable. Second, the criminalization of undocumented immigrants and the militarization of their control not only reproduce these conditions of vulnerability but also in themselves generate vast new opportunities for accumulation. The private immigrant detention complex is a boom industry. Undocumented immigrants constitute the fastest growing sector of the US prison population and are detained in private detention centers and deported by private companies contracted out by the US state. As of 2010, there were 270 immigration detention centers that caged on any given day more than 30,000 immigrants and annually locked up some 400,000 individuals, compared to just a few dozen people in immigrant detention each day prior to the 1980s[19]—that is, prior to the launching of capitalist globalization and the new transnational systems of labor recruitment and control associated with it.

Under Obama, more immigrants were detained and deported than at any time in the previous half century. Detentions and deportations then escalated further under Trump, thus continuing the pattern in place since the 1980s. Some detention centers housed entire families, so that children were behind bars with their parents. Since detainment facilities and deportation logistics are subcontracted to private companies, capital has a vested interest in the criminalization of immigrants and in the militarization of control over immigrants—and more broadly, therefore, a vested interest in contributing to the neofascist anti-immigrant movement.

A month after SB1070 became law, Wayne Calabrese, the president of Geo Group, held a conference call with investors and explained his company's aspirations. "Opportunities at the federal level are going to continue apace as a result of what's happening," he said, referring to the Arizona law. "Those people coming across the border being caught are going to have to be detained and that to me at least suggests there's going to be enhanced opportunities for what we do." The 2005 annual report of the CCA stated with regard to the profit-making opportunities opened up by the prison-industrial complex:

> Our growth is generally dependent upon our ability to obtain new contracts to develop and manage new correctional and detention facilities … The demand for our facilities and services could be adversely affected by the relaxation of enforcement efforts, leniency in conviction and sentencing practices or through the decriminalization of certain activities that are currently proscribed by our criminal laws.[20]

The day after Donald Trump's November 2016 electoral victory, the CCA stock price soared 40 percent on the strength of Trump's promise to deport millions of immigrants.[21]

By the second decade of the twenty-first century, more than 350,000 immigrants were going through privately run prisons for the undocumented each year and record numbers were being deported, even though the absolute number of immigrants had declined. The United States spends more on immigration enforcement than all other enforcement activities of the federal government combined, including the FBI; the Drug Enforcement Administration; and the Bureau of Alcohol, Tobacco, Firearms and Explosives.

THE IMMIGRANT JUSTICE MOVEMENT

As anti-immigrant scapegoating and racism heightened in the latter part of the twentieth century, so too did resistance on the part of immigrants and their supporters alongside labor struggles in which immigrant workers have played an ever-more prominent role. In the United States, an immigrant justice movement dates back decades and had been building as part of the Central American solidarity movement of the 1980s. In 1986, under pressure from this movement, the US Congress passed the Immigration Reform and Control Act, which set up a onetime amnesty process for several million undocumented immigrants but also set up new "guest worker" (read: peonage labor) programs, penalized employers for hiring undocumented worker and required them to check the immigration status of every worker, and expanded border militarization and control over immigrant communities. As journalist and immigrant rights activist David Bacon has noted, the Immigration Reform and Control Act "set in place the basic dividing line in the modern immigrant rights movement" between a moderate wing and a radical wing.[22]

The immigrant justice movement exploded into mass protests in the United States in spring 2006,[23] triggered by the introduction in the US Senate of a draconian piece of draft legislation, known as the Sensenbrenner Bill for the name of the sponsoring senator, that would have criminalized undocumented immigrants and their supporters. These mass protests of spring 2006 mobilized tens of millions of immigrants and their allies and helped defeat the Sensenbrenner Bill, but also sparked an escalation of state repression and racist nativism and fuelled the neofascist anti-immigrant movement. Particularly frightening to ruling groups was a general strike by immigrants on May Day 2016, El Gran Paro Americano 2006/Un Día Sin Inmigrantes (the Great American Strike/A Day Without an Immigrant), that paralyzed the economy in cities where immigrants formed a significant portion of the workforce.[24] The backlash involved, among other things, stepped-up raids on immigrant workplaces and communities; mass deportations; an increase in the number of federal immigration enforcement agents; the deputizing of local police forces as enforcement agents; the further militarization of the United States–Mexico border; anti-immigrant hysteria in the mass media; and the introduction at the local, state, and federal levels of a slew of discriminatory anti-immigrant legislative initiatives.

In the face of what can only be described as a terror campaign against immigrant communities, a split occurred: the more "moderate" or liberal wing of the leadership pursued a strategy of seeking allies in the halls of power and limiting mass mobilization to a pressure mechanism on elites to open up space at the table for the Latino/a establishment, while the more radical, grassroots-oriented wing insisted on building a mass movement for immigrant rights and social justice from the ground up. The liberal camp sought allies in Congress, among the Democrats, organized labor, and mainstream civil rights and public advocacy organizations to negotiate more favorable immigrant reform legislation. This camp was willing to sacrifice the interests of some immigrants in order to win concessions from mainstream allies, such as forsaking full legalization for all immigrants in exchange for dubious "paths to citizenship" and compromising over such issues such as "guest workers programs," which have been condemned as indentured servitude and have been shown to place the labor movement in a more vulnerable position.

The radical grassroots camp was not against lobbying or attempting to penetrate the halls of power, but it insisted on prioritizing a permanent mass movement from below that subordinated alliances with liberals to the interests of the disenfranchised majority of immigrant workers and their families. This camp also insisted on the need to link the immigrant rights movement more openly and closely with other popular, labor, and resistance struggles around the world for global justice.

These distinct strategies represent, in the broader analysis, two different class projects within the multiclass community of immigrants and their supporters: the former, those middle class strata who aspire to remove racist and legal impediments to their own class status; the latter, a mass immigrant working class that faces not only racism and legal discrimination but also the acute labor exploitation and survival struggles imposed on them by a rapacious global capitalism. On the one side, noted Bacon, were "well-financed advocacy organizations in Washington, DC, with links to the Democratic Party and the business community. They formulate and negotiate immigration reform proposals that combine labor supply programs and increased enforcement against the undocumented." On the other side were "organizations based in immigrant communities and among labor and political activists, who defend undocumented immigrants, and who resist proposals for greater enforcement and labor programs with diminished rights."[25]

This dividing line was played out from 2006 until 2016 in a succession of "comprehensive immigration reform" bills that were introduced into Congress. Although none passed, almost all of them involved a greatly expanded militarization of the border ("securing the border"), the expansion of "guest worker" programs, and the introduction and expansion of other repressive state controls over immigrant communities and work centers in exchange for extremely limited concessions with regard to the legalization of a small portion of the more than 12 million undocumented immigrants.

While Democratic Party and Latino establishment organizations and leaders pushed the comprehensive immigration reform strategy, the grassroots immigrant justice movement expanded struggles in a variety of fronts. Tens of thousands of young immigrants known as the "DREAMers" marched, held sits ins, performed collective civil disobedience, lobbied, and wrote letters around the struggle for the DREAM Act (Development, Relief, and Education for Alien Minors Act), which would allow undocumented students graduating from high school to apply for permanent residence if they complete two years of college or two years of service in the US military. Immigrant workers centers sprung up in every locale across the United States where immigrant workers were present, and many of them became organized into the National Day Laborer Organizing Network and the National Domestic Workers Alliance. The Binational Front of Indigenous Organizations worked transnationally among immigrant sending communities in Mexico and immigrant workers communities in the United States. The Dignity Campaign was a loose coalition of local and national immigrant justice and fair trade organizations proposing alternatives to comprehensive immigration reform bills that stressed "border enforcement" and criminalization of immigrant communities and encouraged the movement to see immigration in global context and to draw out the connections between trade policies, displacement, and migration.

Both the immigrant justice struggle and the anti-immigrant backlash came together in spring and summer of 2014 during the so-called "invasion" of Central American children, a fabricated story and a classic example of how a "moral panic" is generated by the moral entrepreneurs of the state and dominant groups and manipulated from above.[26] As Bacon has shown, the "story" began when US immigration officials gave photos to a Tea Party media outlet in Texas showing children in immigration detention centers, in what appeared to be a well-planned strategy to whip up a "moral panic," to place the immigrant justice movement onto the defensive, to undermine immigration reform in Congress, and above all to legitimate a new spiral of militarization and criminalization.[27]

Fanned by propaganda from the anti-immigrant movement, for several months the mainstream media plastered the public with sensationalist stories of an invasion by Central American children. These sensationalist accounts provided no context with regard to the roots of such migration in the long history of US intervention in the region, the devastating US counterinsurgency wars followed by free trade, neoliberal policies, and renewed militarization that have left the region in economic devastation, social violence, and despair. The media also ignored that there was nothing "new" about the surge; such migration had been taking place for years and steadily increasing since 2000. The "moral panic" gave anti-immigrant forces the opportunity to stage some of the most vile racist public demonstrations in recent years.

The election of the openly racist and anti-immigrant Donald Trump to the presidency in 2016 resulted in a sharp escalation of anti-immigrant hysteria as part of the Trump regime's strategy to scapegoat immigrants for the crisis. But beyond scapegoating, the criminalization of immigrants, the increase in raids and detentions, and "build the wall" rhetoric were part of a larger strategy to disarticulate political organization and resistance among immigrant communities. It was not surprising that the wave of detentions and deportation of immigrants from Mexico and Central America as Trump took office targeted in particular labor and community activists among the undocumented immigrant community. US rulers appeared to be pushing forward with the effort to replace the system of superexploitation of undocumented immigrant labor with a mass "guest worker program" that would be more efficient in combining superexploitation with super control. Indeed, while the detention and deportation of undocumented immigrant workers in California escalated in the second decade of the twenty-first century, the use of "guest workers" in that state's $47 billion agricultural industry increased by 500 percent from 2011 to 2017.[28]

CONCLUSION: WORKING CLASS HEGEMONY, GLOBAL CITIZENSHIP, AND UNIVERSAL HUMAN RIGHTS

Criminalization and militarized control over immigrant labor reflects a broader militarization of the global economy. Beyond the United States, major sectors of the transnational capitalist class are becoming dependent on local, regional, and global violence, conflict, and inequalities, and in fact push for such conflict through their influence on states and in political and cultural systems. This militarized accumulation is characteristic of the entire global economy. We are increasingly living in a global war economy, and certain countries, such as the United States and Israel, are key gears in this machinery. Militarized accumulation to control and contain the downtrodden and marginalized and to sustain accumulation in the face of crisis lends itself to fascist political tendencies, or what I have referred to as twenty-first-century fascism.[29] A key element of this global war economy is the transnational immigrant detention and repression complex.

A mass immigrant rights movement is at the cutting edge of the struggle against transnational corporate exploitation. Granting full citizenship rights to the hundreds of millions of immigrants around the world would undermine the division of the global working class into immigrants and citizens. That division is a central component of the new class relations of global capitalism, predicated on a casualized and "flexible" mass of workers who can be hired and fired at will; are de-unionized; and face precarious work conditions, job instability, a rollback of benefits, and downward pressures on wages.

The strategic challenge of the immigrant justice movement in the United States as elsewhere is how to achieve the hegemony of the mass worker base within the movement. The expanding crisis of global capitalism opens up grave dangers—for immigrants and for all of humanity—but also opens up opportunities. It is not to the political parties of the status quo (e.g., the Democratic Party in the United States), to the transnational capitalist class, or to the halls of establishment power but to the mass base of this movement—the communities of poor immigrant workers and their families who swell the cities and rural towns of the world—to whom we must turn to reverse the anti-immigrant onslaught.

More broadly (and this idea might clash with progressives who for decades have fought for citizenship rights for all), the whole notion of *national* citizenship needs to be questioned. Borders are not in the interests of the global working class; they should be torn down. So long as the rights we associate with citizenship are seen to adhere to a limited group of people who belong to a nation, there will always be those who fall outside of the nation and are excluded from these rights; there will always be *others*. We must consider citizenship rights as universal human rights for all people who for whatever reason happen to reside in a particular territory. We must replace the whole concept of national citizenship with that of global citizenship. This is a truly revolutionary rallying cry. And it is the only one that can assure justice and equality for all.

SEVEN

GLOBAL CAPITALISM AND THE RESTRUCTURING OF EDUCATION

PRODUCING GLOBAL ECONOMY WORKERS AND SUPPRESSING CRITICAL THINKING

W orld capitalism has been undergoing a process in recent decades of *capitalist globalization*, or profound restructuring and expansion. What type of "human capital" does the emerging global capitalist system require in order for it to function (which is to say, in order for capital accumulation to overcome the technical and political impediments to its continuous expansion)? For one, it needs a cadre of organic intellectuals[1] who do the overall thinking and strategizing for the system and a small army of technocrats and administrators who can resolve problems of system maintenance and development. At the same time, this system needs a very large army of people who will supply nothing but their labor and who are not disposed or equipped to think critically and reflexively on the nature of their existence or that of a system sustained on great inequalities and ever more repressive and ubiquitous social control. Finally, it needs a mass of humanity as surplus labor, let us say a few billion people or so, who can serve as a *reserve* supply of manual and other forms of low-skilled and flexible labor in agriculture, industry, and services; who can be carefully controlled at all times; and who can be discarded when they are no longer needed.

What kind of an educational system would be able to deliver such a mass of humanity endowed with (or lacking) the sets of skills, knowledge, and mental faculties to meet these requirements? Certainly, there would be a core of elite centers of education where the organic intellectuals who administer the system and engage in its ongoing design would study and train. Below it would be a tier of educational institutions producing every sort of vocational and technocratic expert, what Robert Reich once referred to as "symbolic analysts"[2] and others as "knowledge workers," meaning that these people would be trained in the use and manipulation of symbols, whether as engineers, computer programmers, scientists, or financial analysts. In exchange for their services and their obedience, they would be rewarded with comfortable lifestyles.

Then there would be the 80 percent, that mass of humanity increasingly "precariatized" and thrown into the ranks of surplus labor, for which basic numeracy and literacy skills are all that is required in order to supply labor for the system, yet whose potential for critical thinking would pose a serious threat. This tier in the educational system would be quite restricted in its content if not in its provision, serving the dual function of supplying the numeracy, literacy, and technical knowledge necessary to be servile workers while suppressing the development of critical thinking that could contribute to mounting a challenge to global capitalism and imposing punitive social control. In fact, this is just the kind of educational system that the transnational elite has promoted worldwide in recent years.

THE TRIFURCATION OF HUMANITY: THE 1 PERCENT, THE 20 PERCENT, AND THE 80 PERCENT

On the eve of the 2015 annual World Economic Forum meeting in Davos, Switzerland, an event attended exclusively by the cream of the transnational business, political, and cultural elite (it costs about $40,000 to attend, and at that, one must be invited), the development NGO Oxfam released a report on global inequality, aptly titled "Wealth: Having It All and Wanting More."[3] The report observed that the wealthiest 1 percent of humanity owned 48 percent of the world's wealth in 2014, up from 44 percent in 2009, and that under current trends, this 1 percent would own more than 50 percent by the next year. The obscenity of such concentrations of wealth becomes truly apparent when seen in the context of expanding inequality. The report identified the world's richest eighty billionaires among this 1 percent, whose wealth increased from $1.3 trillion in 2010 to $1.9 trillion in 2014, an increase of $600 billion in just four years, or by 50 percent in nominal terms. The wealth of these eighty billionaires was more than all of the wealth owned by the bottom half of the world's population. At the same time, this bottom half of humanity saw its wealth decrease by 50 percent during this same period. In other words, there was a direct transfer of hundreds of billions of dollars from the poorest half of humanity to the richest eighty people on the planet.

While the report characterized such inequality as "simply staggering," it is noteworthy that this polarization of wealth between the bottom half of humanity and the richest eighty people on earth (all but seven of whom are men) according to Oxfam actually accelerated since the 2008 financial collapse, so it would seem that the crisis has made the rich many times richer and the poor many times more poor. It is similarly worth noting that the world's top billionaires and the 1 percent are concentrated in the financial and insurance sector. (Warren Buffett and Michael Bloomberg led the way, followed by the likes of George Soros, a Saudi prince, several Russian oligarchs, a Brazilian, and a Colombian.) A major portion of these richest were also concentrated in the pharmaceutical and health care sectors, and here Indian and Chinese billionaires led the way, together with ones from Turkey, Russia, Switzerland, and elsewhere. Such immense concentrations of wealth translate in manifold ways into political influence: according to Oxfam, the financial and pharmaceutical sectors spent in recent years close to $1 billion lobbying in the United States alone.

The Occupy Wall Street movement of 2011–12 brought to worldwide attention the concentration of the world's wealth in the hands of the 1 percent with its famous rallying cry, "We are the 99 percent!" However, an equally if not more significant division of the world's population with regard to political and sociological analysis is between that better off—if not necessarily outright wealthy—20 percent of humanity whose basic material needs are met, that enjoys the fruits of the global cornucopia and that generally enjoys conditions of security and stability, in contrast to the bottom 80 percent of the world's people who face escalating poverty, depravation, insecurity, and precariousness. The Oxfam report noted that the richest 20 percent of humanity owned 94.5 percent of the world's wealth in 2014 while the remaining 80 percent had to make do with just 5.5 percent of that wealth. In other words, the world, in simplified terms, faces a trifurcated structure of the 1 percent, the 20 percent, and the 80 percent.

The global elite has taken note of these extreme inequalities, as evidenced in the inordinate attention received by French economist Thomas Piketty's 2014 study, *Capital in the Twenty-First Century*,[4] and is concerned that such polarization threatens to undermine growth and may lead to instability and even to rebellion. But there is little or no discussion among the 1 percent about any fundamental redistribution of wealth and power downward; instead, the elite has turned to expanding the mechanisms of ideological and cultural hegemony as well as repression. Both coercive and consensual domination are practiced and constructed in and through educational systems alongside the media and culture industries and the political and policing systems. This mass of humanity is to be seduced by the promise of petty (and generally banal) consumption and entertainment backed by the threat of coercion and repression (terror) should dissatisfaction lead to rebellion.

So what type of a worldwide educational system would this 1 percent, the global ruling class, presumably attempt to construct in the face of such a trifurcation of humanity? I was asked to ponder just such a question for my participation in a 2015 conference on elite education: to discuss my theory of global capitalism and how a focus on global political economy may shed light on the matter of the worldwide educational system in these neoliberal times.[5] To understand the implications of globalization for elites and power relations worldwide, including global capital's changing needs with regard to educational systems, we must turn to the political economy of global capitalism as a qualitatively new epoch in the ongoing and open-ended evolution of the world capitalist system.

CAPITALIST GLOBALIZATION AND CRISIS

Capitalism experiences major episodes of crisis about every 40–50 years as obstacles emerge to ongoing accumulation and profit-making.[6] These are "structural" or "restructuring crises" because the system must be restructured in order to overcome the crisis. As opportunities for capitalists to profitably invest gradually dry up, the system seeks to open up new outlets for surplus capital, typically through violence, whether structural or direct. Structural adjustment programs imposed on the former Third World countries, austerity measures, "free trade" agreements, and capital flight are examples of structural violence (a recent example was Greece's struggle with the European Union-International Monetary Fund-private banking complex troika), while US wars of intervention in the Middle East, the militarization of borders, and the construction of prison-industrial complexes are forms of direct violence. Both forms of violence have the simultaneous function of opening up new opportunities for capitalist *expansion* and *control* in the face of stagnation.

Structural crises of capitalism, along with their economic dimension, involve social upheavals, political and military conflict, and ideological and cultural change. The last major crisis of world capitalism prior to the 2008 global financial collapse began in the late 1960s and hit hard in the early 1970s. The year 1968 was a turning point: In the United States, Martin Luther King Jr. was assassinated in the midst of expanding Black and Chicano liberation movements, the countercultural and the anti-war movements, and escalating militant worker struggles. The Tlatelolco massacre of students took place in Mexico City that same year, at a time of great campesino, worker, and student upheavals across the country. Further away, other major upheavals from below were taking place that year: the Prague Spring, the uprising of students and workers in Paris, the height of the Cultural Revolution in China, the Tet Offensive in Vietnam, which marked the beginning of the first major defeat for US imperialism, and the spread of anti-colonial and armed liberation movements throughout Africa and Latin America.

All this reflected a crisis of hegemony for the system—a crisis in its political and cultural domination. Then came the economic dimension. By 1973, the US government had to abandon the gold standard; the recently formed Organization of Petroleum Exporting Countries (OPEC) imposed its oil embargo, which sent shock waves through the world economy; and stagflation (stagnation plus inflation) set in everywhere. This was, in a nutshell, a severe structural crisis of world capitalism—a crisis of twentieth century nation-state capitalism. By the early 1970s a prerevolutionary situation was percolating in many countries and regions. The popular classes were able to resist attempts by the dominant groups to shift the burden of the 1970s crises on to their shoulders.

As the crisis intensified, these dominant groups sought ways to liberate themselves from the social democratic, redistributive "class compromise" arrangements of previous decades. Analytically speaking, capital sought to free itself of any reciprocal responsibility to labor in the capitalist system, and capitalist states sought to shed themselves of the social welfare systems that were established in preceeding decades. Elites in the rich countries also sought ways to integrate emergent Third World elites into the system.[7] These dominant groups launched the "neoliberal counterrevolution," an attempt to roll back the social welfare state, to re-subordinate labor, and to reconstitute their hegemony at the global level through a newfound transnational mobility of capital and a transformation of the interstate system.

The model of "savage" global capitalism that took hold in the late twentieth century involved a new capital–labor relation based on the deregulation, informalization, deunionization, and flexibilization of labor as more and more workers have swelled the ranks of the *precariat* (a proletariat existing in permanently precarious conditions).[8] "Free trade" agreements and neoliberal policies have played a key role in the subordination of labor worldwide and the creation of this global flexible labor market. The new model of global capitalism has also involved a renewed round of extensive and intensive expansion of the system. The former "socialist" countries and the revolutionary states of the Third World were integrated into the world market in the late twentieth century. But even more than extensive expansion, the system has undergone *intensive* expansion involving the commodification of spheres of society previously outside of the logic of exchange value such as social services, utilities, public lands, infrastructure, health, and education, so that these spheres have become sources of accumulation and the unloading of surplus capital. Let us put this into historic context.

The capitalist system has gone through successive waves of expansion and transformation since its bloody inception in 1492 with the conquest of the Americas. Each epoch has seen the reorganization of political and social institutions, the rise of new class agents and technologies on the heels of major structural crises, which has resulted in new waves of outward expansion through wars of conquest, imperialism, and colonialism that bring more of humanity and of the planet into the orbit of capital. In the dialectical and historical materialist approach, the distinct and varied social institutions, such as the educational system, are connected with one another, grounded in political economy (i.e., in the process of the production and reproduction of our material existence), and experience ongoing transformation in consort with the changing nature of the social order. Each epoch of world capitalism therefore has had implications for the major institutions that comprise society.

The mercantile era spanned the sixteenth, seventeenth, and early eighteenth centuries, during which a world market was created. This was followed by an epoch of classical competitive capitalism inaugurated with the French Revolution of 1789 that brought in its wake the first industrial revolution, the definitive triumph of the bourgeoisie as a ruling class, and the consolidation of the nation-state and the interstate system as the political form of the capitalist system. Competitive capitalism gave way to the rise of corporate capital, powerful national monopolies, and capitalist classes in the core capitalist countries, which organized themselves around protected national markets and engaged in a new round of imperialist expansion and interstate competition over world markets, resources, and labor reserves. It took two world wars and mass social struggles around the world for corporate capitalism to stabilize around a new "social structure of accumulation," a pattern of accumulation involving a distinct and identifiable set of institutions, social norms, and political structures that facilitate a period of expanded accumulation.[9]

But the Fordist–Keynesian social structure of accumulation that took hold following World War II, with its mechanisms of redistribution, state intervention to regulate the market, and "class compromise," entered into a deep structural crisis in the 1970s. Emergent transnational capital responded to that crisis of the 1970s by "going global," giving way to the current epoch of global capitalism. One key distinctive feature of the global epoch of world capitalism is that the system has all but exhausted possibilities for *extensive* expansion as the whole world has been brought into the orbit of capital, so that globalization involves an *intensive* expansion that is reaching depths not seen in previous epochs. The life-world itself, to use Habermas's phrase,[10] becomes colonized by capital, and the educational system is one institution for this colonization.

TRANSNATIONAL CAPITAL, THE TRANSNATIONAL STATE, AND COMMODIFICATION OF EDUCATION

Global capitalism involves a rearticulation of social power relations around the world. This new epoch is characterized above all by the rise of truly transnational capital and the integration of every country and region into a new globalized system of production, finances, and services. We have seen a sequence in the rise of the global economy. Production was the first to transnationalize, starting in the late 1970s, epitomized by the "global assembly line" and the spread of *maquiladoras* (sweat shops) and *zonas francas* (free trade zones) based on the superexploitation of cheap, often young female, workers. Next to transnationalize were national banking and financial systems, in the 1990s and early twenty-first century, following the deregulation of banking and financial markets in most countries around the world and the creation of countless new "financial instruments," or tradable forms of finance. There is no longer such a thing as a national financial system. Given its fungible nature and its virtually complete digitalization, money moves almost frictionless through the financial circuits of the global economy and plays a key integrative function. Transnational finance capital has become the hegemonic fraction of capital on a world scale; it determines the circuits of capital and has subordinated productive capital to itself, not to mention the subordination of governments, political systems, social institutions, and households.

More recent is the transnationalization of services. By the second decade of the twenty-first century, in fact, the major thrust of "free trade" negotiations such as the Trade in Services Agreement was aimed at removing remaining national regulation and public control of services, including finance, utilities, infrastructure, transportation, health, and education. Capitalist globalization has been a process of ongoing liberation of transnational capital from the nation-state and from popular and working class constraints, of the prerogative of accumulation over any social consideration, and of the progressive "commodification of everything."

But transnational capital is not faceless. A transnational capitalist class (TCC) has emerged as the manifest agent of global capitalism. National capitalist classes began to internationalize early in the twentieth century. As the process accelerated in the post–World War II period, especially following the 1970s crisis, capitals from core countries began to interpenetrate through numerous mechanisms that I and others have documented—among them, through foreign direct and cross-investment; the transnational interlocking of boards of directors; transnational mergers and acquisitions; vast networks of outsourcing, subcontracting, joint ventures, and alliances; and the establishment of tens of thousands of transnational corporate subsidiaries.[11] Multinational corporations gave way to the giant global or transnational corporations that now drive the global economy. The TCC is grounded in emergent global circuits of accumulation rather than national circuits. The TCC has become the hegemonic fraction of the capitalist class on a global scale, and at its apex is transnational finance capital. Power in most countries has gravitated away from local and national fractions of the elite as well as from the popular classes and toward transnationally oriented capitalists and elites.

Transnational fractions of the elite have vied for and in most countries taken state power, whether by elections or other means, and whether through the takeover of existing parties or the creation of entirely new political platforms, backed by powerful corporate business groups. As these transnationally oriented elites have captured national states, they have used political control and cultural and ideological influence that accrues to material domination to push economic restructuring and capitalist globalization, integrating their countries into the new global circuits of accumulation as well as into the global legal and regulatory regime (such as the World Trade Organization) that is still under construction. These neoliberal states have opened up each national territory to transnational corporate plunder of resources, labor, and markets. Neoliberalism, as is well known, involves among other things the deregulation and privatization of services, including educational systems.

As the TCC and its political and bureaucratic allies have pushed capitalist globalization, national states adopt similar sets of neoliberal policies and sign "free trade" agreements in consort with one another and with the supranational and transnational institutions that have designed and facilitated the global capitalist project, among them the World Trade Organization, the International Monetary Fund, the World Bank, the European Union, the United Nations, and the Organization of Economic Cooperation and Development. This increasingly dense network of nation-state institutions and transnational and supranational organizations comprise transnational state apparatuses. The transnational state promotes globalized circuits of accumulation and the power of transnational capital in each country. It is through transnational state apparatuses that the TCC attempts to exercise its class power in each country and in the global system as a whole. Such transnational state institutions as the World Bank and the International Monetary Fund have been at the forefront of the neoliberal restructuring of educational systems, including the commodification of schooling and the privatization of higher education.

THE CHANGING LABOR NEEDS OF THE GLOBAL ECONOMY AND THE NEW PRECARIAT

In the classic study, *Schooling in Capitalist America*,[12] Bowles and Gintis showed how the internal organization of schools corresponded to the internal organization of the capitalist workforce in its structures, norms, and values (their "correspondence theory") and how the school system, with its disciplinary processes, hierarchal relations, and hidden curricula, prepared students for their future role in the capitalist economy. Schools, they argued, played a critical role in capitalist class control of labor and in the reproduction of extant social inequalities.[13]

Bowles and Gintis's essential argument on the relationship between education and the capitalist economy and society remains valid today, but the nature of capitalism (specifically its globalization) and the labor needs of the global economy have changed. Bowles and Gintis argued that there was a contradiction between the needs of accumulation and the needs of social reproduction. The capitalist economy needed a workforce that was highly trained, intelligent, and self-directed. The education required for this workforce also developed people's ability to think and brought together millions of young people under conditions that could encourage struggles for social justice. Today, however, global capitalism needs a workforce with less autonomy and creative abilities and one subject to ever more intense mechanisms of social control in the face of a rising tide of superfluous labor and ever more widespread immiseration and insecurity. The hidden curriculum and the ideological content of mass education around the world remain in place, but the openly and directly repressive elements of education appear to play a heightened role.

Bowles and Gintis analyzed the development of education in the epochs of competitive and monopoly capitalism. The successive waves of the industrial revolution from the late eighteenth century into the early twentieth centuries required a workforce with increasing knowledge and skills. Fordist–Keynesian capitalism needed a mass of semi-skilled and high-skilled workers, whether in the industrial heartlands of the world system or in the urban pockets of import substitution industrialization in the Third World. In addition, Third World elites promoting capitalist developmentalism sought to generate national educational systems often modeled on those of the core countries.

But as globalization has intensified, so too has the dual process of Taylorism and deskilling so strikingly analyzed by Harry Braverman in his classic and quite prescient study, *Labor and Monopoly Capital*,[14] while several waves of the "scientific and technological revolution," especially computer and information technology, have made redundant much skilled and semi-skilled human labor, as Jeremy Rifkin described, two decades after Braveman's study, in his popular book, *The End of Work*, and as Stanley Aronowitz and William DiFazio discuss more recently in *The Jobless Future*.[15] Just as the world's population is increasingly polarized between the 80 and the 20 percent, so too work is increasingly polarized between unskilled and low-skilled labor on the farms and in the factories, office, and service complexes of the global economy as well as in the armed and security forces of the global police state, and on the other hand, high-skilled technical and knowledge workers. It is likely that the revolutions just getting underway in nanotechnology, bioengineering, three-dimensional manufacturing, blockchain, autonomously driven vehicles, the Internet of Things, and robotic and machine intelligence—the revolutionary technologies of the immediate future, the so-called "fourth industrial revolution"—will only heighten this tendency toward bifurcation in the world's workforce between high-skilled tech and knowledge workers and those relegated to McJobs, at best, or simply to surplus labor.[16]

To reiterate: Global capital needs a mass of humanity that has basic numeracy and literacy skills and not much more, alongside high-tech educational training for high skilled and knowledge workers. There are a handful of global elite universities that educate and groom the TCC, its organic intellectuals, and transnationally oriented managerial and technocratic elites such as Harvard, Yale, Cambridge, Oxford, Swiss Federal Institute of Technology, Tokyo University, Indian Institutes of Technology, the Grandes Écoles in France, and so on. Brezis estimates that the top fifty universities around the world recruit 33 percent of transnational political elites and 47 percent of transnational business elites.[17] While most of these global elite universities are located in the United States, the network of elite universities now turn to new transnational student markets to recruit from around the world. Below the elite universities are higher education institutions intended to train people for a mercantile insertion into the upper rungs of the global labor market. Meanwhile, and just as the neoliberal onslaught was in full swing, transnational state institutions such as the Organisation of Economic Co-operation and Development, the European Union, the United Nations, the World Bank, the International Monetary Fund, and the World Trade Organization began calling in the 1990s for universal primary education alongside a shift from public to private secondary education and the privatization and commodification of higher education.

The World Bank has played the lead role in establishing the transnational elite's policy agenda in this regard. Its landmark 2003 report, *Achieving Universal Primary Education by 2015*, called for primary education to become universal worldwide by the year 2015, expanding on the call for such universal education contained in the United Nation's *Millennium Development Goals* promulgated with much fanfare in 2000 at the United Nations Millennium Summit and with the participation of so-called civil society representatives.[18] The Millennium Development Goals put forth a set of eight development goals to be achieved by 2015, among them: a reduction by half the proportion of people living in extreme poverty and who suffer from hunger; universal primary education; a reduction by two-thirds the mortality rate among children under five and by three quarters the maternal mortality rate, halt and reverse the incidence of major diseases, promote gender equality and the empowerment of women, and so on. However, the prescription put forth to achieve these lofty goals was based on a more thoroughgoing privatization of health and educational systems, further freeing up of the market from state regulations, greater trade liberalization and more structural adjustment, and the conversion of agricultural lands into private commercial property—in other words, an intensification of the very capitalist development that has generated the social conditions to be eradicated.[19]

The 2003 World Bank report made clear that an expansion of access and curricular and structural changes in education would be for the purpose of preparing workers for jobs in the global economy and that educational reform would take place within a neoliberal policy framework. It argued that universal primary education when "combined with sound [read: neoliberal] macroeconomic policies" is essential to "globally competitive economies," sustained growth, and increased labor productivity. The report stressed that equitably distributing primary educational opportunity should not be confused with "the redistribution of other assets such as land or capital."[20] It also specified that it was calling for public sector *financing* of primary schooling but not necessarily *provision*. This is important because privatization often takes the form of governments creating markets for the corporate seizure of public education and the provision of public subsidies for privately run schools such as charter schools in the United States and elsewhere. More generally, Ball and Youdell have analyzed the numerous forms of "hidden privatization in public education."[21]

At the same time as the World Bank and other transnational state institutions have called for universal primary education in order to assure the provision of a labor force for global capitalism, they have pushed the privatization of higher education. In its 1998 report, *Higher Education Financing Project*, the World Bank called for higher education programs to be privatized, deregulated, and "oriented to the market rather than public ownership or governmental planning and regulation." The report argued for a substantial increase in university tuition fees, charging full fees for room and board, providing loans for students based on market interest rates together with the subcontracting of private companies to collect student loan repayments, expanding "entrepreneurial training" at universities, offering university research findings to corporate purchases, and generally increasing the number of private institutions with a progressive decrease in public education.[22] The report's author stated in an addendum that

> much of what may look like the agenda of the neoliberal economist may also be more opportunistic than ideological. With taxes increasingly avoidable and otherwise difficult to collect and with competing public needs so compelling on all countries, an increasing reliance on tuition, fees and the unleashed entrepreneurship of the faculty may be the only alternative to a totally debilitating austerity.[23]

This neoliberalization of higher education converts the university worldwide into the domain of the elite and to that 20 percent of global society with the resources to finance their education and to train for taking commanding roles in global society. At the same time, it heightens the ideological role that education plays in inculcating dull minds, respect for authority, obedience, a craving for petty consumption and fantasy—that is, the banal culture of global capitalism and its dehumanizing values.

Neoliberal restructuring and (most importantly) privatization open up educational systems to transnational capital as a new space for accumulation and as a brain trust for transnational capital, which has invaded the university and the educational system more generally, in every sense, from converting education into a for-profit activity, to commissioning and appropriating research (often publicly funded) and generating a major new source of financial speculation through students loans.[24]

Neoliberal restructuring around the world has extended what Sheila Slaughter and Larry L. Leslie called "academic capitalism," or the development of functional linkages between higher education and corporate "knowledge capitalism."[25] In the United States, where Slaughter and Leslie focused their research, the corporate takeover of higher education has involved the bifurcation of the professoriate into a small core of tenured professors and an army of precariatized or contract instructors. Adjunct faculty now teach more than 70 percent of all university courses in the United States.[26] The switch from public funding to tuition-led funding of higher education has contributed to the student debt, which increased more than 400 percent from 2000 to 2013, when it reached $1.2 trillion.[27] These mechanisms of debt bondage lock out would-be surplus labor from access to public higher education and force the poorest to turn to for-profit private "universities" that have proliferated, with enrollment increasing 2017 percent from 2000 to 2014 (compared to 25 percent for public universities and for private nonprofit institutions).[28]

There is a double movement here. Capitalist globalization has involved a shift in the low and unskilled labor-intensive phases of global production circuits from the North to the South at the same time as work in general has become bifurcated into deskilled and high-skills jobs. Thus, the neoliberal program of universal primary education and the privatization and commodification of secondary and higher education is reciprocal to changes in the global division of labor as well as to the transformation in labor and the "end of work."

GLOBAL POLICE STATE AND IDEOLOGICAL HEGEMONY, ON AND OFF THE CAMPUSES

The extreme inequalities of the global political economy cannot easily be contained through consensual mechanisms of social control. The great challenge faced by the system is to contain the real and potential rebellion of the global working class and the surplus population. Relations of inequality and domination in global society include the increasing salience of new transnational class inequalities relative to the older forms of North–South inequality, a resurgence of racial and ethnic hierarchies, and a new class of immigrant workers worldwide denied the rights of citizenship and held in labor peonage. There is the spread of frightening systems of mass social control and repression.[29] The ruling groups have launched farcical wars on drugs, "terrorism," immigrants, and "gangs" (and youth more generally); wars of social control and dispossession waged against the popular and working classes and the surplus labor population, all of which have engulfed social and political institutions, including educational systems.[30] The TCC has taken up this challenge by imposing fear and obedience and assuring the social control of youth, in part, by converting schools into centers for repressive discipline and punitive punishment. The role of schooling in social control is an old theme, but the coupling of the educational system with those of new systems of mass social control and surveillance appears to be reaching depths hitherto unseen.

The US press is full of stories that stretch the imagination on the militarization of public schools, the criminalization of students, and extreme disciplinary punishment as the school-to-prison pipeline becomes ever more institutionalized.[31] Class relations in the United States have historically been highly racialized, and the racialized nature of this criminalization and punitive punishment cannot be overemphasized. In many states, public school students are now thrown into jail for tardiness and absences. According to a complaint filed with the US Department of Justice in June 2013, students in Texas have been taken out of school in handcuffs, held in jail for days at a time, and fined more than $1,000 for missing more than ten days of school. According to the complaint, school grounds are run like a police state, with guards rounding up students during "tardy sweeps," suspending them, and then marking their absences as unexcused even when students have legitimate reasons for absence, such as family emergency or illness.[32] The Pentagon has supplied schools throughout the United States with military-grade weapons and vehicles and even with grenade launchers.[33] Schools have spied on students in their home by supplying laptop computers with webcams that are activated by remote control.[34] The surveillance state has invaded the public school system, especially poor, working class and racially oppressed communities, with closed-circuit television cameras, security checkpoints, full time armed guards, and military recruiters.

This militarization of schools appears to bring about a convergence of school systems serving the working class and racially oppressed communities with the criminal justice system to such an extent that the two systems appear as nothing less than a single institutional continuum.[35] Gilmore has shown how the turn to mass incarceration provided the state with a means of caging surplus labor (disproportionately from racially oppressed communities) and capital with a means of unloading surplus and sustaining accumulation.[36] The regime of repression and punishment in the public school system appears as the juvenile corollary to mass incarceration. As broad swaths of the working class become surplus labor, schools in marginalized communities "prepare" students for prison and "social death" rather than for a life of labor.

Meanwhile, high-stakes standardized testing (itself a lucrative source of corporate accumulation) aims to impose a dull uniformity on curricula, reduce learning to rote memorization, routine, punctuality, and obedience to regimented classrooms while they discipline nonconforming teachers and attack teachers unions. Handwritten essays are not evaluated by experienced educators but by temp workers hired seasonally at low wages and assigned to grade up to forty essays an hour. One for-profit test scoring company, Pearson, operates twenty-one scoring centers around the United States, hiring 14,500 temp scorers during the scoring season.[37] Results are then used to defund and close "nonperforming" schools. Teachers received prepackaged lesson plans that are scripted to prepare for the tests. High-stakes testing leads to the segregation of learning and bifurcation of schools into those catering to the well off and those serving the working class and surplus labor that closely mirrors the new spatial apartheid in urban centers. Punitive standardized testing and the spread of charter schools, admission to which is determined by test performance, facilitates co-optation of promising (and obedient) students from the working class and racially/ethnically oppressed communities into the would-be ranks of the 20 percent as technocratic and knowledge workers.

The hidden curriculum of ideological hegemony, socialization into hierarchy, and conformity and the suppression of critical thinking play a heightened role in global capitalism. "The ideas of the ruling class are in every epoch the ruling ideas," observed Marx famously in *The German Ideology:*

> The class that is the ruling material force of society, is at the same time its ruling intellectual force. . . . The class that has the means of material production at its disposal has control at the same time over the means of mental production, so that thereby, generally speaking, the ideas of those who lack the means of mental production are subject to it. The ruling ideas are nothing more than the ideal expression of the dominant material relationships, the dominant material relationships grasped as ideas.[38]

The "dominant material relationships" of global capitalism are expressed in the ideology of neoliberalism, multiculturalism, individualism, martial masculinity, militarism, and as well in postmodern pessimism. As Argentine scholar Atilio Boron observes in his excellent study on the role of the World Bank and of neoliberalization of education in undermining critical thought:

> It is extremely difficult and costly to escape the formidable intellectual vice of the nefarious combination of neoclassical economics and postmodernism, the result of which has been a deeply conservative and conformist mode of thought imbued with a broad repertoire of subtle mechanisms of ideological control which cut at the very roots the growth of critical thought in the university, not to mention at the level of the mass media and public space in general.[39]

Boron goes on to note that until the mid-twentieth century, public universities predominated in Latin America; indeed, there were almost no private universities of significance. But by 2008, 60 percent of all universities in Latin America were private, accounting for some 40 percent of all student enrollments; and in some countries, such as Brazil, Chile, and Colombia, the number of private universities entirely eclipsed the number of public universities. At the same time, Boron reports, there has been a deleterious deterioration in the quality of education at the public universities, together with defunding, rising student fees, a decline in instructor earnings, and a shift to part-time and contract instructors. Education increased slightly from 1985 to 2005 as a percentage of GNP in most Latin American countries, while during this same time, spending on higher education declined significantly in almost every country and in some cases dropped precipitously.

As the neoliberal commodification of higher education proceeds, "the classic ideal that conceived of education as a process for the cultivation and integral development of the human spirit has been abandoned" and replaced by a crude "mercantile and utilitarian conception of education as training in order to learn the skills that the market demands and to assure the 'employability' of the student." Higher education has become a "service." One of the consequences of the neoliberal takeover of higher education has been, in Boron's words, "the generalized acceptance now enjoyed by the previously bizarre idea that universities should be considered as profitable institutions that generate income generated by the 'sale of their services.'"[40]

Boron calls for "critical and radical thought" *contra* neoliberal ideology diffused through the educational and mass media systems of global capitalism. His call, although aimed at Latin America, is equally appropriate for global society as a whole:

> An observer who came down from Mars might ask, "Why does Latin America need radical thought?" The answer: for a very simply reason; because the situation in Latin America is radically unjust, so absolutely unjust and so much more unjust with each passing year, that if we want to make a contribution to the social life of our countries, to the wellbeing of our peoples, we have no other alternative but to critically rethink our society, to explore "other possible worlds" that allow us to move beyond the crisis and to communicate with the mass of people who make history in a plain, simple, and understandable language.[41]

CONCLUSION: A REVITALIZED PHILOSOPHY OF PRAXIS

A global rebellion against the rule of the TCC has spread since the financial collapse of 2008. Wherever one looks around the world, there is an escalation of popular and grassroots social justice struggles and the rise of new cultures of resistance. At the same time, the crisis has produced a rapid political polarization between a resurgent left and a neofascist right. The far right is often driven by ethnic nationalisms and the manipulation of fear and insecurity experienced by downwardly mobile and precariatized working class communities. These communities have in recent years been targeted for recruitment to neofascist projects by far right forces in a number of countries, including in the United

States, where these forces mobilized behind the Trump candidacy in the 2016 elections and then provided a critical base of support for the Trump presidency. How these struggles play out will depend, in part, on how effectively popular forces from below manage to construct a counterhegemony to that of the transnational ruling bloc. The prospects for such a counterhegemony depend on how the crisis is understood and interpreted by masses of people, which in turn depends, in significant part, on a systemic critique of global capitalism and on organic intellectuals of the popular classes—in the Gramscian sense, as intellectuals who attach themselves to and serve the emancipatory struggles of the popular classes—committed to putting forth such a critique.

Alongside the economic restructuring of capitalist globalization since the 1980s, organic intellectuals of the emerging TCC responded at the cultural level to the popular and revolutionary uprisings of the 1960s and the 1970s with a strategy of "diversity" and "multiculturalism" to reconstruct ideological hegemony. Those uprisings opened up space in higher education for the formerly excluded groups—racially oppressed, women, and poor workers—and diversified what had been a Eurocentric, racist, and sexist curriculum hostile to the oppressed. As the corporate, political, and cultural elite came to embrace "diversity" and "multiculturalism," their strategy aimed to neuter through co-optation the demands for social justice and anti-capitalist transformation. Dominant groups would now welcome representation in the institutions of capital and power but would suppress, violently if necessary, struggles to overthrow capital or simply curb its prerogatives. Some among the historically oppressed groups gained representation in the institutions of power; others aspired to do so. They condemned oppression but banished *exploitation* from the popular vocabulary.

In Latin America, the dominant groups violently repressed the "Indio Insurreccionista" (the insurrectionary Indian) who demanded control over land and resources and encouraged the "Indio Permitido" who would be allowed to seek cultural pluralism and political representation but was not to question the capitalist social order and its structure of property and class power.[42] On US university campuses, cultural and identity politics took over. Dominant groups now praise, even champion, opposition to racism as personal injury and "micro-aggression" that eclipses any critique of the macro-aggressions of capitalism and the link between racial oppression and class exploitation—what Aviva Chomsky terms "the politics of the left-wing of neoliberalism." She points out that university administrators are attempting now to absorb into "the market oriented system of higher education" a new upsurge of student activism in the United States that has placed climate change, inequality, immigrant rights, and opposition to mass incarceration at the forefront of campus struggles.[43] Yet the term *neoliberalism* has become a stand-in for *capitalism*. Critique of neoliberalism as a set of policies (liberalization, privatization, deregulation, and so on) and an accompanying ideology that has facilitated capitalist globalization cannot substitute for a critique of global capitalism.

A critical part of the construction of any counterhegemonic project will take place in schools and university campuses around the world. Throughout the Americas, my own focal point of scholar-activism, teachers have led the struggle against neoliberal educational reform, the privatization of education, the defunding and closure of schools, the de-unionization of the profession, and state repression of students. They have stood alongside the remarkable student mobilizations in Mexico, Chile, Brazil, the United States, and elsewhere. There is a need to infuse student struggles and workers uprisings with radical global political economy theory and analysis that can contribute to the practices of global social justice and emancipatory struggles, that is, to what Antonio Gramsci called a *philosophy of praxis*.

EIGHT

DAVOS MAN COMES TO THE THIRD WORLD

THE TRANSNATIONAL STATE AND THE BRICS

It is commonplace these days for observers to see the prominent role of the BRICS bloc of nations (Brazil, Russia, India, China, and South Africa) in international affairs as a Southern challenge to global capitalism and the power of the rich countries of the former First World. Scholars, journalists, and Left activists have applauded the rise of the BRICS as a new bloc from the Global South that offers a progressive, even anti-imperialist option for humanity.[1] "Not since the days of the Non-Aligned Movement and its demand for a New International Economic Order in the 1970s has the world seen such a coordinated challenge to western supremacy in the world economy from developing countries," claimed Indian scholar Radhika Desai in 2013, following plans announced in April of that year to establish a BRICS development bank.[2] Brazilian political scientist and activist Roberto Mangabiera Unger went so far as to recommend that the global Left seek a partnership with the BRICS governments in order to build a Left alternative to global capitalism.[3]

There is no doubt that, seen from the perspective of a world of national economies and international markets and through the lens of the interstate system, the BRICS as a collective constitutes an economic and political powerhouse with the potential to reshape global processes. However, the larger issue behind the BRICS debate is this: Through what theoretical-analytical lens do we view world political and economic developments? How we understand these dynamics is crucial to struggles for political and social change, especially at this time of acute global crisis. Many interpretations of the BRICS share an approach known in international relations theory as *realism*, whereby world politics are seen in terms of the struggle among nation-states for status and power in a competitive interstate system. Even as some commentators have begun to question unqualified enthusiasm for the BRICS as a progressive alternative,[4] these accounts remain mired in a tenacious realism whereby the nature of what is debated is the extent to which the BRICS as nations are challenging the prevailing international order. But if we want to understand the BRICS phenomenon, we need to shift the entire focus toward a global capitalism perspective that breaks with such a nation-state/interstate framework.

The global capitalism perspective sees the world, not in terms of nation-states struggling for hegemony through competition in this twenty-first century, but rather in terms of transnational social and class forces that pursue their interests through national states and other institutions. Can the conflicts and competition that rage in the global system be explained through a framework of competing nation-states and struggles for national hegemony? Interstate dynamics certainly involve tension and conflict that require explanation, but we must move beyond the surface phenomena that are most visible in such tension and conflict to get at the underlying essence of how social and class forces are organized in the global political economy and how these forces express themselves through the interstate system.

The BRICS are deeply implicated in global capitalism and its defining features as a new epoch in the world capitalist system. The first of these features is the rise of truly transnational capital. The world economy of international market integration, in which nation-states were linked to one another through trade and financial flows, has given way to a global economy characterized by the emergence of a globalized production and financial system driven by transnational corporations and banks. The BRICS have integrated into these globalized production and financial structures, and the policies that the bloc has pursued seek to deepen this integration.

A second feature is the rise of a transnational capitalist class (TCC), consisting of those who own and manage the transnational corporations and financial institutions that drive the global economy. The TCC is transnational because it is grounded in global circuits of accumulation, marketing, and finance unbound from particular national territories and because its interests lie in global rather than local accumulation. The leading capitalists and elites in the BRICS countries have sought to expand these globalized circuits over earlier national circuits. A third feature is the rise of a transnational state that functions to impose capitalist domination beyond national borders. As we will see, the BRICS are enmeshed in transnational state apparatuses.

Finally, hegemony and imperialism within global capitalism are no longer about nation-states dominating colonies or other nation-states but rather about transnational capitalist groups, including those from countries that were previously colonized, asserting their social power and structural domination through the varied institutions of the transnational state to control the production and appropriation of wealth around the world through the reproduction of these transnational class relations.

Most analyses of the BRICS and of interstate dynamics remain stubbornly trapped in the realist perspective. Yet there are now TCC groups in almost every country of the world—certainly they are present and entrenched in the states of the BRICS countries—whose interests lie in strengthening their own national and regional standing as a staging platform for advancing global integration. This process does generate international and North–South tensions, but such tensions are not in fundamental contradiction with global capitalism or with TCC groups from the North. Yet they are in fundamental contradiction with the global working and popular classes, including those in the BRICS countries.

THE ECOSYSTEM OF GLOBAL CAPITALISM

The term *BRICS* was first coined in 2001 by Jim O'Neill, a Goldman Sachs analyst who described the BRICS countries as those with the most potential for growth in the first half of the twenty-first century based on demography, the size of potential markets, recent growth rates, and the embrace of globalization.[5] O'Neill suggested that a more prominent role for the BRIC (at that time South Africa had not yet been added) countries in global economic and political management could help stabilize the system. The report by Goldman Sachs, which is perhaps the most predatory financial institution on the planet, stressed that transnational investors would find new opportunities in the BRICS countries.

In O'Neill's view, China was to become the most important exporter of manufactured goods, India of services, and Russia and Brazil of raw materials. The group met for its first summit in 2009 in Russia and has since held annual summits. In 2016, the BRICS had a population of about three billion people, a total estimated GDP of some $20 trillion, and around $5 trillion of foreign exchange reserves. Shortly after O'Neill's report was published, academics and journalists began to take up the notion of an emergent BRICS bloc, edged on by the opposition of the BRICS (and many other governments) to renewed interventionism in the early twenty-first century, especially the US invasion and occupation of Iraq, and by the erosion of the neoliberal Washington consensus.

According to the Third World Network, these countries subsequently began to see themselves as a group "largely because of foreign investor and media perceptions."[6] In his study *The Poorer Nations*, Indian academic Vijay Prashad locates the rise of the BRICS in the demise of what he calls the "Third World project" as neoliberalism pushed by the former First World countries became hegemonic. He traces this project to the series of international meetings between the former First World and Third World states that took place in the 1970s, known as the North–South dialogue, to achieve the objective of a more balanced New International Economic Order. This dialogue between the developed and the developing countries made little headway and then collapsed at the International Meeting on Cooperation and Development that took place in Cancun in 1981, simply known as the Cancun Summit, seen as both the last gasp of the Third World project as well as the moment when the Reagan and Thatcher governments definitively launched the neoliberal project. Representatives from a number of Southern countries then attempted to pick up the pieces of the shattered Third World project through the Southern Commission that they established following the Cancun Summit to develop South–South cooperation and to resuscitate a "Southern agenda." But this commission broke up in dismal failure on the eve of the 1990 Iraqi invasion of Kuwait and the first Gulf War. Prashad traces the rise of the BRICS a decade later to these earlier efforts at South–South cooperation.[7]

Prashad acknowledges that dominant capitalist class and elite interests emerging in the former Third World during the late twentieth century sought to find common ground with their Northern counterparts in global market integration and in suppression of the aspirations of the popular masses. Nonetheless, he is enthusiastic over the prospects of BRICS elites carrying through on the promise of a revived "Third World project" or Southern development paradigm—a stance that appears to stem from nostalgia for the "anticolonial moment" of the mid-twentieth century than from any evidence. In an exchange with me several years ago, Prashad characterized my work as an "ethnography of Davos Man," in reference to the cream of the global corporate and political elite that come together each year at the annual meetings of the World Economic Forum in Davos, Switzerland.[8] He debated with me the extent to which the old Third World elites have become part of the global elite and the TCC. For him, competition with and antagonism to metropolitan-based capital remains a major feature of the dynamics between the BRICS and the core countries; indeed, he suggested that there are fundamental contradictions between the Group of 7 (G7) countries and the BRICS countries.

But does Davos Man represent the old First World elites, or does it represent global elites, that is, an emergent TCC and its political agents and state allies? And is the BRICS an effort by Third World elites to contest the power of Davos Man? Differences among them notwithstanding, all of the BRICS are countries with powerful capitalist classes that control these countries. BRICS governments' discourse is often radical, populist, and antisystemic in tone—what Bond refers to as "talk left, walk right."[9] But it is their actions that we must be concerned with and the structures and processes that lie beneath those actions. Only by a stretch of the imagination can one argue that the BRICS is a multistate bloc representing a socialist or a popular class alternative to the global capitalist system. The BRICS capitalist classes and a majority of state elites within the BRICS countries are seeking not a withdrawal from but rather greater integration into global capitalism and heightened association with transnational capital. This is reflected in the major planks of the BRICS platform: incentives for foreign investment, infrastructural projects, trade integration, recapitalization of the international financial institutions, and implementation of macroeconomic policy prescriptions.[10]

A study of capitalist groups (along with leading state managers) in the BRICS countries makes clear that these groups have been experiencing ongoing integration into the circuits of transnational capital and that these capitalist groups are increasingly part of the TCC.[11] BRICS politics have sought to further pry open the global system so that BRICS elites might participate in it. Some of these efforts do clash with the G7, but BRICS proposals have the effect of extending global capitalism and contributing to its stabilization, and in the process, of further transnationalizing the dominant groups in these countries. Far from indicating polarized or antagonistic interests, the BRICS economic and political protagonism has for the most part been aimed at constructing a more expansive and balanced global capitalism.

The relationship between politics and economics is a complex and often contentious vector of analysis. Important lessons from Latin America help us understand this relationship as regards the BRICS. Latin American Marxists showed how a number of left-populist revolutions in that region in the 1960s and the 1970s, such as that led by Juan Velasco Alvarado in Peru in 1968, were less anti-capitalist challenges than efforts to bring about more modern class relations in the face of the tenacity of the antiquated, often semi-feudal oligarchies that ruled the continent and who were holding back the development of capitalism.[12] These governments did introduce some popular and working class policies, yet they essentially aimed to modernize the domination of capital.

In a similar way, and transposing the analogy from the level of individual Latin American countries to that of the global system, the BRICS politics aim to force those elites from the older centers of world capitalism into a more balanced and integrated global capitalism. For instance, China repeatedly proposed in the wake of the 2008 collapse not that the Chinese currency, the renminbi, become the new world currency to replace the dollar, but that the International Monetary Fund issue a truly world currency not tied to any nation-state.[13] Such a truly transnational currency would help save the global economy from the dangers of continued reliance on the US dollar, an atavistic residue from an earlier era of US dominance in a world system of national capitalisms and hegemonic nation-states. And when Donald Trump announced in the early months of his presidency a withdrawal of US leadership and a "go it alone" policy, China announced that it would take the leadership on behalf of the world capitalist system to sustain and push forth globalization—an announcement that was cheered by the Davos elite.[14]

In the previous epoch of world capitalism, anticolonial, nationally oriented industrialization, and nationalist elites had interests often in contradiction with those of metropolitan capital and (later) with globalizing capital. Third World elite groups turned to using their own local states and to promoting local accumulation in their aspirations for core status or to acquire capital and power. (They had mass movements from below pressuring them to do so as well.) This was so because of the structure of the world capitalist system in previous epochs, a structure generated by the particular form in which capital spread outward from its original heartland through colonialism and imperialism.

As we moved into the epoch of global capitalism beginning in the late twentieth century, transnational capitalists and globalizing elites in the former Third World—and from the former First World—found that they could increasingly aspire to detach themselves from local dependency, that is, the need to generate a national market and assure the social reproduction of local popular and working classes. These elites found that they could instead use the global economy to accumulate capital, status, and power. This process of globalization did not resolve (and in fact aggravated) legitimacy crises of local states both North and South; such is the contradictory and crisis-ridden nature of global capitalism. Yet, as international relations scholar Matthew Stephen points out, "the continuation of geopolitical rivalries in the form of particular 'flash-points' amongst the major powers (the Middle East, Taiwan, Korea, the Sino-India border dispute) mostly represents isolated hangovers from the process of exclusive territorial state formation, rather than a defining feature of contemporary politico-economic rivalries."[15]

Let us explore the historical context further. The global capitalist system developed out of the historical structures of world capitalism. The system's centuries-long expansion out of its European birthplace and later on out of other metropolitan centers means that agents from those regions disproportionately dominate emerging global structures. There is no doubt that Davos Man is moving toward an ever-greater integration of transnationally oriented elites from across the globe. Even if elites who originate in historically metropolitan countries predominate in a snapshot of the TCC and the transnational elite, elites from around the world are rapidly joining the ranks of Davos Man. The old metropolitan elites who have moved to globalize do not accumulate their capital, nor do they reproduce their status and power, from older national economies or circuits of accumulation but from new transnational ones that are open to investors from around the world and from which dense networks have emerged that cut across national and regional lines. What we see is a fusion of capitals from numerous national origins through multiple and overlapping mechanisms and networks, into webs of transnational capital, what former Goldman

Sachs CEO Richard Gnodde refers to as "the ecosystem of global capital."[16] In this ecosystem, blocs emerge where countries in the Global South that share a desire for expansion in the global economy find solidarity among one another in trying to open up space within Western-dominated institutions for their own class formation as contingents of the TCC. Certainly the TCC in the former Third World needs the state for its class development and to enter competitively into global circuits. Yet the picture that emerges is less one of the BRICS states confronting metropolitan capital than of transnational capital colonizing the state in new ways.

Even a cursory glance at the empirical evidence shows that BRICS capitalists are deeply integrated into the TCC, and that integration is rapidly expanding. By the second decade of the twenty-first century, Southern firms accounted for more than one-third of worldwide foreign direct investment (FDI) flows.[17] China led the way among the BRICS: between 1991 and 2003, China's FDI increased tenfold and then increased 13.7 times from 2004 to 2013, from $45 billion to $613 billion.[18] From 2000 to 2016, India's annual FDI outflow grew from $1.7 billion to $140 billion.[19] "Global business investment now flows increasingly from south to north and south to south, as emerging economies invest in the rich world and in less developed countries," reported *The Economist*. The magazine noted that such companies as Brazil's Embraer, Mexico's Cemex, Tata Group and Mittal Steel Company in India, and China's Lenovo, among others, are global corporations with operations in the hundreds of billions of dollars that span every continent.[20] Cemex is in fact the largest producer of cement in the world and Mittal, with more than 330,000 employees in sixty countries and factories on five continents, is the largest steel producer in the world. (In 2007 Lakshmi Mittal became the fifth richest man in the world.)[21] In her study on the TCC in Mexico, sociologist Alejandra Salas-Porras finds that the transnationally oriented fraction of the Mexican corporate and political community integrated increasingly into regional and global corporate networks since the 1980s and that leading Mexican transnational capitalists sit on numerous boards of directors of corporations from elsewhere in the world. "Their [these Mexican transnational capitalists] fate depends increasingly on the performance of such firms in global markets and not necessarily on the Mexican market," she notes. "As the domestic market loses strategic interest for some Mexican corporations, they also lose interest in the corporate network and become more interested in global interlocking."[22]

The evidence also suggests that the disproportionate power that metropolitan elites exercise in the global system is wielded in the interests of transnational capital. First World elites no longer need to build up a domestic labor aristocracy in pursuit of their class and group interests, and the Mexican multibillionaire Carlos Slim—the second richest man in the world in 2017—has inconceivably more social power than the mass of US workers, as do the Middle Eastern or Chinese elites that control sovereign wealth funds and invest trillions of dollars around the world. Let us now take a closer look at the underlying transnational capitalist essence of what appears on the surface to be national and North–South rivalry.

NORTHERN AGRICULTURAL SUBSIDIES AND UNITED STATES–CHINA TRADE

Brazil has led the charge within the BRICS that Northern agricultural subsidies unfairly undermine the competitiveness of Brazilian and other Southern country agricultural exports. Yet Southern opposition to the subsidy regime for agriculture in the North has constituted not opposition to capitalist globalization but a policy that has stood in the way of such globalization. Brazil has sought more, not less, globalization; it wants to see a global free market in agricultural commodities. What happens when we shift the frame of analysis from interstate relations to transnational class relations? In Brazil, who would benefit from the lifting of Northern agricultural subsidies? Above all, it would benefit the soy barons and other giant agro-industrial exporters that dominate Brazilian agriculture. And who are these barons and exporters? A study of the Brazilian economy reveals that they are agribusiness interests in Brazil that bring together Brazilian capitalists and land barons with the giant transnational corporations that drive global agribusiness, and their ownership and cross-investment structures bring together individual and institutional investors from around the world, such as Monsanto, ADM, and Cargill.[23] Simply put, "Brazilian" agricultural exports are transnational capital agricultural exports. Adopting a nation-state-centric framework of analysis makes this look like a Brazilian national conflict with powerful Northern countries. If Brazil got its way, it would not have curtailed but have furthered capitalist globalization and would have advanced the interests of transnational capital.

Cargill is the largest exporter of US and Brazilian soybeans. Cargill, ADM, and Argentine-based Bunge finance 60 percent of soy produced in Brazil, while Monsanto controls soy-seed manufacturing in both countries.[24] Brazil-based capitalists, in turn, are heavily invested in these companies. This globalized soy agro-industrial complex uses Brazil as a base with which to conquer and control world soy markets. The Brazilian government's aggressive program of agricultural trade liberalization, waged through the World Trade Organization, is not in defense of "Brazilian" interests against Northern or imperial capital but on behalf of a transnationalized soy agro-industrial complex. The Brazilian state acted in the way we would expect as a component of the transnational state, conceived in analytical abstraction as a web of institutional networks that include national states and international and supranational institutions through which the TCC and its political agents and allies organize global capitalism and the conditions for transnational accumulation in pursuit of their class and groups interests.

Brazil took its case against US farm subsidies and European Union sugar subsidies to the World Trade Organization in 2004, which ruled in Brazil's favor; the ruling suggests that the World Trade Organization, far from being an instrument of US or European "imperialism,"[25] is an effective instrument of the transnational state. What appear as international struggles for global hegemony or South struggles against the North are better seen as struggles by emerging transnational capitalists and elites outside of the original transatlantic and Trilateral core (North America, Western Europe, and Japan) to break into the ranks of the global elite and develop a capacity to influence global policy formation, manage global crises, and participate in ongoing global restructuring. The BRICS national economic strategy is structured around global integration. Nationalism becomes a strategy for local contingents of the TCC seeking space in the global capitalist order in association with transnational capital from abroad.

Those who posit growing international conflict between the traditional core countries and rising powers in the former Third World point most often to China and its alleged conflict with the United States over global influence. Geopolitical analysis as conjunctural analysis must be informed by structural analysis. The policies of the Chinese (as well as the other BRICS states) have been aimed at integration into global production chains in association with transnational capital. By 2005, China's stock of FDI to GDP was 36 percent (compared to 1.5 percent for Japan and 5 percent for India), with half of its foreign sales and nearly a third of its industrial output generated by transnational corporations.[26] Moreover, the giant Chinese companies (ranging from the oil and chemical sectors to auto, electronics, telecommunications, and finance) have associated with transnational corporations from around the world in the form of mergers and acquisitions, shared stock, cross-investment, joint ventures, subcontracting, and so on, both inside China and around the world. Inside China, for instance, some 80 percent of large-scale supermarkets had merged with foreign companies by 2008.[27] There is simply no evidence of "Chinese" companies in fierce rivalry with "US" and other "Western" companies over international control. Rather, the picture is one of competition among transnational conglomerates that integrate Chinese companies. That Chinese firms have more secure access to the Chinese state than other firms does not imply the state conflict that observers posit, because these firms are integrated into transnational capitalist networks and access the Chinese state on behalf of the amalgamated interests of the groups into which they are inserted.

Similarly, these same commentators point to a growing US trade deficit and an inverse accumulation by China of international dollar reserves and then conclude that the two states are locked in competition over international trade and hegemony.[28] But we cannot possibly understand United States–China trade dynamics without observing that 40–70 percent of world trade in the early twenty-first century was intrafirm or associational, that some 40 percent of exports from China came from transnational corporations based in that country, and that much of the remaining 60 percent was accounted for by associational forms involving Chinese and transnational investors. These transnational class and social relations are concealed behind nation-state data and behind the foggy glasses of outdated paradigms. When we focus on the production, ownership structures, class, and social relations that lie behind nation-state trade data, we are in a better position to search for causal explanations for global political and economic dynamics.

The international division of labor characterized by the concentration of finance, technology, and research and development in traditional core countries and low-wage assembly (along with raw materials) in traditional peripheral countries is giving way to a global division of labor in which core and peripheral productive activities are dispersed as much within as among countries. Contrary to the expectations of nation-state-centric perspectives, transnational corporations originating in traditionally core countries no longer jealously retain their research and development operations in their countries of origin. The United Nations Conference on Trade and Development dedicated its 2005 annual World Investment Report to the rapid internationalization of research and development by transnational corporations.[29] Applied Materials, a leading solar technology company headquartered in California, shifts components for its solar panels all over the world and then assembles them at distinct final market destinations. The company decided in 2009, however, to open a major research and development center in Western China that is the size of ten football fields and employs 400 engineers.[30] Moreover, many companies that previously produced in the traditional core countries were investing in new facilities in these "emerging economies" to achieve proximity to expanding local markets.

Does this mean that there are no political tensions in international forums or between Western-dominated international institutions and Southern elites? To the contrary, this is a moment of mounting worldwide political tension that is expressed in multiple forms, including in interstate relations. These forums are highly undemocratic and are dominated by the old colonial powers as a political residue of an earlier era. But here is the key point: these international political tensions—sometimes geopolitical—do not indicate underlying structural contradictions between rival national or regional capitalist groups and economic blocs. The transnational integration of these national economies and their capitalist groups created common class interests in an expanding global economy. And besides, as I observed above, capitalist groups from these countries form part of transnational conglomerates in competition with one another. The inextricable mixing of capitals globally through financial flows simply undermines the material basis for the development of powerful national capitalist groups in contradiction with the global capitalist economy and the TCC.

Interstate conflict in the new era has generally taken place in the past two decades between the centers of military power in the global system and those states where nationally oriented elites still exercised enough control to impede integration into global capitalist circuits, such as in Iraq prior to the 2003 US invasion or North Korea; those states where social and political instability threatened the global capitalist order, such as the Horn of Africa; or those states where subordinate classes exercised enough influence over the state to result in state policies that threaten global capitalist interests, such as Venezuela and other South American countries that turned to the left in the early twenty-first century.

Where there are growing geopolitical and even military tensions, such as in the South China Sea or NATO's eastern flank with Russia, there is simply no evidence to characterize these antagonisms as conflicts among rival economic groups and national capitalist classes. They are better explained as expressing quandaries of state legitimacy and the efforts by state elites to reproduce their privileged status within the unity of a global capitalism in crisis. What are more accurately termed *transnational conflicts*, I have always insisted, spring from three wells of international tension: the pressures for legitimacy at the level of the nation-state; the clash between distinct fractions among capitalists and elites with differing degrees of transnationalization and dependence on the (national) state in each nation-state and their tussles over policy; and threats to the global order from popular or unruly social forces from below.

THE TRANSNATIONAL STATE AND FREE TRADE AGREEMENTS

The transnational state as a conceptual abstraction—that is, an analytical tool—provides a better explanation for the agency of BRICS within the global capitalist system than a variety of realist notions, among them, of interstate competition, North–South confrontation, or struggles for nation-state hegemony. Examples abound as to how the TCC exercises in class power through transnational state apparatuses, but these examples are blind-sighted out of view by the realist framework. This framework, for instance, views trade liberalization in North–South national terms, so that regional agreements such as the North American Free Trade Agreement (NAFTA) or the Central American Free Trade Agreement in the Americas, or multilateral World Trade Organization negotiations, are interpreted as instances of Northern or core country domination and exploitation of the South. Free trade agreements have indeed opened up the world to transnational corporate plunder, concentrating power further in the hands of the TCC, dispossessing local communities, and deepening polarization between the rich and the poor within and across countries. But powerful agents within the South who were as much a part of the global power structure and who benefitted as much from liberalization as their Northern counterparts also promoted these agreements.

The reluctance of the US and EU governments to eliminate agricultural subsidies in recent years during World Trade Organization negotiations were seen as Northern attempts to protect its own agricultural producers while gaining access to Southern agriculture and markets and hence to maintain its domination in the international system. Yet farmers in the North did not benefit from free trade agreements and faced the same takeover, as did their Southern counterparts, by the leviathanlike transnational agro-industrial corporations that have come to dominate the world food system, from laboratory to farm to supermarket, such as Cargill, Monsanto, and ADM. Southern governments such as Brazil and India that, in calling for an end to Northern agricultural subsidies, supposedly championed the interests of the South over the North, were not protecting the interests of small farmers and local rural communities in their own countries any more than Northern states did. As part of capitalist globalization, these same governments steadily facilitated the transformation of their national agricultural systems into corporate dominated capitalist agriculture. Brazil, for example, is the second largest exporter of soy in the world, and its soy industry is thoroughly enmeshed in the global corporate agro-industrial complex, in the hands of large-scale producers, suppliers, processors, and exporters who themselves are part of the global corporate food system.

Many leftist critics saw the NAFTA as a US takeover of Mexico along the lines of classical theories of imperialism and dependency.[31] The NAFTA is a casebook study of the ravages of capitalist globalization on the popular classes in the countryside, including what remains of the peasantry, of small and medium market producers and rural communities. An estimated 1.3 million families were forced off the land in the years after NAFTA went into effect in 1994 as the Mexican market became flooded with cheap corn from the United States. US farmers did not reap the benefits of NAFTA; transnational corporate agro-industry did, along with a handful of powerful economic agents on both sides of the border. From NAFTA into the twenty-first century, Mexican agro-export businesses grew rapidly. In Mexico, the winners were the Mexican members of the TCC. Patel has shown how consumers in Mexico did *not* benefit from cheaper corn imported from the United States. Rather, the price of tortillas (the Mexican staple) *actually rose* in the wake of NAFTA even as bulk corn prices dropped. This was because NAFTA helped Mexican transnational capitalists to gain monopoly control of the corn-tortilla market. Just two companies, GIMSA and MINSA, together control 97 percent of the industrial corn flour market.[32] GIMSA, which is owned by Gruma SA, a multibillion-dollar Mexican-based global corporation that also dominates the tortilla market in the United States under the label Mission Foods, accounted for 70 percent of the market. Alongside the displacement of millions of small producers, the Mexican government increased its subsidies for these large ("efficient") corn millers and simultaneously scaled back credit for small rural and urban producers and social programs involving food subsidies for the poor, who traditionally consumed local hand-made tortillas.

In sum, the corn-tortilla circuit went from one based on small, local corn and tortilla producers to a transnational commodity chain involving industrially produced and US-state subsidized corn and industrially produced and Mexican-state subsidized tortilla production and distribution on both sides of the border. We can see here how transnational conglomerates of corn production and processing on both sides of the border were the beneficiaries of NAFTA while both the US and the Mexican states acted to facilitate transnational accumulation through the approval of NAFTA, the subsidization of transnational corporate production, the conversion of peasant agriculture into transnational agribusiness, and neoliberal austerity. This is not a picture of US neo-colonization of Mexico as much as it is one of transnational corporate colonization of both countries, facilitated by the two national states functioning as components of transnational state apparatuses.

The Mexican state and political system were wracked by fierce and even bloody struggles between national and transnational fractions of the elite in the 1980s and 1990s as the country integrated into the global economy. During these struggles, global elites from outside Mexico and transnational state institutions supported transnationally oriented fractions in their effort to gain control of the Mexican state and to become the reigning group in control of the ruling party, the Institutional Revolutionary Party. This transnational fraction of the Mexican elite triumphed definitively with the election to the presidency of one of its key representatives, Carlos Salinas de Gortari, in the fraud-tainted vote of 1988. These class dynamics constituted the broader context for the Mexican state's promotion of NAFTA, which was aimed at the transformation of the Mexican agricultural system that had come into existence with the Mexican revolution of 1910 and involved a significant portion of peasant, collective, and small-scale production for the domestic market, into a globally integrated system based on large-scale export-oriented capitalist agriculture. It is noteworthy that NAFTA itself was heavily pushed by transnational groups within the Mexican business and political elite. The North American Group of the Trilateral Commission, which played a key role in designing and governing NAFTA, included 12 Mexican members.[33]

Transnationally oriented Mexican government officials who came to power in 1988 called on the World Bank even as they were negotiating NAFTA to assist them in drafting policies to accomplish this transition to transnational corporate agriculture.[34] In fact, the original impetus for Mexico's globalization came from transnationally oriented technocrats from within the Mexican state under the Salinas administration in consort with supranational organizations such as the World Bank. Subsequently, they mobilized powerful economic groups among the Mexican business community. These sectors of the capitalist class became organized in the 1980s into the Altacomulco group and were able to make the shift from national into transnational circuits of accumulation and go on to lead powerful Mexican-based transnational corporations. Transnational state apparatuses in such cases actually take the lead in organizing and globalizing local dominant groups. This transnationalization of the Mexican state and of significant portions of the Mexican capitalist class is a process that cannot be understood in terms of outdated neocolonial analyses of US imperialism and Mexican dependence.

The agricultural trade liberalization pushed by Northern states and the transnational agro-industrial corporate lobby shifts wealth not to First World farmers but to transnational capital; to the giant corporations that control marketing and agro-industrial processing while also reorganizing the value structure in such a way that cheap processed foods are available to better off urban strata in both North and South. While it is true that US "farmers" may enjoy a higher standard of living than many of their Third World counterparts, they do not have more security and are completely controlled by corporate dictates. Rather than independent farmers, they are more accurately seen as employees of the corporate agribusiness giants or as rural workers, in which capital exercises indirect control over the means of production, determining what must be produced, how it must be produced, and under what terms output is to be marketed … provided that their farms do not go into foreclosure.

The BRICS (and other "emerging markets" such as Mexico) provide new investment outlets for overaccumulated transnational capital. Yet as this happens, local BRICS capitalists (and this holds true for local capitalists more generally) jump on the bandwagon of new patterns of transnational accumulation. In a sense, they hitch a ride on to global capitalism and in this way become swept up into transnational class formation. There is no clearer case of this than the transnationalization of Central American capitalists, which has taken place in the past decades in two waves. The first wave took place in the aftermath of the 1980s wars of revolution and counterinsurgency and as neoliberalism in the 1990s opened up the region to transnational capital, especially in the form of transnational corporation investment in the *maquiladora* assembly industry, tourism, nontraditional agricultural exports, retail, and finance. But as this took place, local capitalist groups that were previously grounded in protected national industries and traditional agro-exports co-invested with transnational corporations from abroad and transnationalized themselves.[35] The second wave took place into the second decade of the twenty-first century and through the expansion of agrofuel and other "flexicrops" in the region. This wave brought together transnational bankers and investor groups such as Goldman Sachs and the Carlyle Group, with many of the major local investor groups in Central America.[36]

In the wake of the 2008 financial collapse, US-based companies, according to one report, were looking increasingly to China, India, Brazil, and other so-called "emerging economies," not primarily as cheap labor for re-export but as "potential consumers for American produced goods and services." This shift, "which has been underway for several years but has intensified sharply during the downturn, comes as vast numbers of families in these emerging economies are moving into cities and spending like never before to improve their living standards."[37] The tendency toward a global decentralization of consumer markets reflects a "rebalancing" in the global economy, in which consumer markets are less concentrated in the North and more geographically spread around the world. This does not mean that the world is become less unequal, but rather that North and South refer increasingly to social rather than geographic location, in terms of transnational class relations rather than membership in particular nation-states.

CONCLUSION: CAPITALIST GLOBALIZATION
AS WORLD-HISTORIC CONTEXT

The legacy of the postcolonial struggles and Third World efforts at national industrialization meant that many former Third World countries entered the globalization age with significant state sectors. The BRICS countries stand apart from their G7 counterparts in that, to varying degrees, they have significant state sectors—although South Africa (and to a lesser extent, Brazil) have privatized much of the public sector, Russia has privatized much of its once formidable state sector (or entered into partnership with private capital), and India and even China are in the process of doing so. Neoliberal programs involved the privatization of much of these former state holdings in the late twentieth and early twenty-first centuries, but some sectors, often oil and finance, remained state held in a number of countries, which has led some commentators to suggest that the BRICS represent a genuine alternative to neoliberal globalization.[38] At the same time, several countries such as China and the oil exporters of the Middle East have set up "sovereign wealth funds"—that is, state held investment companies—that involve several trillion dollars. Many have argued that the rise of such powerful state corporations in the international arena signaled a "decoupling" from the US and Western economy.

Yet historian Jerry Harris has shown that these state corporations have not turned inward to build up protected national or regional economies but have thoroughly integrated into transnational corporate circuits. The sovereign wealth funds have invested billions buying stocks in banks, securities houses, and asset management firms, among them Barclays, Blackstone, Carlyle, Citigroup, Deutsche Bank, HSBC, Merrill Lynch, Morgan Stanley, UBS, the London Stock Exchange, and NASDAQ. He terms this phenomenon *transnational state capitalism*; the activities of the sovereign wealth funds and other state corporations underscore "the statist nature of the Third World TCC." These state corporations undertook a wave of investment in "emerging market" equities and in other investments abroad. He adds that many of these sovereign wealth funds have invested in stock exchanges in the United States, Europe, and elsewhere: "The drive to combine stock markets responds to the financial needs of the TCC, who want to trade shares anywhere, invest across asset classes and do it faster."[39]

The case of China is revealing. Some have claimed that China is competing with Western capitalists, but in fact transnational capital is heavily co-invested in China's leading state corporations. For instance, in 2007 Warren Buffet had invested $500 million in the China National Petroleum Corporation, the world's fifth largest oil-producing company. The corporation had co-investments and joint ventures around the world with virtually all the major private transnational oil companies and was able to enter the Iraqi oil market with the assistance of the US occupiers.[40] There has been a substantial fusion of Chinese and transnational finance capital. In the early twenty-first century, transnational banks became minority holders in major Chinese financial institutions, and Chinese banks likewise invested in private financial institutions around the world. These same webs of association with transnational capital hold true for Russian state (as well as private) corporations.

Global capitalism remains characterized by wide and expanding inequalities, whether measured within countries or among countries in North–South terms, and grossly asymmetric power relations adhere to interstate relations. Such historical political asymmetries in international relations have not been dismantled, and stand in a widening disjuncture with capitalist globalization and global class relations. But this cannot blind us to analysis that moves beyond a nation-state/interstate framework. Breaking with nation-state-centric analysis does not mean abandoning analysis of national-level processes and phenomena or interstate dynamics. It does mean, however, that we view transnational capitalism as the world-historic context in which these play themselves out.

It is not possible to understand anything about global society without studying a concrete region and its particular circumstances—a part of a totality, in its relation to that totality. To evoke globalization as an explanation for historic changes and contemporary dynamics does not mean that the *particular* events or changes identified with the process are happening all over the world, much less in the same ways. It does mean that the events or changes are understood as a consequence of globalized power relations and social structures. Distinct national and regional histories and configurations of social forces as they have historically evolved mean that each country and region undergoes a distinct experience under globalization.

If the BRICS do not represent an alternative to global capitalism and the domination of the TCC, they do signal the shift toward a more multipolar and balanced interstate system within the global capitalist order. The BRICS played a crucial role in averting a US missile strike against Syria in 2013 (only to have the Trump government launch such a strike and escalate US intervention in 2017) and have spoken out strongly for Palestinian rights, Iranian sovereignty in the face of US–Israeli hostility, and other international political positions that push toward a more balanced interstate regime. But such a multipolar interstate system remains part of a brutal, exploitative, global capitalist world in which the BRICS capitalists and states are as committed to control and repression of the global working class as their Northern counterparts. As South African political scientist and activist Patrick Bond has emphasized, all five BRICS have been hit in recent years by an explosion of mass struggles from below against rising capitalist exploitation and state repression and corruption.[41] Our analyses carry political implications: by misreading the BRICS policies, critical scholars and the global left run the risk of becoming cheerleaders for repressive states and transnational capitalists in the "emerging" South. We would be better off by a denouement of the BRICS states and by siding with "BRICS from below" struggles of popular and working class forces.

NINE

GLOBAL POLICE STATE

A global police state is emerging as world capitalism descends into a crisis that is unprecedented in its magnitude, its global reach, the extent of ecological degradation and social deterioration, and the sheer scale of the means of violence that is now deployed around the world. *Global police state* refers to three interrelated developments. First is the ever more omnipresent systems of mass social control, repression, and warfare promoted by the ruling groups to contain the real and the potential rebellion of the global working class and surplus humanity. Second is how the global economy is itself based more and more on the development and deployment of these systems of warfare, social control, and repression simply as a means of making profit and continuing to accumulate capital in the face of stagnation (what I term *militarized accumulation*, or *accumulation by repression*). And third is the increasing move towards political systems that can be characterized as twenty-first-century fascism, or even in a broader sense, as totalitarian.

In referring to the global police state, I want to underscore the increasing convergence around global capitalism's political need for social control and repression and its economic need to perpetuate accumulation in the face of overaccumulation and stagnation. Transnational capital has subordinated virtually the entire world's population to its logic and its domination. In this sense, the world's people live under a dictatorship of the transnational capitalist class (TCC). I mean here dictatorship in the literal (etymological) sense of the word, such that transnational capital dictates the conditions under which billions of people carry out their lives in the global economy and society. In this sense, it is a more encompassing, powerful, omnipresent, and deadly dictatorship than any other in history. At the same time, however, I mean dictatorship in the more

183

figurative sense that, absent a change of course, we are moving toward a political dictatorship of the TCC as it imposes and sustains its rule through a global police state.

This dictatorship is reactive. We are seeing a breakdown worldwide of global capitalist hegemony. If the global working class and oppressed peoples were simply passive, there would be no need for such repression and control. The Italian socialist Antonio Gramsci developed the concept of *hegemony* to refer to the attainment by ruling groups of stable forms of rule based on "consensual" domination. Gramsci's notion of hegemony posits distinct forms of domination: coercive domination and consensual domination. Hegemony is a class relationship in which the ruling group manages to gain the "active consent" of subordinate classes as part of a larger project of class rule or domination. It involves the subordinate classes internalizing the moral and cultural values, the codes of practical conduct, and the worldview of the dominant classes or groups—in sum, the internalization by the oppressed of the social logic of the system of domination itself. In distinction to an outright dictatorship or military regime, force and coercion in a hegemonic order are ever-present but may take a back seat to ideological control and other forms of co-optation. But now the revolt of the oppressed and exploited populations around the world is leading to the breakdown of consensual means of domination and compels the TCC to impose increasingly coercive and repressive forms of rule.

THE CRISIS OF GLOBAL CAPITALISM

The crisis of global capitalism shares aspects of earlier systemwide structural crises, such as those of the 1880s, the 1930s, and the 1970s. But there are six interrelated dimensions to the current crisis that I believe set it apart from these earlier ones and suggest that a simple restructuring of the system will not lead to its restabilization; our very survival now requires a revolution against global capitalism. These six dimensions, in broad strokes, present a "big picture" context in which a global police state is emerging, and as I discuss in the next section, they are all linked structurally to capitalism's Achilles' heel, overaccumulation,

First, the system is fast reaching the ecological limits of its reproduction. We have reached several tipping points in what environmental scientists refer to as nine crucial planetary boundaries. We have already exceeded these boundaries in three of them—climate change, the nitrogen cycle, and diversity loss.[1] There have been five previous mass extinctions in earth's history. While all of them were due to natural causes, for the first time ever, human conduct is intersecting with and fundamentally altering the earth system. "We are deciding, without quite meaning to, which evolutionary pathways will remain open and which will forever be closed," observes Elizabeth Kolbert in her best seller, *The Sixth Extinction*.[2] These ecological dimensions of global crisis cannot be overstated and have been brought to the forefront of the global agenda by the worldwide environmental justice movement. Communities around the world have come under escalating repression as they face off against transnational corporate plunder of their environment.

Capitalism cannot be held solely responsible for the ecological crisis. The human–nature contradiction has deep roots in civilization itself. The ancient Sumerian empires, for example, collapsed after the population oversalinized their crop soil. The Mayan city-state network collapsed around 800 AD because of deforestation. And the former Soviet Union wreaked havoc on the environment.[3] However, given capital's implacable impulse to accumulate profit and its accelerated commodification of nature, it is difficult to image that the environmental catastrophe can be resolved within the capitalist system. "Green capitalism" appears as an oxymoron, as capitalism's attempt to turn the ecological crisis into a profit-making opportunity.

Second, the level of global social polarization and inequality is unprecedented. The richest 1 percent of humanity in 2016 controlled more than 50 percent of the world's wealth, and 20 percent controlled 95 percent of that wealth, while the remaining 80 percent had to make do with just 5 percent. These escalating inequalities fuel capitalism's chronic problem of overaccumulation: the TCC cannot find productive outlets to unload the enormous amounts of surplus it has accumulated, leading to chronic stagnation in the world economy. These extreme levels of social polarization present a challenge of social control to dominant groups. They strive to purchase the loyalty of that 20 percent, while at the same time dividing the 80 percent, co-opting some into a hegemonic bloc and repressing the rest.

As Trumpism in the United States and the rise of far-right and neofascist movements in Europe so well illustrate, co-optation also involves the manipulation of fear and insecurity among the downwardly mobile so that social anxiety is channeled toward scapegoated communities. This psychosocial mechanism of displacing mass anxieties is not new, but it appears to be increasing around the world in the face of the structural destabilization of capitalist globalization. Scapegoated communities are under siege, such as the Rohingya in Myanmar, the Muslim minority in India, the Kurds in Turkey, southern African immigrants in South Africa, and Syrian and Iraqi refugees and other immigrants in Europe. As with its twentieth century predecessor, twenty-first-century fascism hinges on such manipulation of social anxiety at a time of acute capitalist crisis. And as I discuss below, extreme inequality requires extreme violence and repression that lend themselves to projects of twenty-first-century fascism.

Third, the sheer magnitude of the means of violence and social control is unprecedented, as well as the magnitude and concentrated control over the means of global communication and the production and circulation of symbols, images, and knowledge. Computerized wars, drone warfare, robot soldiers, bunker-buster bombs, satellite surveillance, data mining, spatial control technology, and so forth have changed the face of warfare, and more generally, of systems of social control and repression. Warfare has become normalized and sanitized for those not directly on the receiving end of armed aggression. And moreover, we have arrived at the panoptical surveillance society, a point brought home by Edward Snowden's revelations in 2013, and the age of thought control by those who control global flows of communication and symbolic production.

Fourth, we are reaching limits to the extensive expansion of capitalism, in the sense that there are no longer any new territories of significance to integrate into world capitalism, and new spaces to commodify are drying up. The capitalist system is by its nature expansionary. The system is like riding a bicycle: when you stop pedaling, you fall over. If the capitalist system stops expanding, it faces collapse. In each earlier structural crisis, the system went through a new round of extensive expansion—from waves of colonial conquest in earlier centuries, to the integration in the late twentieth and early twenty-first centuries of the former socialist countries, China, India, and other areas that had been marginally outside the system. Today, however, there are no longer any new territories to integrate into world capitalism. At the same time, the privatization of education, health, utilities, basic services, and public lands are turning those spaces in global society that were outside of capital's control into "spaces of capital," so that intensive expansion is reaching depths never before seen. What is there left to commodify? Where can the system now expand? New spaces have to be violently cracked open, and the peoples in these spaces must be repressed by the global police state.

Fifth, there is the rise of a vast surplus population inhabiting a "planet of slums," pushed out of the productive economy, thrown into the margins, and subject to sophisticated systems of social control and to destruction, into a mortal cycle of dispossess–exploit–exclude. Let us recall: crises provide capital with the opportunity to accelerate the process of forcing greater productivity out of fewer workers. The processes by which surplus labor is generated have accelerated under globalization. Spatial reorganization has helped transnational capital to break the territorial-bound power of organized labor and impose new capital–labor relations based on fragmentation, flexibilization, and the cheapening of labor. These developments, combined with a massive new round of primitive accumulation and displacement of hundreds of millions, have given rise to a new global army of superfluous labor that goes well beyond the traditional reserve army of labor that Marx discussed.

Global capitalism has no direct use for surplus humanity. But indirectly, it holds wages down everywhere and makes new systems of twenty-first-century slavery possible. These systems range from prison labor, to the forced recruitment at gunpoint by warlords contracted by global corporations of miners to dig up valuable minerals in the Congo, slave labor recently revealed in the Brazilian timber industry, thousands of slaves in the Southeast Asia fishing industry, and virtually enslaved sweatshop workers and exploited immigrant communities held in bonded labor.[4] As I mentioned previously, this would not be a problem for capital if surplus humanity passively resigned itself to death. But dominant groups face the challenge of how to contain both the real and potential rebellion of surplus humanity. In addition, surplus humanity cannot consume, and so as their ranks expand the problem of overaccumulation becomes exacerbated.

Sixth, there is an acute political contradiction in global capitalism: economic globalization takes places within a system of political authority based in the nation-state. Transnational state apparatuses are incipient and have not been able to play the role of "hegemon," or a leading nation-state with enough power and authority to organize and stabilize the system, much less to impose regulations on transnational capital. This contradiction generates a host of dilemmas for states and the transnational elite. Governments under capitalism gain their legitimacy by appearing to achieve or to work toward employment, stability, and greater prosperity—that is, by meeting the "general social interest." Yet in the age of capitalist globalization, governments are dependent on attracting to the national territory transnational corporate investment, which requires providing capital with all the incentives associated with neoliberalism—downward pressure on wages, deregulation, austerity, and on so—that aggravate inequality, impoverishment, and insecurity for working classes.

In other words, nation-states face a contradiction between the need to promote transnational capital accumulation in their territories and their need to achieve political legitimacy. As a result, states around the world have been experiencing spiraling crises of legitimacy. Managers of the capitalist state need to generate conditions for a reactivation of transnational accumulation, yet they also must respond to mass popular pressures from below that push them in the opposite direction. This situation generates bewildering and seemingly contradictory politics and also helps explain the rise of far-right and neofascist forces that espouse rhetoric of nationalism and protectionism even as they continue to promote neoliberalism.

OVERACCUMULATION: CAPITALISM'S ACHILLES' HEEL

The turn toward a global police state is structurally rooted in perhaps the fundamental contradiction of capitalism: overaccumulation, which is interwoven with all six dimensions of global crisis discussed above. The polarization of income and wealth is endemic to capitalism: the capitalist class owns the means of producing wealth and therefore appropriates as profits as much as possible of the wealth that society collectively produces, so that even as the system churns out more and more wealth, the mass of workers cannot actually consume that wealth. The gap grows between what is produced and what the market can absorb. If capitalists cannot actually sell (or "unload") the products of their plantations, factories, and offices, then they cannot make profit. Left unchecked, expanding social polarization results in crisis—in stagnation, recessions, depressions, social upheavals, and war. "In these crises there breaks out an epidemic

that, in all earlier epochs, would have seemed an absurdity—the epidemic of overproduction," wrote Marx and Engels in *The Communist
Manifesto*. "Society suddenly finds itself put back into a state of momentary barbarism . . . And why? Because there is too much civilization, too
much means of subsistence, too much industry, too much commerce."[5]

Globalization has greatly exacerbated overaccumulation. As capital
went global from the 1970s and on, the emerging TCC was able to get
around state intervention in the capitalist market and undermine the redistributive programs that mass struggles of poor and working people
had forced on the system in the twentieth century. The extreme concentration of the planet's wealth in the hands of the few and the accelerated
impoverishment and dispossession of the majority means that the TCC
cannot find productive outlets to unload enormous amounts of surplus it
has accumulated. A series of lesser jolts to the global economy, from the
Mexico peso crisis of 1995, to the Asian financial meltdown of 1997–
1999 and its spread to several other regions, and then the dot-com busts
and global recession of 2000–2001, were preludes to the 2008 collapse of
the global financial system. The Great Recession—the worst crisis since
the 1930s—marked the onset of a deep structural crisis of overaccumulation. As uninvested capital accumulates, enormous pressures build up to
find outlets for unloading the surplus. Capitalist groups pressure states to
create new opportunities for profit-making. By the twenty-first century,
the TCC turned primarily to three mechanisms in order to sustain global
accumulation in the face of overaccumulation: financial speculation, the
plunder of public finances, and state-organized militarized accumulation.

Deregulation of the financial industry and the creation of a globally
integrated financial system in recent decades has allowed the TCC to
unload trillions of dollars into speculation. The sequence of speculative
waves in the global casino since the 1980s included real estate investments in the emerging global property market that inflated property values in one locality after another; wild stock market speculation leading
to periodic booms and busts (most notably the bursting of the dot-com
bubble in 2001); the phenomenal escalation of hedge-fund flows; currency speculation; and every imaginable derivative, ranging from swaps
and futures markets to collateralized debt obligations, asset pyramiding,
and Ponzi schemes.

US treasury bailouts of the Wall Street-based banks following the
2008 collapse, which was triggered by speculation in the housing mar-

ket, went to bail out individual and institutional investors from around the world. According to a 2011 report by the US government's General Accounting Office, the US Federal Reserve undertook a whopping $16 trillion in secret bailouts between 2007 and 2010 to banks and corporations from around the world.[6] But then the banks and institutional investors simply recycled trillions of dollars they received in bailout money into new speculative activities in global commodities markets, especially energy and food markets, which provoked a spike in world prices in 2007 and 2008 and sparked "food riots" around the world.

As opportunity for speculative investment in one sector dries up, the TCC simply turns to another sector to unload its surplus. The latest outlet for surplus capital at the time of writing (late 2017) seems to be the overvalued technology or information technology sector (although the stock market as a whole was grossly inflated). Institutional investors, especially speculative hedge and mutual funds, poured billions of dollars into the tech sector since the 2008 Great Recession, turning it into a major new outlet for uninvested capital in the face of stagnation. Investment in the information technology sector jumped from $17 billion in 1970s to $175 billion in 1990, then to $496 billion in 2000, on the eve of the bursting of the turn-of-the century dot-com bubble, but then climbed up again to new heights after 2008, reaching $674 billion as 2017 drew to a close.[7]

The gap between the productive economy (what the media calls the "real economy") and "fictitious capital" (that is, money thrown into circulation without any base in commodities or in productive activity) has reached mind-boggling levels. Gross world product, or the total value of goods and services produced worldwide, for instance, stood at some $75 trillion in 2015, whereas currency speculation alone amounted to $5.3 trillion a day that year and the global derivatives market was estimated at an astonishing $1.2 quadrillion.[8] The "real economy" has also been kept sputtering along by the expansion of credit to consumers and to governments, especially in the Global North and among new middle and professional layers and high-income groups in the Global South, to sustain spending and consumption. In the United States, which has long been the "market of last resort" for the global economy, household debt is higher than it has been since the end of World War II. US households owed in 2016 nearly $13 trillion in student loans, credit card debt, auto loans, and mortgages. In just about every country in the Organisation for Economic

Co-operation and Development, the ratio of income to household debt remains historically high and has steadily deteriorated since 2008.[9]

The TCC has also turned to raiding and sacking public finance, which has been reconfigured through austerity, bailouts, corporate subsidies, government debt, and the global bond market as governments transfer wealth directly and indirectly from working people to the TCC. The global bond market—an indicator of total government debt worldwide—had already reached $100 trillion by 2011.[10] Governments issue bonds to investors in order to close government budget deficits and also to subsidize private accumulation so as to keep the economy going. They then have to pay back these bonds (with interest) by extracting taxes from current and future wages of the working class. Already by the late twentieth century, state income brought in by bonds often just went right back to creditors. Thus, the reconfiguration of state finances amounts over time to a transfer of wealth from global labor to transnational capital; a claim by transnational capital on future wages and a shift in the burden of the crisis to the working and popular classes.

In the perverse world of predatory transnational finance, capital debt and deficits themselves became new sources of financial speculation that allow the TCC to raid and sack public budgets. Governments facing insolvency in the wake of the Great Recession turned to bond emissions in order to stay afloat, which allowed transnational investors to unload surplus into these sovereign debt markets that they themselves helped to create. Gone are the times that such bonds are bought and held to maturity. They are bought and sold by individual and institutional investors in frenzied twenty-four-hour worldwide trading and bet on continuously through such mechanisms as credit default swaps that shift their values and make bond markets a high-stakes gamble of volatility and risk for investors. Moreover, conservative politicians have presented rising public debt as caused by working people living beyond their means to legitimate the call for social spending cuts and austerity. The toxic mixture of public finance and private transnational finance capital in this age of global capitalism constitutes a new battlefield in which the global rich are waging a war against the global poor and working classes. This becomes a critical part of the story of global police state as resistance to this financial pillage mounts around the world.

Yet such financial pillage cannot resolve the crisis of overaccumulation and ends up aggravating it in the long run as the transfer of wealth from workers to the TCC further constricts the market. Data for 2010 showed that companies from the United States were sitting on $1.8 trillion in uninvested cash. Corporate profits have been at near record highs at the same time that corporate investment declined.[11] As we progressed into the twenty-first century, massive concentrations of transnational finance capital were destabilizing the system, and global capitalism ran up against the limits of financial fixes. The result is ever-greater underlying instability in the global economy.

MILITARIZED ACCUMULATION
AND ACCUMULATION BY REPRESSION

Yet there is another mechanism that has sustained the global economy and that pushes the system toward a global police state: militarized accumulation. While it is true that unprecedented global inequalities can only be sustained by ever more repressive and ubiquitous systems of social control and repression, it is equally evident that quite apart from political considerations, the TCC has acquired a vested interest in war, conflict, and repression as a means of accumulation. As war and state-sponsored repression become increasingly privatized, the interests of a broad array of capitalist groups shift the political, social, and ideological climate toward generating and sustaining social conflict —such as in the Middle East—and in expanding systems of warfare, repression, surveillance, and social control. The so-called wars on drugs and terrorism; the undeclared wars on immigrants, refugees, and gangs (and poor, dark-skinned, and working class youth more generally); the construction of border walls, immigrant detention centers, prison-industrial complexes, and systems of mass surveillance; and the spread of private security guard and mercenary companies have all become major sources of profit-making.

A cursory glance at US news headlines in the first few months of the Trump government illustrated this militarized accumulation. The day after Donald Trump's electoral victory, the stock price of Corrections Corporation of America (rebranded in 2016 as CoreCivic), the largest for-profit immigrant detention and prison company in the United States, soared 40 percent, given Trump's promise to deport millions of immigrants. The stock price of another leading private prison and immigrant detention company, GEO Group, saw its stock prices triple in the first few months of the Trump regime. (The company had contributed $250,000 to Trump's inauguration and was then awarded with a $110 million contract to build a new immigrant detention center in California.)[12] Military contractors such as Raytheon and Lockheed Martin report spikes each time there is a new flare-up in the Middle East conflict. Within hours of the April 6, 2017, US Tomahawk missile bombardment of Syria, the company that builds those missiles, Raytheon, reported an increase in its stock value by $1 billion. Hundreds of private firms from around the world put in bids to construct Trump's infamous United States–Mexico border wall.[13]

The attacks of September 11, 2001, were a turning point in the construction of a global police state. The United States state took advantage of those attacks to militarize the global economy, while it and other states around the world passed draconian "anti-terrorist" security legislation and escalated military ("defense") spending.[14] The Pentagon budget increased 91 percent in real terms between 1998 and 2011, and even apart from special war appropriations, it increased by nearly 50 percent in real terms during this period. In the decade from 2001 to 2011, military industry profits nearly quadrupled. Worldwide, total defense outlays (military, intelligence agencies, Homeland Security/Defense) grew by 50 percent from 2006 to 2015, from $1.4 trillion to $2.03 trillion.[15] The "war on terrorism," with its escalation of military spending and repression alongside social austerity, has collateral political and ideological functions. It legitimates the new transnational social control systems and the creation of the global police state in the name of security. It allows states to criminalize social movements, resistance struggles, and "undesirable" populations.

The circuits of militarized accumulation coercively open up opportunities for capital accumulation worldwide, either on the heels of military force or through states' contracting out to transnational corporate capital the production and execution of social control and warfare. Hence the generation of conflicts and the repression of social movements and vulnerable populations around the world becomes an accumulation strategy that conjoins with political objectives and may even trump those objectives. By way of example, companies such as CoreCivic and GEO Group are traded on the Wall Street stock exchange, which means that investors from anywhere around the world may buy and sell their stock, and in this way develop a stake in immigrant repression quite removed from, if not entirely independent, of the more pointed political and ideological objectives of this repression. The type of permanent global warfare we now face involves both low- and high-intensity wars, "humanitarian missions," "drug interdiction operations," "anti-crime sweeps," undocumented immigrant roundups, and so on.

Few developments in recent decades have been so functional to the global capitalist assault on the working and oppressed peoples of the Americas (and so illustrative of accumulation by repression) than the so-called "war on drugs." Dominant accounts portray the drug wars as a heroic struggle by the US, Mexican, and other governments in the Americas against depraved mafia cartels and criminal gangs, typically mystifying and sensationalizing the havoc as "senseless violence." Yet these wars constitute the axis around which the vast program of militarized accumulation and capitalist globalization revolves in Mexico, Colombia, and elsewhere in the Western hemisphere, a multipronged instrument of the TCC for primitive accumulation. "The war on drugs is a long-term fix to capitalism's woes," observes journalist Dawn Paley, "combining terror with policymaking in a seasoned neoliberal mix, cracking open social worlds and territories once unavailable to globalized capitalism."[16] Since the late 1990s, the United States has invested several tens of billions of dollars in the "war on drugs" in Latin America. Yet this war in Colombia, Mexico, and Central America has been exposed as a vast program of militarized accumulation and capitalist globalization that links the transnational military–industrial–security complex with neoliberal reform and repression of social movements.[17] And in the United States, as documented in Michelle Alexander's bestseller, *The New Jim Crow*, the farcical war on drugs has been a mechanism for the mass incarceration of surplus African-American, Chicano, and poor white labor.[18]

As spin-off effects of military spending flow through the open veins of the global economy—that is, the integrated network structures of the global production, services, and financial system—it becomes increasingly difficult to distinguish between military and nonmilitary dimensions of a global war economy. In this regard (and crucial to the global police state) is the development of new technologies associated with digitalization and what is now referred to as the *fourth industrial revolution*. The tech sector is now at the cutting edge of capitalist globalization and is driving the digitalization of the entire global economy.[19] Computer and information technology, first introduced in the 1980s, provided the original technological basis for globalization. In recent years, there has been another wave of technological development that has brought us to the verge of the fourth industrial revolution, based on robotics, three-dimensional printing, the Internet of Things, artificial intelligence and machine learning, bio- and nanotechnology, quantum and cloud computing, new forms of energy storage, and autonomous vehicles.

Karl Marx famously declared in *The Communist Manifesto* that "all that is solid melts into air" under the dizzying pace of change wrought by capitalism. Now the world economy stands at the brink of another period of massive restructuring. At the heart of this restructuring is the digital economy based on more advanced information technology; on the collection, processing, and analysis of data; and on the application of digitalization to every aspect of global society, including war and repression. Computer and information technology has revolutionized warfare and the modalities of state-organized militarized accumulation, including the military application of vast new technologies and the further fusion of private accumulation with state militarization. The new systems of warfare and repression made possible by more advanced digitalization include artificial intelligence-powered automated weaponry such as unmanned attack and transportation vehicles, robot soldiers, a new generation of "superdrones," microwave guns that immobilize, cyber attack and info-warfare, biometric identification, biological weapons, state data mining, and global electronic surveillance that allows for the tracking and control of every movement. Militarized accumulation and accumulation by repression, already a centerpiece of global capitalism, may become ever more important as it fuses with new fourth industrial revolution technologies, not just as a means of maintaining control but as expanding outlets for accumulated surplus that stave off economic collapse.

Digitalization makes possible the creation of a global police state. Dominant groups apply the new technologies to mass social control in the face of resistance among the precariatized and the marginalized. The dual functions of accumulation and social control are played out in the militarization of civil society and the crossover between the military and the civilian application of advanced weapons, tracking, and security and surveillance systems. The result is permanent low-intensity warfare against communities in rebellion as theaters of conflict spread from active war zones to urban and rural localities around the world.

The profound reconfiguration of space facilitated by digitalization is captured by the notion of global green zoning. "Green zone" refers to the nearly impenetrable area in central Baghdad that US occupation forces established in the wake of the 2003 invasion of Iraq. The command center of the occupation and select Iraqi elite inside that green zone were protected from the violence and chaos that engulfed the country. Urban areas around the world are now green zoned through gentrification, gated communities, surveillance systems, and state and private violence. Inside the world's green zones, elites and privileged middle and professional strata avail themselves of privatized social services, consumption, and entertainment. They can work and communicate through Internet and satellite, sealed off under the protection of armies of soldiers, police, and private security forces.

Green zoning takes on distinct forms in each locality. While on sabbatical in 2015, I witnessed such zoning in Palestine in the form of Israeli military checkpoints, Jewish settler-only roads, and the apartheid wall. In Mexico City, the most exclusive residential areas in the upscale Santa Fe district are accessible only by helicopter and private gated roads. In Johannesburg, a surreal drive through the exclusive Sandton City area reveals rows of mansions that appear as military compounds, with private armed towers and electrical and barbed-wire fences. In Cairo, I toured satellite cities ringing the impoverished center and inner suburbs where the country's elite could live out their aspirations and fantasies. They sport gated residential complexes with spotless green lawns, private leisure and shopping centers, and English-language international schools under the protection of military checkpoints and private security police.

Outside of the global green zones, warfare and police containment have become normalized and sanitized for those not directly at the receiving end of armed aggression. *Militainment*—portraying and even glamorizing war and violence as entertaining spectacles through Hollywood films and television police shows, computer gaming and corporate "news" channels—may be the epitome of sadistic capitalism. It desensitizes, bringing about complacency and indifference. In between the green zones and outright warfare are prison industrial complexes, immigrant and refugee repression and control systems, the criminalization of outcast communities, campaigns of social cleansing of the poor, and capitalist schooling. The omnipresent media and cultural apparatuses of the corporate economy, in particular, aim to colonize the mind—to undermine the ability to think critically and outside the dominant worldview. A neofascist culture emerges through militarism, misogyny, extreme masculinization, and racism. Such a culture generates a climate conducive to mass violence, often directed against the racially oppressed, ethnically persecuted, women, and poor, vulnerable communities.

The rise of the digital economy and the blurring of the boundaries between the military and the civilian sectors appear to fuse three fractions of capital around a combined process of financial speculation and militarized accumulation into which the TCC is unloading billions of dollars in surplus accumulated capital as it hedges its bets on investment opportunities in a global police state. Financial capital supplies the credit for investment in the technology sector and in the technologies of the global police state. Technology firms develop and provide the new digital technologies that are now of central importance to the global economy. Ever since National Security Agency whistleblower Edward Snowden came forward in 2013, there has been a torrent of revelations on the collusion of the giant technology firms with the US and other governments in the construction of a global police state. And the military–industrial–security complex applies this technology, as it becomes an outlet for unloading surplus and making profit through the control and repression of rebellious populations. This bloc of transnational capital has accrued enormous influence in the halls of power in Washington and other political centers around the world.

Absent a change of course forced on the system by mass mobilization and popular struggle from below, mounting crisis will cement the digital economy with the global police state. The new technological revolution promises to increase the ranks of surplus humanity and also impose greater competitive pressures on the TCC, thus heightening its need to impose more oppressive and authoritarian forms of labor discipline on the global working class. The more the global economy comes to depend on militarization and conflict, the greater the drive to war and the higher the stakes for humanity. There is a built-in war drive to the current course of capitalist globalization. Historically, wars have pulled the capitalist system out of crisis while they have also served to deflect attention from political tensions and problems of legitimacy.

THE SPECTER OF TWENTY-FIRST-CENTURY FASCISM

Fascism, whether in its classical twentieth century form or possible variants of twenty-first century neofascism, is a particular response to capitalist crisis. Trumpism in the United States, BREXIT (UK withdrawal from the European Union) in the United Kingdom, and the increasing influence of neofascist and authoritarian parties and movements throughout Europe and around the world represent a far-right response to crises of global capitalism. Twenty-first-century fascism shares a number of features with its twentieth century predecessor, but there are also key differences. Above all, fascism in the twentieth century involved the fusion of reactionary political power with national capital. In distinction, twenty-first-century fascism involves the fusion of transnational capital with reactionary and repressive political power—an expression of the dictatorship of transnational capital. In both cases, however, fascism is a response to deep structural crises of capitalism, such as that of the 1930s and the one that began with the financial meltdown of 2008.

The fascist projects that came to power in the 1930s in Germany, Italy, and Spain, as well as those that vied unsuccessfully to seize power, such as in the United States, had as a fundamental objective crushing powerful working class and socialist movements. But in the United States, Europe, and elsewhere, the left and the organized working class are at a historically weak point. In these cases, twenty-first-century fascism appears to be a preemptive strike at working classes and at the spread of mass resistance through the expansion of a police state. In addition, twenty-first century fascism is centrally aimed at coercive exclusion of surplus humanity. States abandon efforts to secure legitimacy among this surplus population and instead turn to a host of control mechanisms, including criminalizing the poor and the dispossessed, with tendencies toward genocide in some cases. As I have discussed above, the mechanisms of coercive exclusion include mass incarceration and the spread of prison-industrial complexes, pervasive policing, anti-immigrant legislation, and the manipulation of space in new ways so that both gated communities and ghettos are controlled by armies of private security guards and technologically advanced surveillance systems; ubiquitous, often paramilitarized policing; and mobilization of the culture industries and state ideological apparatuses to dehumanize victims of global capitalism as dangerous, depraved, and culturally degenerate.

The dictatorship of transnational capital involves newfound ability to achieve political domination through control over the means of intellectual production, the mass media, the educational system, and the culture industries. There is a much more profound and complete penetration of capital and its logic into the spheres of culture and community (indeed, into the life world itself). Corporate marketing strategies depoliticize through the manipulation of desire and libido. The danger is that the grievances and frustrated aspirations of the excluded become channeled into petty consumption and flight into fantasy rather than into placing political demands on the system through collective mobilization. The mechanisms of cultural hegemony together with panoptical surveillance and new social control technologies would probably allow twenty-first-century fascist projects to rely more on selective than generalized repression—unless a revolt from below comes to actually threaten the rule of the TCC. Systems of mass incarceration and green zoning may replace the concentration camps of twentieth century fascism. The new modalities of social control and ideological domination blur boundaries, so that there may be a constitutional and normalized neofascism, with formal representative institutions, a constitution, political parties and elections—all while the political system is tightly controlled by transnational capital and its representatives, and any dissent that actually threatens the system is neutralized if not liquidated.

Twenty-first-century fascist projects seek to organize a mass base among historically privileged sectors of the global working class, such as white workers in the Global North and middle layers in the Global South, that are experiencing heightened insecurity and the specter of downward mobility. As with its twentieth century predecessor, the project hinges on the psychosocial mechanism of displacing mass fear and anxiety at a time of acute capitalist crisis toward scapegoated communities, such as immigrant workers, Muslims, and refugees in the United States and Europe. Far-right forces do so through a discursive repertoire of xenophobia, mystifying ideologies that involve race/culture supremacy, an idealized and mythical past, millennialism, and a militaristic and masculinist culture that normalizes and even glamorizes war, social violence, and domination.

Classical twentieth century fascism in Germany (and Spain and Italy to a lesser extent) did offer the material benefits of employment and social wages to a portion of the working class even as it unleashed genocide on those outside the chosen group. There is now little possibility in the United States or elsewhere of providing such benefits, so that the "wages of fascism" appear to be entirely psychological. In this regard, the ideology of twenty-first-century fascism rests on irrationality—a promise to deliver security and restore stability that is emotive, not rational. It is a project that does not and need not distinguish between the truth and the lie.[20] The Trump regime's public discourse of populism and nationalism, for example, bore no relation to its actual policies. In its first year, Trumponomics involved deregulation, the virtual smashing of the regulatory state—slashing social spending, dismantling what remained of the welfare state, privatizations, tax breaks to corporations and the rich, and an expansion of state subsidies to capital—in short, neoliberalism on steroids.

An essential condition for twentieth and twenty-first-century fascism is the spread of fascist movements in civil society and their fusion at some point with reactionary political power in the state. Let us recall that civil and political society are a unity; there can be no stable or hegemonic project without a correspondence between the two. In the United States, fascist movements have been rapidly expanding since the turn of the century in civil society and in the political system through the right wing of the Republican Party. Trump proved to be a charismatic figure able to galvanize and embolden disparate neofascist forces, from white supremacists, white nationalists, militia, neo-Nazis, and Klans to the Oath Keepers, the Patriot Movement, Christian fundamentalists, and anti-immigrant vigilante groups. Encouraged by Trump's imperial bravado, his populist and nationalist rhetoric, and his openly racist discourse, and predicated in part on whipping up anti-immigrant, anti-Muslim, and xenophobic sentiment, they began to cross-pollinate to a degree not seen in decades as they gained a toehold in the Trump White House and in state and local governments around the country.[21] Paramilitarism spread within many of these organizations and overlapped with state repressive agencies. This fusion of fascist movements in civil society with reactionary political power in the state sets fascism apart from right-wing authoritarianism that is also spreading around the world.

It is a mistake to view twenty-first-century fascism as a political development outside of the "normal" progression of global capitalism in this time of acute crisis. Trumpism and other far-right movements did not represent a break with capitalist globalization but rather the recomposition of political forces as the crisis deepened. Despite the rhetoric of nationalism and protectionism, Trumpism and similar movements in Europe and elsewhere were not departures from but incarnations of an emerging dictatorship of the transnational capitalist class. To paraphrase the great Prussian military strategist, Carl von Clausewitz, who famously said that "war is the extension of politics by other means," Trumpism (and to varying degrees other far-right movements around the world) were the extension of capitalist globalization by other means, namely by an expanding global police state and a neofascist mobilization.

Twenty-first-century fascism and the global police state are characterized by a triangulation of far-right, authoritarian, and neofascist forces in civil society; reactionary political power in the state; and transnational corporate capital, especially speculative finance capital, the military–industrial–security complex, and the extractive industries, all three of which are in turn dependent on and interwoven with high-tech or digital capital. The extractive and energy complexes must dislodge communities and appropriate their resources, which make them most prone to supporting or even promoting repressive and neofascist political arrangements. Capital accumulation in the military–industrial–security complex depends on never-ending wars and on systems of repression. Financial accumulation requires ever greater austerity that is hard, if not impossible, to impose through consensual mechanisms.

How these three sectors of capital came together in the United States with state and paramilitary forces was abundantly demonstrated in 2016 in a military-style counterinsurgency against indigenous activists and their allies who were peacefully protesting the construction of the Dakota Access Pipeline in lands near the Standing Rock Sioux reservation in North Dakota. Bankrolled by a consortium of banks that included Wells Fargo and Bank of America, the private Fortune 500 oil and gas company building the pipeline, Energy Transfer Partners, hired a mercenary and security firm known as TigerSwan, which originated as a Pentagon and State Department contractor for the Middle East wars. TigerSwan was charged with organizing a counterinsurgency campaign against the protesters in coordination with the company and with local, state, and federal law enforcement agencies, including National Guard troops. "Aggressive intelligence preparation of the battlefield and active coordination between intelligence and security elements are now a proven method of defeating pipeline insurgents," stated TigerSwan, in calling the anti-pipeline protesters "jihadist fighters" and the protest area a "battlefield." The "less than lethal" arsenal unleashed by the public–private counterinsurgency apparatus included rubber bullets, bean bag pellets, Long Range Acoustic Devices, water cannons, attack dogs, predator drones, metadata imaging, counterintelligence, and psyops.[22] While the Standing Rock ordeal is a chilling case study in paramilitarization of the global police state, such operations against social justice movements are now routine around the world.

Twenty-first-century fascism cannot be understood as a nation-state project in this age of global capitalism. It is more analytically and conceptually accurate to talk of a *global police state*. The global order as a unity is increasingly repressive and authoritarian, and particular forms of exceptional national states or national polities, including twenty-first-century fascism, develop on the basis of particular national and regional histories, social and class forces, and political conditions and conjunctures. Yet the militarization of cities, politics, and culture in such countries as the United States and Israel; the spread of neofascist movements in North America and Europe; and the rise of authoritarian regimes in Turkey, the Philippines, and Honduras are inseparable from these countries' entanglement in webs of global wars and the militarized global accumulation, or global war economy. The powers in the international system must secure social control and defend the global order in each particular national territory lest the global order itself become threatened.

CONCLUSION: FASCISTS, REFORMISTS, INTELLECTUALS, AND THE GLOBAL WORKING CLASS

Great storm clouds are brewing. As I write these lines in late 2017, it seemed that the tempest is upon us. We stand before the gates of hell, and if those gates are opened it may well involve prolonged civil wars, the passage to a more openly militarized global police state, and a third world war. Yet we must not lose sight of the fact that an expanding global police state to suppress dissent and maintain social control is driven by contradictions that are tearing apart global capitalism. If the system were doing well, there would be no need for war or a global police state. Trumpism and other far-right, authoritarian, and neofascist responses around the world must be seen as reactive to the global revolt of the popular and working classes. In the United States, the repression against Occupy Wall Street, Black Lives Matter, the Dakota Access Pipeline water protectors, and other social movements and popular struggles in recent years signals an increasing breakdown of control and erosion of the ruling group's hegemony. Beyond the United States, a global rebellion against the TCC has been spreading since the financial collapse of 2008.

But this rebellion has not been able to press forward for several reasons that we need to carefully ponder as this global battle against the specter of twenty-first-century fascism heats up. Let us recall that crises present us with grave dangers but also with opportunities to challenge the dominant system and advance emancipatory projects from below. To take advantage of these opportunities, the "left" intellectual class—and I refer here especially to the United States—must shake itself loose of crippling identity politics and strive to become organic intellectuals in the service of the mass movements from below. With the apparent triumph of global capitalism in the 1990s following the collapse of the old Soviet bloc, the defeat of Third World nationalist and revolutionary projects, and the withdrawal of the Left into postmodern identity politics and other forms of accommodation with the prevailing social order, many intellectuals who previously identified with anti-capitalist movements and emancipatory projects seemed to cede a certain defeatism before global capitalism. The decline of the Left and socialist movements worldwide in the late twentieth century led to a degeneration of intellectual critique as well.

The intellectual elite turned to a postmodernism that celebrated a world of "differences" and endless fragmentation, out of which came the new identity politics in which capitalism became "just another" among the multiplicity of oppressive systems. This postmodern identity politics should not be confused with struggles against particular forms of exploitation and oppression that different groups face. There can be no general emancipation without liberation from these particular forms of repression (ethnic, gender, sexual, and so on). It is equally true that all these particular forms of oppression are grounded in the larger social order of global capitalism. Yet the postmodern narratives alienated a whole generation of young people in the late twentieth and early twenty-first centuries from embracing a desperately needed Marxist critique of capitalism at the moment of its globalization. Identity politics cannot aspire to more than symbolic vindication, diversity (often meaning diversity in the ruling bloc), nondiscrimination in the dominant social institutions, and equitable inclusion and representation *within* global capitalism. The transnational elite was all too willing to embrace such a politics of "diversity" and "multiculturalism" because it proved effective in channeling mass struggles into nonthreatening demands for inclusion if not into outright co-optation. Vital rebellion is breaking out everywhere; in order to move beyond the multiplicity of fragmented struggles and spontaneity, we need more than ever a revitalized Marxist critique of global capitalism that involves a critique of the liberalism of the transnational elite.

The most urgent task right now may be a united front against fascism and global war, but that task cannot be addressed without a set of principles and goals, and a vision of what we are struggling for, beyond what we are struggling against. For the fight back to be successful, it needs to have a sharp analysis of global capitalism and of its crisis, a clear vision of an emancipatory project around which resistance forces can unite. This means moving beyond the view that emancipatory struggles involve a resistance in civil society but not a campaign to overthrow the capitalist state, which involves the development of political organizations and projects alongside mass social movements. Ultimately, we need a *transnational ecosocialist project*. What would be the agent of any such project? This must be the new global working class that labors in the factories, farms, offices, and service sectors of global capitalism. But we must have a new conception of the global working class—one that highlights immigrant labor, female labor, part-time, temporary, contract, and precariatized workers, ethnically diverse workers, as well as surplus humanity, those that have been structurally marginalized. Some would say that talking about the global working class is a distraction from the fight against neofascism. But it is the opposite: only by building up the organization of the global working class and placing its multitude of struggles at the center of the fight back can we win.

This raises the matter of the liberal and reformist elite. The unwillingness of the transnational elite to challenge the predation and rapaciousness of global capital has opened the way for the far-right response to crisis. In the United States, the betrayal of the liberal elite was as much to blame for Trumpism as were the far-right forces that mobilized the white population around a program of racist scapegoating, misogyny, and the manipulation of fear and economic destabilization. Bolstered by the betrayal of the intellectuals, the liberal elite's brand of identity politics has served to eclipse the language of the working and popular classes and of anti-capitalism. It helped to derail ongoing revolts from below and to push white workers (here I refer specifically to the United States) into an "identity" of white nationalism, which helped the neofascist right to organize them politically.[23]

As part of its very genesis, capitalism splintered the exploited classes along ethnic/racial lines so that capitalism has been immanently racialized, at least in its still Western core. I want to stress that in the United States and Europe (and elsewhere as well), an ecosocialism that does not place anti-racism in front and center is a dead end. Yet an anti-racism that does not involve a critique of and struggle against capitalism can only go so far, has already shown diminishing returns, and will ultimately serve the liberal elite, if not the far-right, at the expense of the poor majority of victims of racism.

Many among the transnational elite will be unlikely to object to twenty-first-century fascism in political power if that is what it takes to beat down challenges from below and maintain control. Yet the more far-sighted among these elites will seek reform, perhaps even radical reform, in the interests of saving the system from itself. Their reform program should be embraced to the extent that it attenuates the worst depredations of global capitalism and pulls us back from war and fascism. But the popular and working class agenda must not be subordinated to that of the reformist elite. Popular class forces must exercise leadership within a broad antifascist alliance. The global working class does need broad alliances, including with reformist elements among the transnational elite. Yet the reform of capitalism has historically come less from enlightened elites than from mass struggles from below that forced elites to reform. The best way to achieve a reform of capitalism is a struggle against it. If reformism from above fails and if the Left is not able to seize the initiative, the road may be open for twenty-first-century global fascism founded on the global police state.

TEN

REFLECTIONS ON A BRAVE NEW WORLD

A TECTONIC SHIFT IN WORLD CAPITALISM

A Great Transition[1] to a just and sustainable world requires as its starting point an accurate understanding of how the system in which we live, capitalism, has evolved in recent decades. A "brave new world" of globalized capitalism burst forth in the latter decades of the twentieth century. At first glance, the system may look familiar: capitalism continues to be driven by the endless accumulation of capital, with the attendant outward expansion, polarization, crises, and wars. But all systems exist in a perpetual state of development, transformation, and eventual demise, giving rise to new organizational forms, and capitalism is no exception. Each successive epoch in its centuries-long existence has brought the reorganization of political and social institutions and the rise of new agents and technologies on the heels of major crises. Waves of outward expansion through wars of conquest, colonialism, and imperialism have brought more of humanity and of nature into the orbit of capital. This widening and deepening enclosure has ushered in the new epoch of global capitalism.

In its first stage, capitalism emerged from its feudal cocoon in Europe during the so-called Age of Discovery, symbolized by the bloody conquest of the Americas starting in 1492. This epoch spanned the creation of the colonial and interstate systems, the emergence of the transatlantic economy, and the intensification of trade between West and East.

The second stage, defined by the industrial revolution, encompassed the forging of the modern nation-state and the rise to power of the bourgeoisie, symbolized by the American Revolution of 1776 and the French Revolution of 1789. The third stage, the rise of national corporate capitalism in the late nineteenth century, brought a new wave of imperialist conquest, powerful national financial and industrial corporations, the consolidation of nation-states and national markets, and the integration of these national markets into a single world market.

Many observers of twenty-first century capitalism continue to analyze it through the lens of this outdated national corporate stage. However, it has become clear that we are now in the throes of another major transformation of world capitalism, a transition to a qualitatively new transnational—or global—stage. The turning point in this epochal shift came during the global recession in the 1970s following the oil crisis and the collapse of the Bretton Woods system, the international financial structure set up after World War II. Capitalism was able to transcend that crisis by "going global," leveraging globalization processes into a vast restructuring and integration of the world economy. From this dynamic emerged truly transnational capital, along with the rise of a transnational capitalist class and transnational state apparatuses.

Global capitalism, however, now faces an unprecedented crisis—at once ecological, social, economic, and political. To avert a collapse of civilization, we cannot rely on outdated modes of analysis, but instead must ask the right questions. What is new about global capitalism? Where are its fissures? What is its structure of power? And what viable forms of struggle from below for system change does this new epoch offer?

THE NEW GLOBAL ECONOMY

The hallmark of the new epoch has been the rise of truly *transnational* capital with its integration of every country and much of humanity into a new globalized system of production, finance, and services. The latter decades of the twentieth century saw technological revolutions, particularly in communications and information technology, but also in transportation, marketing, management, and automation as well, that expedited innovative cross-border patterns of accumulation and supranational economies of scale. Capitalists achieved a newfound global mobility in a dual sense. First, the new technologies enabled the global organization of the economy. Second, policymakers across the globe eliminated obstacles to the free movement of capital through deregulation, free trade agreements, and integration processes, such as that of the European Union.

To be sure, capitalism has always been a *world* system—it was never simply national or regional. It expanded from the onset, ultimately engulfing the entire world, and depending throughout its existence on a web of worldwide trade relations. National development has always been conditioned by the larger worldwide system of trade and finance and on the international division of labor that colonialism brought about. The new transnational phase, however, entails a shift from a *world economy* to a *global economy*.

In earlier epochs, each country developed a national economy linked to each other through trade and financial flows (or payments) in an integrated international market. The current epoch has seen the globalization of the production process itself. Global capital mobility has allowed capitalists to reorganize production worldwide to maximize profit-making opportunities. Capitalists can now freely search for the cheapest labor, lowest taxes, and laxest regulatory environments. National production systems have become fragmented and integrated externally into new globalized circuits of accumulation.[2]

Previously, for instance, auto companies in the United States produced cars from start to finish, with the exception of the procurement abroad of some raw materials, and then exported them to other countries. The circuit of accumulation was national, save for the final export and foreign payment. Now, instead, the process of producing a car has been decentralized and fragmented into dozens of different phases that are scattered across many countries around the world. Often, individual parts are manufactured in several different countries, assembly may be stretched out over others, and management may be coordinated from a central computer terminal unconnected to actual production sites or to the country of domicile of the corporation.

The globalization of the production process thus breaks down and functionally integrates what were previously national circuits into new global circuits of accumulation. As the global economy emerged, production was the first to transnationalize, starting in the late 1970s, epitomized by the rise of the global assembly line and the spread of modern-day sweatshops in free trade zones around the world. Next, following a wave of financial deregulation in most countries around the world, national banking and financial systems transnationalized in the 1990s and 2000s. Indeed, a national financial system no longer exists. The transnationalization of services has since followed through a new wave of international trade-in-service and other agreements that have expedited the decentralized provision across borders of services as well as the privatization of health care, telecommunications, and other industries.

There is a qualitative difference between the world of the early twentieth century and that of today. Global capitalism does not consist of the aggregation of "national" economies, but their integration into a greater transnational whole. With the global economy comes a more organic integration of social life worldwide. Even the most remote communities are now linked into the new circuits of global economy and society through vast decentralized networks of production and distribution, as well as by global communications and other integrative technologies and cultural flows increasingly fostering those networks.

But all is not well in the global village. Economic globalization entails the fragmentation and decentralization of complex production chains and the worldwide dispersal and functional integration of the different segments in these chains. Yet this fragmentation and decentralization is countered by a reverse movement: the centralization and concentration of worldwide economic management, control, and decision-making power in a handful of ever more powerful transnational corporations (TNCs).

THE TRANSNATIONAL CAPITALIST CLASS

Transnational capital is not faceless. A transnational capitalist class (TCC), made up of the owners and managers of transnational capital, has emerged as the agent of global capitalism. Its interests lie in promoting global, not national, circuits of accumulation. Among the many developments facilitating this cross-integration of capitalist groups around the world into a TCC, the massive expansion of TNCs and the spread of their affiliates plays a major role, along with transnational ownership of these companies' capital shares. Other important developments include the phenomenal growth in foreign direct investment; an equally phenomenal increase in cross-border mergers and acquisitions; the interlocking of boards of directors; the spread of cross-border joint ventures and strategic alliances of all sorts; the spread to most countries of the world of stock exchanges trading TNC shares; and increasing global outsourcing and subcontracting networks. The giant corporate conglomerates that drive the global economy have ceased to be corporations of a particular country and have increasingly come to represent transnational capital.

It is difficult to overstate the extent to which capital has become transnationally integrated, concentrated, and centralized in the TCC. One 2011 analysis of the share ownerships of 43,000 TNCs identified a core of 1,318 with interlocking ownerships that tied the TNCs in this core tightly to one another. Each of these core TNCs had ties to two or more other companies, with an average number of twenty. Although they represented only 20 percent of global operating revenues, these 1,318 TNCs appeared to collectively own through their shares the majority of the world's largest blue chip and manufacturing firms. This core accounted for 20 percent of global operating revenue; the world's largest blue chip and manufacturing firms accounted for another 60 percent. And since the core, according to the report, exercises effective control over the TNC structure, it in effect exercises control over 80 percent of the world's revenue.

Moreover, much of this web is woven around a "super-entity" of 147 even more tightly knit companies—all of their ownership is held by other members of the super-entity—that controls 40 percent of the total wealth in the network.[3] In effect, less than 1 percent of the companies control 40 percent of the entire network. The top 100 corporations have an average of twenty holding companies each, domiciled in low-tax jurisdictions around the world; more than 500 affiliates, each spread over many countries; and supply chains that span the globe. These corporate colossi are clustered in the banking and financial sector, "fourth industrial revolution" technology companies (especially information technology, automation, and telecommunications), energy, and the military–industrial–engineering–security complex.[4] This congruent concentration and centralization suggests that the global economy is acquiring the character of a planned oligopoly, with centralized planning taking place within the inner network of TNC nodes. In particular, the transnational capitalist class has gained enormous structural power over states and political processes in its pursuit of global corporate interests.

Greece provides a textbook case of how the structural power of transnational capital subsumes the direct power of states (and of working classes and leftist governments that do win state power). The leftist Syriza party won office (but not power) in early 2015 through an anti-austerity program that came on the heels of several years of mass protest by Greek workers of the debt crisis imposed on the country by transnational investors, exerting control through the European Union. Once in office, the Syriza government caved under enormous pressure from the "troika"—the European Central Bank, the German government, and the International Monetary Fund, acting as a collective representative of the TCC. The troika made emergency loans to avoid default and resultant isolation from global financial markets conditional on further austerity and the sale to transnational investors of what remained of the Greek public sector.

The linkage between globalized capitalism, economic control, and political domination is critical to the coalescence of the new power structure. The TCC has been trying to position itself, with limited success, as a new global ruling class. Capitalists and ruling elites first sought to transnationalize in an effort to break the power that the working classes had achieved in their respective countries through the mass popular movements and anti-colonial struggles of the post–World War II period, culminating in the tumultuous decade of the 1960s. Going global allowed the emerging TCC and its political and bureaucratic agents in states and international agencies to dismantle the diverse forms of redistributive or "social" capitalism that had come into being in the wake of the 1930s Great Depression, such as the New Deal in the United States and social democracy in Western Europe. In this way, globalization weakened the power of labor at the national level. What followed is a well-known story: decreased levels of unionization, the onset of austerity and privatization, and the spread of new systems of labor control. New work arrangements are increasingly "flexible," meaning that workers are often forced to give up full-time tenured employment for part-time, temporary, informal, and contract work.

Technology has also played a key role in these new social and political relations of global capitalism. The transnational capitalist class has been able to draw on computer and information technology in its political campaign to open the world to transnational capital through "free trade," integration agreements, and neoliberal policies. The digital revolution also made possible the global integration of national financial systems and new forms of money, such as hedge funds or secondary derivative markets. It has similarly enabled the frictionless and instantaneous movement of money in its diverse forms around the world, bringing about what political economists refer to as the financialization of the global economy. Any fixed asset—a factory, an agro-industrial complex, even real estate—can be converted into a new form of digitized money capital and traded around the world, rendering fluid the ownership of capital and the class relations associated with it.

Such mobility allows transnational financial capital to appropriate, circulate, and redistribute wealth all around the world in unprecedentedly flexible ways, bestowing a frightening power upon global financial markets, as shown in Greece and elsewhere. Those who struggle to confront capitalist exploitation face an amorphous, moving target. In earlier epochs of capitalism, the process of exploitation, or the appropriation of wealth by capitalist from workers, was seen as a direct relation. Today, however, financialized tangible and intangible wealth moves instantaneously through the open veins of the global financial system and is endlessly appropriated and re-appropriated in evolving forms. Hence, the global working class faces the TCC in bewildering new ways. For example, whereas conventional fleet-owning taxi companies may have exploited taxi drivers, Uber drivers from India to Mexico are exploited by shareholders around the world in this "platform" company that produces nothing yet has a valuation of $40 billion.

The coming fusion of this globally integrated financial system with emergent technology points to troubling prospects ahead. The entire industrial revolution enhanced productivity by a factor of about 100, whereas the information and communication revolution enhanced it by a factor of many times greater in just the first few years of its introduction.[5] Now, cutting-edge technologies—including three-dimensional printing, artificial intelligence and machine learning, robotics, the Internet of Things, nano- and biotechnology, new materials, energy storage, and quantum computing—join physical, digital, and biological worlds. The TCC has started to "weaponize" these new technologies both figuratively (in that the TCC uses their productive power as a weapon in its class warfare) and literally (insofar as these technologies are applied to new systems of transnational warfare and social control, such as robot soldiers and omnipresent surveillance).

INTIMATIONS OF A TRANSNATIONAL STATE

How does the TCC organize itself to pursue its interests around the world? How do the class and social relations of global capitalism become institutionalized? What is the system's political authority structure? Despite the rhetoric of market fundamentalism, the capitalist system cannot be sustained through market relations alone. Capitalism requires the state in order to function. But national governments do not exercise the transnational political authority that global capitalism requires. It is through transnational state apparatuses that global elites attempt to convert the structural power of the global economy into supranational political authority. The transnational state is not unrelated to the concept of global governance (a notion first put forward by the World Bank and now championed by the World Economic Forum), but it is by no means synonymous with global government. Nor is it the same as consensual processes of transnational governance.

As transnational factions of national elites emerged in the latter decades of the twentieth century, they organized politically. They vied for, and in most countries won, state power, whether through elections or other means, such as foreign (mostly US) political and military intervention. These transnationally oriented elites used this power to implement policies favorable to integration into the global economy. As the TCC and its political and bureaucratic allies pushed capitalist globalization, nation-states came to adopt similar sets of neoliberal policies and to sign free trade agreements in consort with one another and with the supranational and transnational institutions that have designed and facilitated the global capitalist project, such as the World Trade Organization, the International Monetary Fund, the World Bank, the European Union, the United Nations system, and the Organisation of Economic Cooperation and Development. These organizations, together with nation-states in which transnationally oriented elites have come to power, form an increasingly dense institutional network that constitutes a transnational state.

As a side note, there is a mounting backlash against capitalist globalization among the popular and working classes and more nationally oriented sectors of the elite, as well as from right-wing populism, as evidenced in the 2016 referendum on UK withdrawal from the European Union (BREXIT) and the rise of right-wing populist movements throughout Europe that call for a withdrawal from globalization processes. These developments in no way belie the thesis of a transnational state;

rather, they underscore the highly conflictive nature of global capitalism and uncertainty as to further globalization in the face of the explosive contradictions and the widespread opposition that it generates. On the other hand, despite its nationalist rhetoric, the Trump regime in the United States was not opposed to capitalist globalization but in fact pursued a program of neoliberalism on steroids and "globalization by other means."[6] When Trump did impose tariffs on imported steel and aluminum in March 2018, he was opposed by much of the TCC and the political elite in the United States, including even by sectors of the steel industry that relied on cheaper imported steel for the production of intermediate and finished steel products. Indeed, support for the tariffs came principally from trade union bureaucrats; Trump's move was really about appeasing his restless working class social base. Recall, as well, that Obama, Bush, and Clinton, all closely identified with neoliberal globalization, also imposed tariffs at one point or another in their administrations.

This transnational state promotes globalized accumulation circuits over local and national ones. The TCC attempts, through transnational state apparatuses, to exercise its power in individual countries and in the global system as a whole, the transnational state functioning as a collective authority of the TCC. For instance, the International Monetary Fund, the World Bank, and other transnational state institutions imposed structural adjustment programs and free trade agreements on one country after another in the wake of capitalist globalization. These programs included the privatization of public sectors, trade liberalization, and investment guarantees for TNCs, with the intended effects of undermining the power of labor and popular movements, while heightening the influence of transnationally oriented capitalists and elites in each country. Other agencies of the transnational state, such as the United Nations Development Program, along with the nongovernmental organizations they fund, critique poverty and espouse a discourse of "needs," "consensus," "inclusion," and "citizen participation" even as they often promote market "solutions" and the corporate-driven capitalist globalization that generates poverty, inequality, and marginality in the first place.

The transnational state faces a contradictory mandate. On the one hand, it sets out to promote the conditions for capitalist globalization; on the other, it tries to resolve the myriad problems created by globalization: economic crisis, poverty, environmental degradation, chronic political instability, and military conflict. The transnational state has had great difficulty addressing these issues because of the dispersal of formal political authority across many national states. Transnational state apparatuses are fragmentary, with no center or formal constitution and no transnational enforcement capacity. But the inability of the transnational state to regulate and stabilize global capitalism is also due to the TCC's blind pursuit of immediate profits over the general and long-term interests of the system.

In the past, capitalists faced constraints on the national level to unbridled profit-making. National governments, pressured by mass mobilization, could draw on a set of policy instruments, such as tax, wage, public works, regulatory, social welfare, and other measures, to attenuate the worst effects of capitalism. These policies helped offset what political economists refer to as the "internal contradictions" of the capitalist system. The most pressing of these contradictions is that of overaccumulation and social polarization, in which wealth accumulates at one end of the pole and misery and impoverishment at the other. At the world level, colonialism and imperialism resulted in a transfer of wealth from the poor to the rich countries that offset the worst social contradictions in the latter while exacerbating them in the former, a cause of the endemic instability of the Global South relative to the Global North. In the present, transnational capital's liberation from the nation-state has enhanced its structural power over oppositional forces struggling within the bounds of the nation-state. As a result, there has been an unprecedented polarization of wealth between the haves and have-nots, which in turn aggravates these internal contradictions and generates escalating social conflict and crises of state legitimacy.

The more enlightened elite representatives of the TCC now clamor for a more powerful transnational state to resolve the more and more outmoded disjuncture between a globalizing economy and a nation-state-based system of political authority. They seek transnational governance mechanisms that would allow the global ruling class to rein in the anarchy of the system in the interests of saving global capitalism from itself and from radical challenges from below. Such reformism from above proposes limited redistribution, regulation of global markets, and "green capitalism."

To gain legitimacy, any would-be ruling class must present its own project as representative of the whole of society. To advance that agenda requires that the TCC attempt to resolve the most pressing problems of the social order and to reconcile antagonistic social interests while at the same time securing its own hegemony and ensuring that its long-term interests remain paramount. To achieve these goals, enlightened transnational elites must have at their disposal more effective transnational state apparatuses—that is, an effective system of "global governance" from above.[7] Leadership groups among the transnational corporate and political elite come together each year in the activities of the World Economic Forum, which holds its famed annual meeting in Davos, Switzerland. In 2008, forum founder and Executive Chairman Klaus Schwab called for a renovated "global leadership" and a new "global corporate citizenship" on the part of TNC executives, entailing engagement on major world issues in order to ensure the sustainability of the global marketplace.[8] Following the perceived inability of existing transnational state institutions to respond to the economic meltdown in 2009, the World Economic Forum published a major report that called for a new form of global corporate rule.[9] At the core of the project is remaking the United Nations system into a hybrid corporate–government entity run by TNC executives in "partnership" with governments.

As the transnational elite seeks a stronger transnational state in order to stabilize the global capitalist system, the division of the world into some 200 competing nation-states is not propitious for building global working-class unity. Victories in popular struggles from below in any one country or region can and often do become diverted and even undone by the structural power of transnational capital (as seen in Greece) and the direct political and military domination this structural power affords the dominant groups. Nation-states act as population containment zones, allowing the TCC to maintain a system of differential wages and pit working classes in each country against one another—the so-called "race to the bottom." National cultural and ideological systems, as well as ethnic differences within nation-states, exacerbate this competition and undermine transnational working-class consciousness.

THE MEAN STREETS OF GLOBAL CAPITALISM

The Occupy Wall Street movement in the United States called attention to unprecedented global inequality with its cry of the "99 percent versus the 1 percent." The divide is indeed quite stark: in 2015, the top 1 percent of humanity had more wealth than the remaining 99 percent. Moreover, the top 20 percent of humanity controlled some 95 percent of the world's wealth, while the remaining 80 percent had to make do with just 5 percent.[10] This divide of global society into haves and have-nots has created a new global social apartheid, evident not just between rich and poor countries but within each country, as transnational social and class inequalities grow in importance compared to geographically conceived North–South inequalities. The heightened structural power achieved by the TCC through globalization has enabled it to undermine redistributive policies and to impose a new labor regime on the global working class based on flexibilization and precariatization, or proletarianization under conditions of permanent insecurity and precariousness. The International Labor Organization reported that nearly 1.5 billion workers around the world, or some 50 percent of the global workforce, were in "vulnerable" employment arrangements in 2014, including informal, flexible, part-time, contract, migrant, and itinerant work arrangements.[11]

Globalization has brought a vast new round of global enclosures, as hundreds of millions have been uprooted from the Third World countryside and turned into internal and transnational migrants. Some of the uprooted millions are superexploited through incorporation into the global factories, farms, and offices as precarious labor, while others are marginalized and converted into surplus humanity, relegated to a "planet of slums."[12] Surplus humanity is of no *direct* use to capital. However, in the larger picture, surplus labor is crucial to global capitalism insofar as it places downward pressure on wages everywhere and allows transnational capital to impose discipline over those who remain active in the labor market.

The current technological revolution is expected to increase this surplus labor population exponentially. The "jobless future" resulting from the "rise of robots" capable of replacing human workers is a ubiquitous topic among academics, journalists, and politicians. Millions of people expelled from formal employment have managed to scratch out a living through Uber and other "platform companies" as informal and "self-employed" workers. But for how long? For example, Uber has announced it would replace one million drivers with autonomously driven vehicles.[13] FoxComm, the Taiwanese-based conglomerate that assembles iPads and other electronic devices, announced in 2012 following a wave of strikes by its workers in mainland China that it would replace 1 million workers with robots. As productivity increases, the system sheds more and more workers. In 1990, the top three carmakers in Detroit had a market capitalization of $36 billion and 1.2 million employees. In 2014, the top three firms in Silicon Valley, with a market capitalization of over $1 trillion, had only 137,000 employees.[14]

The polarization of income and the rising tide of surplus labor together aggravate overaccumulation. The global market cannot absorb the ever-rising output of the global economy as the ranks of the surplus population swell and wealth is concentrated among shrinking high-income sectors of global society. As productive outlets dry up for unloading accumulated surplus, the TCC has turned to four mechanisms to continue accumulating in the face of stagnation. The first consists of frenzied financial speculation. The global economy has become one big casino for transnational finance capital, as the gap between the productive economy and "fictitious capital" grows ever wider. Gross world product, or the total value of goods and services produced worldwide, stood at some $75 trillion in 2015, whereas currency speculation alone amounted to $5.3 trillion a day that year and the global derivatives market was estimated at a mind-boggling $1.2 quadrillion.[15]

The second mechanism relies on raiding and sacking public budgets. Public finance is reconfigured through austerity, bailouts, government debt, and the global bond market. A third is the expansion of credit to consumers and to governments, especially in the Global North, to sustain spending and consumption. In the United States, for instance, which has long been the "market of last resort" for the global economy, household debt is higher than it has been for almost all of postwar history. US households owed in 2016 nearly $13 trillion in student loans, credit card debt, auto loans, and mortgages. Meanwhile, the global bond market—an indicator of total government debt worldwide—had already reached $100 trillion by 2011.[16]

Militarized accumulation provides the third mechanism. Unprecedented inequalities can be sustained only by ever more repressive and ubiquitous systems of social control. Yet quite apart from political considerations, the powers-that-be have acquired a vested interest in war, conflict, and repression as a means of accumulation. The so-called wars on drugs, terrorism, and immigrants; the construction of border walls, immigrant detention centers, and ever-growing prisons; the installation of mass surveillance systems; and the hiring of private security guard and mercenary companies have all become major new sources of profit-making.

As war and state-sponsored repression become increasingly privatized, the interests of a broad array of capitalist groups shift the political, social, and ideological climate toward generating and sustaining social conflict—such as in Syria—and in expanding systems of warfare, repression, surveillance, and social control. This impulse to militarized accumulation in turn generates a militaristic politics and a martial (and with it, masculinist and misogynist) culture. The day after Donald Trump's electoral victory, the stock price of CoreCivic, the largest for-profit immigrant detention and prison company in the United States, soared 49 percent, thanks to Trump's promise to arrest and deport 10 million undocumented immigrants.[17] Military contractors such as Raytheon and Lockheed Martin report spikes in their stock prices each time there is a new flare-up in the Middle East conflict.[18] We now appear to be mired in a permanent global war economy.

Global apartheid cushions a tiny percentage of humanity through the creation of "green zones" cordoned off in each locale around the world, in which elites and the better off are insulated by new systems of spatial reorganization, social control, and policing. The term "green zone" refers to the nearly impenetrable area in central Baghdad that US occupation forces established in the wake of the 2003 invasion of Iraq. The command center of the occupation and select Iraqi elite inside that green zone were protected from the violence and chaos that engulfed the country. Urban areas around the world are now "green-zoned" through gentrification, gated communities, surveillance systems, and state and private violence. Inside the world's green zones, privileged strata avail themselves of privatized social services, consumption, and entertainment. They can work and communicate through Internet and satellite sealed off under the protection of armies of soldiers, police, and private security forces. Here, racial and ethnic oppression combine with class domination in a crushing embrace.

While the wave of technological innovation now underway may hold great promise for the long run, under global capitalism, the social and political implications of new technologies—developed within the logic of capital and its implacable drive to accumulate—point to great peril. In particular, these new technologies will aggravate the forces driving overaccumulation and surplus humanity. They will enable the TCC and its agents to create nightmarish new systems of social control, hegemony, and repression, systems that can be used to constrain and contain rebellion of the global working class, oppositional movements, and the excluded masses. Criminalization, often racialized, and militarized control become mechanisms of preemptive containment, converging with the drive toward militarized accumulation with the potential to create a global police state. Already, we may be seeing the breakdown of consensual domination and a rise of coercive systems of social control as strategies for surplus population management.

Within the nation-state, those most marginalized or superexploited are scapegoated, such as Blacks and immigrants in the United States, Muslims and lower castes in India, or Middle Eastern refugees in Europe. Making these groups scapegoats serves to symbolically condense and then redirect anxieties associated with economic blight and social disorganization. Scapegoating helps the political representatives of the ruling groups to organize political coalitions and construct consensus around a repressive order. The vast new powers of cultural hegemony open up possibilities for channeling grievances and frustrated aspirations into individualized and depoliticized escapism and consumerist fantasies.

The spiraling crisis of global capitalism has reached a crossroads. Either there will be a radical reform of the system (if not its overthrow), or there will be a sharp turn toward twenty-first century fascism, the fusion of reactionary political power with transnational capital. The project of twenty-first century fascism is to organize a mass base among historically privileged sectors of the global working class, such as white workers in the Global North and middle classes in the Global South. Both sectors are experiencing heightened insecurity and the specter of downward mobility. Far-right forces pursue militarism, a racist mobilization against scapegoats, and shifts from social welfare to social control states, bolstered by mystifying ideologies rooted in race/culture supremacy and an idealized past. Neofascist culture normalizes—even glamorizes—war, social violence, and domination. The failure of elite reformism through the transnational elite's unwillingness to challenge global capital's rapaciousness has opened a path for the far-right response to crisis.

TRANSFORMING THE GLOBAL SYSTEM?

Structural crises of capitalism—a label that suggests that the only way out of these crises is to restructure the system—occur about every forty to fifty years. The structural crisis of the 1930s was overcome first by World War II and later on by a Keynesian emphasis on state investment, whereas that of the 1970s was overcome through globalization. The financial collapse of 2008 marked the start of a new structural crisis that now threatens to become systemic as we approach the ecological limits to capitalism's reproduction, and human-induced environmental change threatens to bring about the sixth mass extinction in our planet's history and devastating climate disruption.

Rather than restructuring capitalism yet again, it is time to transcend it. A broad-based shift to ecosocialism must underpin any transition to a just and sustainable future. Achieving ecological equilibrium and an environment favorable to life is incompatible with capitalism's expansive and destructive logic. Non-ecological socialism is a dead end, and a nonsocialist ecology cannot confront the present ecological crisis. Here the matters of power and of agency are of critical importance. Who holds power in global society? What are the collective agencies that could bring about a transition to ecosocialism? What elements among the transnational elite may come around to such a transition?

Moving beyond the nightmare of barbarization and the limitations of a reformist path requires a redistribution of power downward and a transformation toward a system in which social need and rational planning trump private profit and the anarchy of market forces. This means a battle for political power, to wrest control from the TCC. Such a battle requires mass mobilization from below on a transnational scale, as well as a viable political program and political organizations with a capacity for transnational coordination of local and national struggles.

As mass struggles for radical change broke out in an emerging global civil society from the 1960s into the twenty-first century, transnational elites came to see the conquest of civil society, beyond mere control of the state, as the key to constructing the hegemony of global capitalism. Transnational state agencies, corporations, and corporate-funded foundations poured billions of dollars into financing vast transnational networks of NGOs.[19] This strategy has helped the transnational elite to secure its hegemony in global civil society by channeling the demands of mass social movements into institutional arenas that do not transgress the logic of the system.[20]

Even when their stated mission is to be oppositional, NGOs tend to be less mobilizers than service providers, replacing mass struggles and social movements with professional bodies that administer programs and advocate rather than organize. They do not, for instance, encourage strikes, demonstrations, or civil disobedience, much less revolutionary movements, and they eschew organizing along class lines. NGOs substitute the language—and along with it, the practice—of class and social struggle with that of "civic engagement" and "consensus-building." To be sure, there are thousands of NGOs that do not fit this description, and many undertake vital work to further struggles for social justice. Yet for the most part, the global network of NGOs functions to produce and reproduce a reformist version of global capitalism, while the conservative ones push to sustain hegemony around the current path of capitalist globalization. Policy reform—especially that involving income redistribution; transnational state regulation of global markets; labor, women's, and ethnic rights; human rights; and climate change action—is important in the road toward a viable future.[21] Yet NGOs often seek to establish the hegemony of a mild reformist path over transformative projects that radically challenge the system and its power structure.

To be sure, a rupture with global capitalism must gain force in part out of such efforts to bring about a reform of the system. What is crucial, though, is for popular class and ecosocialist-oriented forces to advance an alternative vision for global society that goes beyond reformism and for this vision to achieve hegemony.[22] In this way, the formula for moving beyond global capitalism and toward a just and sustainable future can evolve out of the convergence of radically transformative projects from below and transnational elite reformism from above.

The financial collapse of 2008 was followed by a global revolt that reached a crescendo in 2011. That revolt showed how resistance has become transnational in a way that we have hitherto never seen, made possible by the same global communications and information technologies that have allowed capital to globalize. These examples include the globally coordinated peasant/farmer movement, Vía Campesino; an emerging worldwide coordination of women's movements through the #MeToo and other channels; the IndustriALL Global Union founded in 2012; ongoing cross-border labor organizing among US, Mexican, and Canadian workers and trade unionists; the international spread of the Occupy Wall Street movement in 2011 and 2012; and the Arab Spring that started in Tunisia in 2011 and spread throughout North Africa and the Middle East, even though it has taken a tragic turn.

Globalization and displacement generated deeper organic linkages between the oppressed and exploited across national and regional borders, giving rise to an emerging global working class that must become a major agent of any Great Transition. Yet the global revolt is spread unevenly and faces many challenges, including the predominance of national and local forms of consciousness in the absence of any unifying transformational project and forms of organic coordination across national and regional lines. An accurate reading of the new global capitalism is vital because only praxis, the unity of theory and practice, can bring about such a transition. Understanding the social forces and their political and cultural agents that shape global society is essential for building the systemic movement for a transition to ecosocialism.

APPENDIX

SEPTEMBER 2017 INTERVIEW WITH THE JOURNAL
E-INTERNATIONAL RELATIONS

Where do you see the most exciting research and debates occurring in your field?

Robinson: Actually I think we need to go *afield* in this time of rapid worldwide change if we are to understand our individual fields in the broader context. What has most concerned me in recent years is the crisis of global capitalism. There has been a proliferation of critical research and debates related to the crisis that acquire ever-more relevance as the world moves full steam toward a breakdown of the post–World War II order, the rise of right-wing populist and also neofascist movements (Trumpism, BREXIT, the far right revival in continental Europe, the likes of such strongmen as Rodrigo Duterte in the Philippines), a new nuclear arms race and the threat of major international military conflagration. In such times of social upheaval and political breakdown, it is critical for us to move beyond our traditional area of studies if our research is to remain relevant.

Research on the crisis and on related transformation in the global system has led me to bodies of literature and debate that are for the most part new to me. These include military journals to research how warfare and conflict is changing through the so-called "revolution in military affairs" and "fourth generation warfare." I have been reading works on the fourth industrial revolution to comprehend yet another massive restructuring of the global economy now underway through digitalization, financialization, and automation. I have found a new generation of urban studies and radical geography to be indispensable to understanding and debating the rise of megacities and their networks, the restructuring of space, and new systems of transnational social control (the surveillance state, the rise of a global "homeland security" industry, the new urban militarism, and so on). Of course, the debates around globalization and transnational relations continue to be exciting and cutting edge in the face of current global developments. This includes intense debate on the rise of China and the BRICS, the new digital capitalism, the transnational capitalist class, the revival of aggressive nationalisms, resurgent global revolt, and so on. The post–World War II paradigms—for instance, the triad in international relations theory (liberalism, realism, and traditional Marxism)—are not equipped to explain these developments; neither is constructivism. And this is where I return time and again to the explanatory power of analyzing and theorizing global capitalism as a qualitatively new moment in modern world history.

How has the way you understand the world changed over time, and what (or who) prompted the most significant shifts in your thinking?

Robinson: I came of age politically and intellectually in my late teens as a student in East Africa. I came to Marxism through African Marxists who had participated in the anti-colonial and anti-neocolonial struggles of their day. This was my route as well to theories of imperialism, underdevelopment, dependency, and world systems. Later as a participant in the Nicaraguan revolution of the 1980s and its aftermath in the 1990s, I attempted to make sense of the cycle of national liberation and anti-imperialist revolutions that would come to an end in the face of *fin de siècle* capitalist globalization. The shift in my thinking away from the predominant post–World War II radical theories of Third World liberation and development (but not away from an *unorthodox* Marxism) and toward my theory of global capitalism took place in the 1990s. In that decade I sought explanations for the end of this cycle and for the rise of neoliberalism in the profound transformations of the world political economy and the global system that had become more and more apparent. I undertook extensive readings in international relations theory and global political economy and also turned to a second reading and reconsideration of Marx's political economy. I began to reflect on what seemed to me to be a qualitatively new stage of world capitalism—global capitalism—and came to see as historical what others saw as fixed or immanent structures of world capitalism, such as the nation-state form of world capitalism and the great Center–Periphery, or North–South divide. Along with this reflection came a reconsideration of the validity and utility of taking the nation-state and the interstate system as the primary units and categories of analysis in place of social and class groups in a transnational/global setting. These considerations were evident in my first major theoretical work, *Promoting Polyarchy*, published in 1996, and became more fully developed in my 2004 book, *A Theory of Global Capitalism*.

You have been a vocal proponent of a transnational theory of global capitalism for much of the twenty-first century, yet within Marxist international relations scholarship, the key tenets of this theory remain contested. What would you say are the main misconceptions about your theory of global capitalism, and have there been any critiques that led you to reconsider any of its aspects?

Robinson: I appreciate this question because a response requires that we distinguish between criticism based on a misreading of what I have actually argued and disagreement by those who have seriously engaged with my work. For over twenty years now, some critics have charged that, according to me, the nation-state is becoming irrelevant. These critics also say that my theory of the transnational state posits a collection of entities that "bypasses" or "replaces" the nation-state and that I "do not take the state seriously." This is of course utter nonsense, as anyone who takes the time to study my work knows I have never even remotely suggested such a thing. I no longer bother responding to such gibberish. In my 2014 book, *Global Capitalism and the Crisis of Humanity*, I responded in considerable depth to these and other criticisms, including clarifying and expanding my theory of the transnational state.

Another charge that is hard for me to take seriously is that I have not empirically grounded my claims and have ignored local processes that lead to transnationalization. These critics often cite my 2004 book, *A Theory of Global Capitalism*, or even worse, a single article or a secondary source, yet seem oblivious to my empirical and case study books, such as *Latin America and Global Capitalism*, that operationalize the theory of the transnational capitalist class and the transnational state and show just how valid and explanatory these concepts are.

On the other hand, some critics have pointed out gaps and weaknesses in my arguments and have forced me to think things through, in some cases to qualify more carefully my claims. Critics, for instance, pointed to the difficulty in my theory of accounting for continued *inter*national (distinct from transnational) tensions, the return of aggressive nationalisms, and the relative autonomy of military institutions. In response to these critics, I have recently focused on crises of state legitimacy that derive, at least in part, from the contradiction generated by the disjuncture between a globalizing economy and a nation-state-based system of political authority.

Another set of critics charge that I ignore uneven and combined development and the global Center–Periphery divide. In my 2014 book, in response, I elaborated considerably on how I view spatiality and uneven and combined accumulation in global capitalism. I am calling for a break with the same paradigms whose logic and assumptions much of the criticism is based, so that there is truly a Kuhnian problematic here. I have never argued that there is no longer a Center–Periphery divide. We cannot comprehend this divide in the twenty-first century through nation-state paradigms. I conceive of development and underdevelopment as population groups in a transnational setting, so that there are under-developed/peripheral social groups in Los Angeles where I am based and core social groups in Mexico City and Mumbai. The unit of analysis cannot be the nation-state, notwithstanding the disproportion in national-level development indices that is very real and can be explained historically rather than as a fixed structure of world capitalism.

The theory of global capitalism emphasizes the diachronic, in the sense that I am identifying historical movement underway and showing how my theory helps us to understand the direction of change, whereas many critics focus on the synchronic. There are too many anomalies in the accounts of twenty-first-century global society based on outdated paradigms. My critics rarely if ever respond to me when I point out the anomalies in their argument. This is especially so for the orthodox and often dogmatic Marxists. The dogmatic Marxists operate as though world capitalism remained frozen in its twentieth century form. They dismiss the notion of a transnational capitalist class as "Kautskyist" even though I have pointed out repeatedly why and how my theory shares nothing with the "superimperialism" argument of the early twentieth century German Marxist Karl Kautsky.

Writing in 2008, you seemed to hold out some hope for the counterhegemonic and anti-capitalist potential of Venezuela's Bolivarian Revolution. Given the current malaise facing the Bolivarian government, do you see any viable paths forward for twenty-first century socialism in Venezuela?

Robinson: The Bolivarian revolution is in crisis and its survival is uncertain. It is unbelievably hard to make a revolution. In Venezuela, the easy phase came to an end following the collapse of high oil prices. There are many levels of explanation for the malaise in the revolution. It is certainly true that corruption has alienated part of the revolution's social base. It is true as well that government policies such as the dual exchange rate have undercut the revolution. These policies reflect an alliance between the revolutionary bloc and so-called "patriotic" bourgeoisie (the "Boli-bourgeoisie") and a consequent unwillingness to challenge fundamental class and property relations. The government has done virtually nothing to break the country's dependence on oil. And all of this has unfolded to the drumbeat of a US-supported counterrevolution.

While these factors are relevant, the key point in relation to my theory of global capitalism is that no country in the twenty-first century can extricate itself from global capitalism, including the power of global financial markets, and from its influence on what takes place inside a country, as the Greeks will tell you. The Venezuelan government attempted to develop regional and international counterweights to neoliberal global capitalism. This strategy was entirely correct, but much of it was rolled back when commodity prices collapsed in the wake of the Great Recession and the right-wing counteroffensive in the region. The revolutionary Left in Venezuela (for instance, Marea Socialista) have long called for a more radical challenge to class and property relations inside Venezuela; I share this view. Any attempt to push forward a twenty-first-century socialism, in Venezuela and elsewhere, would certainly need to be grounded in such a challenge. In the long run, national struggles from below must be linked and synchronized with transnational struggles. Despite all the problems, intellectuals committed to global social justice need to cut through the story we are hearing about Venezuela from the corporate media that cheerleads the right-wing opposition. We need to defend the Venezuelan revolution notwithstanding all its problems.

Crises of capitalism and claims that they will mark an end to the system have come and gone. What makes the current crisis different?

Robinson: Several factors about the global crisis suggest it may be systemic, meaning that only a supersession of the system can resolve the crisis, rather than merely structural, meaning that a restructuring of the system can resolve it. One is that global capitalism is reaching the ecological limits to its reproduction. Another factor is that there are limits to extensive and intensive expansion. The capitalist system is like riding a bicycle. If you stop pedaling, you fall over. If capitalism stops expanding, it collapses. Each major crisis in the history of world capitalism has resulted in a new round of extensive expansion through colonialism and imperialism. With the incorporation of the former Soviet bloc and Third World revolutions into global capitalism following the Cold War, there are no longer any countries that remain outside of the system or new territories to conquer and incorporate. We have seen in recent years a massive new round of primitive accumulation around the world through capitalist globalization, but there are limits to this intensive expansion. A third is that nation-states no longer have the ability as in the past to offset capitalism's chronic problem of overaccumulation. Given the global mobility of capital, especially of transnational finance capital, nation-states find it difficult to capture and redistribute surpluses downward. Only a global Keynesianism could accomplish this, but the transnational state does not have such a policymaking or enforcement capacity. All of this points to a possible collapse. Civilizations that were unable to overcome their internal contradictions have collapsed throughout history. Such an outcome is not inevitable. But it is not clear at this point under what circumstances the system can resuscitate itself. Wars have often been the defibrillator to capitalist crisis. My greatest fear is that the tensions generated by the crisis lead to a new global military conflagration.

Scholars such as Patrick Bond have conceptualized the BRICS as "sub-imperialist," while others like Radhika Desai have posited that the BRICS are challenging "western supremacy." What can a critical globalization studies perspective tell us about the role of the BRICS in world order?

Robinson: The notion that the BRICS are a progressive alternative to global capitalism has been thoroughly debunked. Bond co-edited a collection of essays on the matter, *BRICS: An Anti-Capitalist Critique.* As those essays showed, the BRICS capitalist classes and a majority of state and institutional elites within the BRICS countries are seeking not a withdrawal but rather greater integration into global capitalism and a heightened association with transnational capital.

However, the global capitalism perspective differs sharply from Bond's concept of subimperialism. According to Bond, subimperialist countries seek markets and outlets for capital export in neighboring countries as junior partners with transnational capital. By this definition, almost every country in the world could be categorized as subimperialist given that almost every country has transnational capitalist groups that are expanding abroad and that transnational capital produces goods and services in virtually all countries. The rise of the transnational capitalist class in the former Third World is incontrovertible. Thai capitalists seek markets and capital outlets in Vietnam. Nigerian capitalists do so around Africa, including in South Africa. Jordanian capitalists do so in Egypt and Egyptian capitalists do so in Jordan. Are they subimperialist to one another?

Bond sees the world economy as boxed into national economies and capitals, yet the extent of global economic integration and the transnationalization of capital in the twenty-first century undermines any significant analytical purchase to dividing the world's countries into imperialist, subimperialist, and imperialized. Bond sees surpluses as transferred from hinterlands to subimperialist capital cities and from there to imperialist headquarters in the North. This is nearly identical to Andre Gunder Frank's classical dependency theory approach in which the world system is constituted by a string of satellite–metropolis relations through which surpluses flow from peripheral hinterlands through semi-peripheral cities and toward core regions.

The BRICS politics represents a challenge to "Western supremacy" (but *not* global capitalism) insofar as the effort to construct a more expansive and balanced global system and to open up further the global system for transnational capitalists and elites in from their respective countries. Some of these efforts do clash with the G7, but BRICS proposals would have the effect of extending and contributing to the stabilization of global capitalism, and in the process, of further transnationalizing the dominant groups in these countries. Here there is a progressive kernel in the BRICS project. The existing political scaffolding of world capitalism, a legacy of the crumbling post–World War II international order, is hopelessly outdated. The leading capitalist groups from the BRICS countries have joined the ranks of the emerging transnational capitalist class and have acquired a stake in the stability and well-being of global capitalism. But all this has occurred within the framework of an increasingly arcane international political order. If the BRICS do not represent an alternative to global capitalism and the domination of the transnational capitalist class, they do signal the shift toward a more multipolar and balanced interstate system within the global capitalist order.

Throughout your academic career, much of your research has focused on developments in Latin America. As accusations of intellectual colonialism are still very much alive, how can scholars from the "developed" world account for the position of relative power and prosperity that they approach their research from?

Robinson: This is a crucial point. The scholarly agenda set by universities and think tanks in the former First World is financed and heavily shaped by foundations such as Ford that in turn are tied to transnational corporate capital and for that matter to the US State Department or other state entities. These research agendas and conceptual frameworks become hegemonic globally. They frame the research and the university curriculum in Latin America and elsewhere in the former Third World. Yet these agendas are often liberal and even progressive rather than conservative, for hegemony works best when more left and radical elements are not repressed but brought into hegemonic projects.

We have seen how such "intellectual colonialism" works to help defuse more radical demands for system change and the mass mobilization from below that push these demands. As I showed in *Promoting Polyarchy*, the mass movements against the Latin American dictatorships in the 1970s demanded not just a restoration of elite civilian rule and formal political rights but a transformation of the whole social order. The foundations and think tanks they financed jumped on board, producing a veritable academic cottage industry on "democratization" that redefined democracy as process (e.g. procedurally free elections) rather than content (substantive equality through far-reaching change) and provided the intellectual and ideological scaffolding for transitions to neoliberal civilian governments that then pushed capitalist globalization. Prior to that, in the 1970s, the Ford Foundation jumped on board with the mass human rights movement, providing financing, organizing conferences, and bringing Latin America scholars to study in the United States, and in this way, it effectuated a shift in the notion of human rights, purging it of social and economic rights—the right to a decent wage, to health care, education—to a liberal conception of formal civil and political rights.

Later on in the 1990s, the same thing happened with "global civil society." As mass struggles for radical change broke out in an emerging global civil society from the 1960s into the twenty-first century, transnational elites came to see the conquest of civil society, beyond mere control of the state, as the key to constructing the hegemony of global capitalism. Transnational state agencies, corporations, and corporate-funded foundations poured billions of dollars into financing vast transnational networks of NGOs. This strategy has helped the transnational elite to secure *its* hegemony in global civil society by channelling the demands of mass social movements into institutional arenas that do not transgress the logic of the system. Even when their stated mission is to be oppositional, NGOs tend to be less mobilizers than service providers, replacing mass struggles and social movements with professional bodies that administer programs and advocate rather than organize. They do not, for instance, encourage strikes, demonstrations, or civil disobedience, much less revolutionary movements, and they eschew organizing along class lines. As the intellectual and ideological counterpart to this NGOization, the academy in First World churned out new theories of "global civil society" conceived, not as sites of class antagonism and fierce struggles around hegemony and counterhegemony, but as a unified site opposed to the state, just at the time that neoliberalism sought to downsize and privatize the state.

Some academics are intellectual mercenaries, pure and simple. And others are counterhegemonic. But most wittingly or unwittingly become absorbed into intellectual production in function of system maintenance or renewal without transgressing the logic of global capitalism. In this way academics in both the former Third World and First World become organic intellectuals of the prevailing social order. The counterhegemonic intellectuals, if they cannot be co-opted, are not funded and face a host of informal sanctions by academic gatekeepers.

If Hegel's claim that "the truth is the whole" is correct, then are interdisciplinary approaches essential for valuable research? Do you see any value to maintaining siloed disciplinary fields within the Social Sciences and Humanities?

Robinson: Interdisciplinary approaches are absolutely essential. They always were essential, and even more so at a time of rapid social change. I echo Wallerstein's call for a unified historical social science. The only thing we achieve with disciplinary closure is to undermine the ability to understand any dimension of the social world since each dimension can only be comprehended as part of and in relation to the whole.

What is the most important advice you could give to young scholars of sociology, political economy, and international relations?

Robinson: Young scholars should not become fixed on paradigms imparted by their mentors. Don't develop a stake in or rigidity around a particular paradigm that later prevents you from identifying and explaining social change at a time when our traditional points of reference are fast becoming overtaken by developments and outdated. Think beyond the box.

Perhaps more important, humanity is in deep crisis. In such times of crisis, it is incumbent upon us to explore the relevance of academic research to the burning political and social struggles of our epoch. As scholars, we must choose between legitimating the prevailing social order and providing technical solutions to the problems that arise in its maintenance or exposing contradictions in order to reveal how they may be resolved by transcending the existing order. Being a counter-hegemonic academic is difficult, especially for young ones who need to secure employment and tenure. Nonetheless, if we do aspire to become organic intellectuals in the service of the poor majority of humanity, we need to become capable of theorizing the changes that have taken place in the system of capitalism, in this epoch of globalization, and of providing to popular majorities these theoretical insights as inputs for their real-world struggles to develop alternative social relationships and an alternative social logic—the logic of majorities—to that of the market and of transnational capital. It is nonsense to say that the social scientist should be "value-free" because *all* social science is value-laden. It cannot be otherwise.

—

This interview was conducted by Laurence Goodchild. Laurence is Deputy Features Editor at E-International Relations.

NOTES

1: GLOBALIZATION: NINE THESES ON OUR EPOCH

1. The enormous (and growing) body of literature on globalization is too vast to reference here. For summary essays, see Mark Juergensmeyer, Saskia Sassen, and Manfred Steger, eds., *Oxford Handbook of Global Studies* (New York: Oxford University Press, 2018 [forthcoming]). See also Leslie Sklair, *Globalization: Capitalism and Its Alternatives* (New York: Oxford University Press, 2002), and Richard P. Appelbaum and William I. Robinson, eds., *Critical Globalization Studies* (New York: Routledge, 2005).

2. As will become clear throughout this book, the distinction between the global market and a transnationally integrated global production and financial system is crucial. Most Marxists emphasize the former, in what we could call *Market Marxism*. See, for example, Bob Jessop, "The World Market, 'North–South' Relations, and Neoliberalism," *AlternateRoutes: A Journal of Critical Social Research 29* (2018).

3. It is impossible for all social relations to be capitalist; human society would collapse if every single interaction were based on exchange value. More technically, what is taking place is the formal subsumption of all peoples to capital as well as the accelerated shift from formal to real subsumption.

4. Thus, my definition of globalization goes beyond most conceptions that see the process as *quantitative*, involving acceleration in the pace of global interconnections and interdependencies (the objective dimension), along with our awareness of such interconnections (the subjective dimension). For an example of a quantitative conceptualization, see Ronald Robertson, *Globalization: Social Theory and Global Culture* (Newbury Park: Sage, 1992). The *qualitative* definition advanced here incorporates these objective and subjective dimensions but sees quantitative change as giving way to qualitative change. My argument is that the world capitalist system has gone through successive waves of global interconnections, each of which has deepened webs of relations and has further broken down autonomies, but that the current epoch is a *qualitatively* new phase. See Immanuel Wallerstein, *The Modern World System* (New York: Academic Press, 1974), and world system and dependency literature in general for the notion that, in this quantitative conception, there is nothing new in globalization

as worldwide interconnections, and see Eric Wolf's brilliant study, *Europe and the People Without History* (Berkeley: University of California Press, 1982), on how such webs of interconnections span back millennia. The comprehensive textbook by Christopher Chase-Dunn and Bruce Lerro is a very useful reference; see their *Social Change: Globalization from the Stone Age to the Present* (Boulder: Paradigm Publishers, 2014).

5   James O'Connor, "A Red–Green Politics in the United States?" *Capitalism, Nature, Socialism* 5, no. 1 (March 1994): 1–19.

6   On social structures of accumulation, see David M. Kotz, Terrence McDonough, and Michael Reich, *Social Structures of Accumulation: The Political Economy of Growth and Crisis* (Cambridge: Cambridge University Press, 1994).

7   These notions of a global social structure of accumulation, a transnational elite, and a global agenda of this transnational elite are discussed in detail in William I. Robinson, *Promoting Polyarchy: Globalization, U.S. Intervention, and Hegemony* (Cambridge: Cambridge University Press, 1996) and in William I. Robinson, *A Theory of Global Capitalism* (Baltimore: Johns Hopkins University Press, 2004).

8   As far as I know, the term *hyperliberalism* was first used by Robert W. Cox, in "Global Perestroika," *Socialist Register 28* (1992).

9   On this point, see Leslie Sklair, *Globalization: Capitalism and Its Alternatives*.

10 I have documented this process at great length in my two books on Latin America and globalization: *Transnational Conflicts: Central America, Social Change, and Globalization* (London: Verso, 2003) and *Latin America and Global Capitalism* (Baltimore: Johns Hopkins University Press, 2008).

11. Regarding these transnational fractions in the North, see, among several important works, Stephen Gill, *American Hegemony and the Trilateral Commission* (Cambridge: Cambridge University Press, 1990), and Robert W. Cox, *Power, Production, and World Order; Social Forces in the Making of History* (New York: Columbia University Press, 1987). On these fractions in the South, see Robinson, *Promoting Polyarchy*; Robinson, *Transnational Conflicts*; and Robinson, *Latin America and Global Capitalism*.

12. Karl Polanyi, *The Great Transformation* (New York: Rinehart and Company, 1944).

13. Stephen Gill and David Law first discussed the structural power of transnational capital in "Global Hegemony and the Structural Power of Capital," *International Studies Quarterly* 33, no. 4 (December 1989): 475–99.

14. Robert Dahl, *Polyarchy: Participation and Opposition* (New Haven: Yale University Press, 1971).

15. The issues raised by this "thesis" are discussed at great length in Robinson, *Promoting Polyarchy*.

16. UNDP, *Human Development* (New York: Oxford University Press, 1994).

17. Oxfam (London), *Wealth: Having It All and Wanting More*, policy-practice

.oxfam.org.uk/publications/wealth-having-it-all-and-wanting-more
-338125.

18. UNDP, Multidimensional Poverty Index, http://hdr.undp.org/en/content
/multidimensional-poverty-index-mpi.

19. UNDP, *Human Development* (emphasis in original).

20. United States Census Bureau, "Income and Poverty in the United States:
2015," www.census.gov/library/publications/2016/demo/p60-256.html

21. "Shares of Household Income of Quintiles in the United States from
1970 to 2016," Statista, www.statista.com/statistics/203247/shares
-of-household-income-of-quintiles-in-the-us/

22. Nicholas Kristof, "An Idiot's Guide to Inequality," *New York Times*, July
23, 2014.

23. For example, on the specific case of Latinos in the United States, see
William I. Robinson, "The Global Economy and the Latino Populations
in the United States: A World Systems Approach," *Critical Sociology* 19: 2
(1992): 29–59.

24. For one example, see the decadent spread of golf courses and sex tourism in Asia for Asian (male) elites, as discussed in Malee Traisawasdi-
chai, "Chasing the Little White Ball," *The New Internationalist*, no. 263
(January 1995): 16–17. I discuss the global tourist industry and how it has
spread in Latin America through globalization in my book *Latin America
and Global Capitalism*.

25. See, e.g., Mike Zielinski, "Armed and Dangerous: Private Police on the
March," *Covert Action Quarterly*, no. 54 (Fall 1995): 44–50, and Stephen
Graham, *Cities Under Siege: The New Military Urbanism* (London: Verso,
2010).

26. On such urban social and physical restructuring bound up with globalizing processes, see Mike Davis's modern classic, *City of Quartz* (London:
Verso, 1990) and his more recent *Planet of Slums* (London, Verso, 2005).

27. UNDP, Human Development.

28. Alan Tovey, "$1,570,000,000,000: How Much the World Spent on Arms
this Year," *The Telegraph*, December 12, 2016.

29. There is a vast and still burgeoning literature on global environment
and society. Two massive studies from a Marxist perspective offer two
different interpretations of capitalism and the environment: John Bellamy
Foster and Richard York, *The Ecological Rift: Capitalism's War on the Earth*
(New York: Monthly Review Press, 2011), and Jason W. Moore, *Capital-
ism in the Web of Life* (London: Verso, 2015). See also Naomi Klein, *This
Changes Everything: Capitalism and the Climate* (New York: Simon and
Schuster, 2013).

30. See Foster and York, *The Ecological Rift*, 29–30.

2: CRITICAL GLOBALIZATION STUDIES

1. I cannot pursue the discussion here, but I should note that I am breaking with Gramsci when I affirm that all intellectual labor is organic. Gramsci divided intellectuals into "traditional" and "organic," whereas for me all intellectual labor is organic. In addition, much of my discussion here refers to intellectuals ensconced in universities, think tanks, foundations, and NGOs. However, I agree with Gramsci's conviction that revolutionary intellectuals come from working class and popular institutions and social movements labor struggles.

2. Oxfam (London), *Wealth: Having It All and Wanting More*, policy-practice .oxfam.org.uk/publications/wealth-having-it-all-and-wanting-more-338125

3. For a detailed discussion, see William I. Robinson, "Digital Capitalism and Global Police State," *Race & Class* (2018, forthcoming).

4. For testimonials and analysis on how scholars and educators who speak out for Palestinian freedom on US campuses suffer all sorts of McCarthyist academic and political repression, including being fired and blacklisted and receiving death threats, see William I. Robinson and Maryam S. Griffin, eds., *We Will Not Be Silenced: The Academic Repression of Israel's Critics* (London and Oakland: Pluto Press and AK Press, 2017).

5. Max Horkheimer, "Traditional and Critical Theory," in *Critical Theory: Selected Essays*, trans. Matthew J. O'Connell (Toronto: Herder and Herder, 1972), 188–243; Robert W. Cox, "Critical Political Economy," in *International Political Economy: Understanding Global Disorder*, ed. Bjorn Hettne (London: Zed, 1995), 31–45.

6. See, inter alia, Goran Therborn, *Science, Class & Society: On the Formation of Sociology & Historical Materialism* (London: Routledge, 1985); Brian Fay, *Critical Social Science* (Cambridge: Polity Press, 1987); Alan F. Chalmers, *What Is This Thing Called Science?* 3rd ed. (Indianapolis: Hackett, 1982); Jean-Paul Sartre, "A Plea for Intellectuals," in Sartre, *Between Existentialism and Marxism* (London: New Left Books, 1974); William I. Robinson, *Promoting Polyarchy: Globalization, U.S. Intervention, and Hegemony* (Cambridge: Cambridge University Press, 1996).

7. Horkheimer, "Traditional and Critical Theory," 196–97.

8. Bertell Ollman, "Why Dialectics? Why Now?" *Science and Society* 62, no. 3 (1998): 339–57.

9. Sartre, "A Plea for Intellectuals," 238.

10. Karl Marx, as cited in Nancy Fraser, "What's Critical About Critical Theory? The Case of Habermas and Gender," in *Feminism as Critique: On the Politics of Gender*, eds. Seyla Benhabib and Drucilla Cornell (Minneapolis: University of Minnesota Press, 1987), 31.

11. Paul Farmer, *Pathologies of Power: Health, Human Rights, and the New War on the Poor* (Berkeley: University of California Press, 2003).

12. Jean Paul Sartre, "A Plea for Intellectuals," 259. Apropos to the discussion here, Sartre states in the same essay that "*the intellectual is someone*

who meddles in what is not his business and claims to question both received truths and the accepted behavior inspired by them" (230, emphasis in original).

13. Susan George, "If You Want to be Relevant: Advice to the Academic from a Scholar–Activist," in *Critical Globalization Studies*, Richard P. Appelbaum and William I. Robinson, eds. (New York: Routledge, 2005), 8.

14. Michael Burawoy et al., *Global Ethnography: Forces, Connections, and Imaginations in a Postmodern World* (Berkeley: University of California Press, 2000), xiv.

15. Antonio Gramsci, *Selections from the Prison Notebooks* (New York: International Publishers, 1971, 9–10.

16. Gramsci, *Selections from the Prison Notebooks*, 5–23; 52–55.

17. Ronen Palan, "New Trends in Global Political Economy," in *Global Political Economy: Contemporary Theories*, Ronen Palan, ed. (London and New York: Routledge, 2000), 16.

18. Robin Blackburn, ed., *Ideology in Social Science: Readings in Critical Social Theory* (Suffolk, UK: Fontana/Collins, 1972); Immanuel Wallerstein, *Unthinking Social Science: The Limits of 19th Century Paradigms* (Philadelphia: Temple University Press, 2001); Therborn, *Science, Class & Society*.

19. Bertell Ollman, *Alienation*, 2d ed. (Cambridge: Cambridge University Press, 1976).

20. Ollman, "Why Dialectics? Why Now?" 342.

21. Francis Fukuyama, *The End of History and the Last Man* (London: Penguin, 1992).

3: THE NEW GLOBAL ECONOMY AND THE RISE OF A TRANSNATIONAL CAPITALIST CLASS

1. William J. Amelio, "Worldsource or Perish," *Forbes*, August 17, 2007.

2. Most Marxists studying world capitalism would concur with the notion of successive mercantile, competitive, and monopoly stages in the development of world capitalism yet tenaciously cling to the outdated notion that we are still in the monopoly stage. For instance, this is the major premise of the "Monthly Review school" grouped around the New York–based monthly socialist magazine, *Monthly Review*.

3. Note that precapitalist and noncapitalist are distinct. There are still, and there always will be, noncapitalist relations; human life could not exist on purely capitalist/commodity relations.

4. This assertion has been repeatedly distorted by my critics, who claim that I see the nation-state and the interstate system as no longer relevant. For a detailed response to my critics, see the introduction and Chapters 1 and 2 of my book *Global Capitalism and the Crisis of Humanity* (New York: Cambridge University Press, 2014). What I mean by the supersession of the nation-state as the organizing principle of capitalism is that, as the commanding heights of capital have become integrated transnationally,

capital no longer organizes itself into competing national capitals and nation-states that drive capitalist development. In turn, this capitalist development takes place in emergent transnational space and through "rescaling" so that the most significant "spaces of capital" are no longer organized as a nation-state/interstate system.

5.   I have critiqued the nation-state-centric framework of analysis in many publications over the past three decades. See my article "Beyond Nation-State Paradigms: Globalization, Sociology, and the Challenge of Transnational Studies," *Sociological Forum* 13, no. 4 (1998): 561–94. See also my *Global Capitalism and the Crisis of Humanity*.

6.   The former Third World countries did so through dependence on First World multinational corporate investment in their countries. These countries sought to import the materials and technologies and produce cars for their national markets and in no way involved the global decentralization and fragmentation of production I am identifying here.

7.   Peter Dicken, *Global Shift*, 3rd ed. (London and New York: The Guilford Press, 1998), 32.

8.   For a typical Market Marxism account, see Bob Jessop, "The World Market, 'North–South' Relations, and Neoliberalism," *AlternateRoutes: A Journal of Critical Social Research* 29 (2018).

9.   Dicken, *Global Shift*, 2 (emphasis in original).

10. See, inter alia, Klaus Schwab, *The Fourth Industrial Revolution* (Geneva: World Economic Forum, 2016); Martin Ford, *The Rise of the Robots* (New York: Basic Books, 2015).

11. Thomas Marois, "TiSA and the Threat to Public Banks" (Amsterdam: Transnational Institute, April 2017), 1; www.tni.org/en/publication/tisa-and-the-threat-to-public-banks

12. For summaries and assessments of this evidence, see inter alia Robinson, *A Theory of Global Capitalism* (Baltimore: Johns Hopkins University Press, 2004); Leslie Sklair, *The Transnational Capitalist Class* (Oxford: Blackwell, 2001); Leslie Sklair, *Globalization: Capitalism and Its Alternatives* (New York: Oxford University Press, 2002); Jeffrey Kentor, "The Growth of Transnational Corporate Networks, 1962 to 1998," *Journal of World-Systems Research* 11, no. 2 (2005): 262–86; Jeffrey Kentor and Yong Suk Jang, "Yes, There Is a (Growing) Transnational Business Community," *International Sociology* 19, no. 3 (2004): 355–68; United Nations Conference on Trade and Development (UNCTAD), *World Investment Report* (Geneva: United Nations, various years); Peter Dicken, *Global Shift*, 5th ed. (New York: Guilford, 2007); William Carroll, *The Making of a Transnational Capitalist Class: Corporate Power in the 21st Century* (London: Zed, 2010); Clifford L. Staples, "Cross-Border Acquisitions and Board Globalization in the World's Largest TNCs, 1995–2005," *The Sociological Quarterly* 49 (2008): 31–51; Clifford L. Staples, "Board Interlocks and the Study of the Transnational Capitalist Class," *Journal of World-Systems Research* 12,

no. 2 (2006): 309–19; Clifford L. Staples, "The Business Roundtable and the Transnational Capitalist Class," in *Financial Elites and Transnational Business: Who Rules the World?*" Georgina Murray and John Scott, eds. (Camberley, UK, and Northhampton, MA: Edward Elgar Publishing, 2012). See also other essays in *Financial Elites and Transnational Business*.

13. United Nations Conference on Trade and Development (UNCTAD), *Handbook of Statistics 2016* (New York and Geneva: Author, 2016), 192. Of this $1.8 trillion, some $800 billion, or 44 percent, went to developing countries.

14. UNCTAD, *Handbook of Statistics 2016*, 200. Of this total, $8.4 trillion, or some one-third, was located in Third World countries.

15. Susan Strange, *Casino Capitalism* (Manchester: Manchester University Press, 1997).

16. The trade statistics are from UNCTAD, *Handbook of Statistics 2016*, 2, 10. Of the total, $7.4 trillion, or 45 percent, corresponded to Third World countries. Exports as a percentage of world output are from UNCTAD, *Trade and Development Report, 2016* (Geneva: Author, 2016), chart 2.2, "Global Exports as a Share of World Output, 1960–2014," 35.

17. See UNCTAD, *World Investment Report 1999*. For 2006 figures, see "UNCTAD Investment Brief," no. 5 (2006), 1. The 2010 figure is from Malgorzata Jaworek and Marcin Kuzel, "Transnational Corporations in the World Economy: Formation, Development, and Present Position," *Copernican Journal of Finance and Accounting* 4, no. 1 (2015): 57, Table 1.

18. UNCTAD, World Investment Report 2002 for 1982 figure, and World Investment Report 2016 for the 2015 figure.

19. Jaworek and Kuzel, "Transnational Corporations in the World Economy," 57, Table 1, and 65, Table 7.

20. UNCTAD, World Investment Report 2016, 124–25.

21. Nam-Hoon Kang and Sara Johansson, "Cross-Border Mergers and Acquisitions: Their Role in Industrial Globalization," *STI Working Papers 2000/1* (Paris: Organization for Economic Cooperation and Development, 2000).

22. The 1999 figure is from Thompson Financial Securities Data 2000, "Share of Cross-Border Mergers: 1980–99," as reported by Global Policy Forum, table on "Worldwide Mergers and Acquisitions, 1980–99." The 2015 figure is from UNCTAD, *World Investment Report 2016*, 204, Annex Table 3.

23. Thompson Financial Securities Data 2000.

24. William Carroll, *The Making of a Transnational Capitalist Class* (London: Zed, 2010), 98.

25. Dicken, *Global Shift*, 223 (emphasis in original).

26. The term *precariat* was popularized (although not coined) by Guy Standing in *The Precariat: The New Dangerous Class* (New York: Bloombury, 2011). But Standing's social democratic conception is seriously flawed. He suggests that the precariat is "a new class" rather than part of the working class experi-

encing a condition faced by expanding sectors of the working class. He does not conceive of this condition as an instance of the capital–labor relation. He takes a First World/Eurocentric view of the global precariat—what we could call "methodological Westernism"—and appears unable to combine class with racial, ethnic, and cultural analysis. His liberal orientation does not critique *capital* as a relation causal to the rise of the precariat as much as the state as an inadequate regulator of the market and its social consequences.

27. International Labor Organization, *World of Work 2014: Developing With Jobs* (Geneva: Author, 2014).

28. Michael Hardt and Antonio Negri, *Empire* (Cambridge, MA: First Harvard University Press, 2000).

29. Karl Marx and Friedrich Engels, *The Communist Manifesto*, in *The Marx-Engels Reader*, 2d ed., Robert C. Tucker, ed. (New York: W.W. Norton, 1978), 476.

30. Marx and Engels, *The Communist Manifesto*, 82.

31. World Trade Organization, "Facts and Figures," www.wto.org/english /tratop_e/region_e/regfac_e.htm.

4: THE NATION-STATE AND THE TRANSNATIONAL STATE

1. Cited in William I. Robinson, *A Theory of Global Capitalism* (Johns Hopkins University Press, 2004), 85.

2. To reiterate what I said in the previous chapter: My critics have repeatedly distorted this assertion of mine by claiming that I see the nation-state and the interstate system as no longer relevant. For a detailed response to this false claim, see the introduction and Chapters 1 and 2 of my book, *Global Capitalism and the Crisis of Humanity* (New York: Cambridge University Press, 2014).

3. Max Weber, *Economy and Society*, G. Roth and C. Wittich, eds. (Berkeley: University of California Press, 1978), 353–54.

4. For these views, see, for instance, three often cited works: Raymond Vernon, *Sovereignty at Bay: The Multinational Spread of U.S. Enterprises* (London: Longman, 1971); Susan Strange, *The Retreat of the State: The Diffusion of Power in the World Economy* (Cambridge: Cambridge University Press, 1996); and Robert Boyer and Daniel Drache, eds., *States Against Markets: The Limits of Globalization* (London: Routledge, 1996).

5. For this approach, see especially Paul Hirst and Grahame Thompson, *Globalization in Question*, 2d ed. (Oxford: Polity Press, 2009). While many Marxists may not see themselves as inspired by Weber or even know what Weber had to say about the states and markets, I believe many if not most indeed have been influenced by the dualist framework.

6. Bertell Ollman, *Alienation*, 2d ed. (Cambridge: Cambridge University Press, 1976).

7. Karl Marx and Friedrich Engels, *The German Ideology* (New York: International Publishers, 1970[1846]), 80.

8. Concretely, the first nation-states arose as part of bourgeois revolution and the early consolidation of capitalist power in such countries as the Netherlands and England, and then became formalized in the seventeenth-century treaty of Westphalia as the political form that world capitalism would acquire.

9. Nicos Poulantzas, *State, Power, Socialism* (London: Verso, 1978), 129 (emphasis in original).

10. These regional banks are part of the larger international financial system and were created in order to function as more specialized regional international financial institutions, complementary to the Bretton Woods institutions. The International Development Bank was formed in 1960, the African Development Bank in 1966, and the Asian Development Bank in 1966. In 1990 the European Bank for Reconstruction and Development was formed as a fourth regional bank.

11. The structural limitation that world capitalism places on progressive or socialist transformation is not new. What is new is the extent to which space for any local or national autonomy has been constricted by globalization.

12. Philip McMichael, *Development and Social Change* (Thousand Oaks: Pine Forge Press, 1996), 203.

13. I have shown how this has played out in specific cases around the world in many of my books and articles. The most detailed case study is of Central America: William I. Robinson, *Transnational Conflicts: Central America, Social Change, and Globalization* (London: Verso, 2003).

14. Howard M. Wachtel, *The Money Mandarins: The Making of a New Supranational Economic Order* (New York: Pantheon Books, 1986), 15.

15. The backdrop to all these developments was the structural crisis of world capitalism in the 1970s, which involved a declining rate of profit for capital and the heightened power of working and popular classes. The globalization of capital and the rise of a transnational state were responses to these two dimensions of the 1970s crisis. Detailed discussion can be found in my books *A Theory of Global Capitalism* and *Global Capitalism and the Crisis of Humanity*.

16. Susan Strange, *States and Markets* (London: Pinter Press, 1994), 112.

17. Strange, *States and Markets*, 107.

18. Cited in Jeremy Bretcher and Tim Costello, *Global Village or Global Pillage?: Economic Reconstruction from the Bottom Up* (Boston: South End Press, 1994), 30.

19. As cited in Wachtel, *The Money Mandarins*, 25.

20. For discussion, see Robert W. Cox, *Production, Power, and World Order* (New York: Columbia University Press, 1987); Craig N. Murphy, *International Organizations and Industrial Change: Global Governance since 1850* (New York: Oxford University Press, 1994).

21. John Williamson, "Democracy and the 'Washington Consensus'," *World Development* 21 (1993): 1329–36.

22. David Harvey, *The Condition of Postmodernity* (Cambridge, MA and Oxford, UK: Blackwell, 1989), 170.

23. Kofi Annan, 31 January 1998 address by the UN Secretary at the World Economic Forum, Davos, Switzerland, reprinted in part as a paid advertisement by the Pfizer Corporation in *The Economist*, March 28–April 3, 1998, 24.

24. Peter Utting, "UN–Business Partnerships: Whose Agenda Counts? *Third World Network*, July 27, 2002; www.globalpolicy.org/socecon/tncs/2001/0727twn.htm.

25. United Nations Development Program, "What is the United Nations Development Program?" www.un.org/partners/business/undp-htm.

26. See, for instance, Lisa Hayes, "Industry's Growing Influence at the WHO," *Health Action International* (February 15, 2001): 1–4; C. Gerald Fraser, "Skepticism Still Surrounds UN Partnership with Private Sector," *Earth Times News Service* (March 2001): 1–3; Corporate Europe Observatory, "High Time for UN to Break Partnership with the ICC" (newsletter; July 25, 2001): 1–9.

27. World Bank, *The State in a Changing World* (Washington, DC: Author, 1997), 12.

28. Karl Marx, "The Eighteenth Brumaire of Louis Bonaparte," in *The Marx-Engels Reader*, 2d ed., Robert C. Tucker, ed. (New York: W.W. Norton, 1978), 435.

29. "The Problem with Profits," *The Economist*, March 26, 2016.

30. Karl Marx and Frederick Engels, "The Communist Manifesto," in *The Marx-Engels Reader*, 2d ed., Robert C. Tucker, ed. (New York: W.W. Norton, 1978), 482.

5: BEYOND THE THEORY OF IMPERIALISM

1. See, inter alia, David Harvey, *The New Imperialism*, 2d ed. (New York: Oxford University Press, 2005); Ellen Meiksins Wood, *Empire of Capital* (London: Verso, 2003); John B. Foster, "The New Age of Imperialism," *Monthly Review* 55, no. 3 (2003): 1–14; John B. Foster, *Naked Imperialism: U.S. Pursuit of Global Dominance* (New York: Monthly Review, 2006); Peter Gowan, *The Global Gamble: Washington's Faustian Bid for World Dominance* (London: Verso, 1999); Alex Callinicos, *Imperialism and Global Political Economy* (Cambridge: Polity, 2009); Walden Bello, *Dilemmas of Domination: The Unmaking of the American Empire* (New York: Henry Holt, 2005).

2. John Bellamy Foster, "The New Imperialism of Globalized Monopoly Finance Capital," *Monthly Review* 67, no. 3 (July–August 2015): 1. In the same article, Foster misreads my argument entirely and associates it with the early twentieth century German socialist's Karl Kautsky's "ultra-imperialism" or "superimperialism" thesis. Yet my global capitalism approach shares little or nothing with Kautsky's thesis. Kautsky, in his 1914 essay

"Ultra-Imperialism" (available at www.platypus1917.org/wp-content
/uploads/readings/kautskykarl_ultraimperialism1914_NLR05804.pdf),
assumed capital would remain national in its essence and suggested that national capitals would collude internationally instead of compete, whereas my
theory on the TCC emphasizes that competition and conflict among capitals is endemic to the system, but that such competition takes on new forms
in the age of globalization not necessarily expressed as national rivalry.

3. Rudolf Hilferding, *Finance Capital: A Study of the Latest Phase of Capitalist
Development* (London: Routledge, 1981 [1910]), 322. Similarly, Nikolai Bukharin, in the chapter titled "World Economy and the 'National'
State" in his classic study, *Imperialism and World Economy* (New York:
Monthly Review Press, 1973 [1929]), states: "There is a growing discord
between the basis of social economy which has become world-wide and
the peculiar class structure of society, a structure where the ruling class
(the bourgeoisie) itself is split into 'national' groups with contradictory
economic interests, groups which, being opposed to the world proletariat,
are competing among themselves for the division of surplus value created
on a world scale" (106).

4. Michael Klare, "The New Geopolitics," *Monthly Review* 55, no. 3 (2003):
51–56.

5. See, e.g, Doug Henwood, *After the New Economy* (New York: The New
Press, 2003); Gonzalo Pozo-Martin, "A Tougher Gordian Knot: Global-
isation, Imperialism and the Problem of the State," *Cambridge Review of
International Affairs* 19, no. 2 (2006): 223–42.

6. Walden Bello, "The Capitalist Conjuncture: Over-Accumulation, Financial Crises, and the Retreat from Globalization," *Third World Quarterly* 27,
no. 8 (2006): 1345–67; 1346.

7. Ellen Meiksins Wood, *Empire of Capital* (London: Verso, 2003), 33 133
(emphasis added).

8. Harvey, *The New Imperialism*, 29–30.

9. Bertell Ollman, *Alienation*, 2d ed. (Cambridge: Cambridge University
Press, 1976).

10. For a discussion on this matter, see William I. Robinson, *Promoting
Polyarchy: Globalization, U.S. Intervention, and Hegemony* (Cambridge:
Cambridge University Press, 1996), Chapter 1.

11. See, inter alia, Goran Therborn, *Science, Class and Society: On the Forma-
tion of Sociology and Historical Materialism* (London: Verso, 1985 [1976]);
Irving M. Zeitlin, *Ideology and the Development of Sociological Theory*, 7th ed.
(Englewood Cliffs: Prentice Hall, 2000).

12. Harvey, *The New Imperialism*, 26.

13. Harvey, *The New Imperialism*, 32.

14. Henri Lefebvre, *The Production of Space* (Oxford: Blackwell, 1991).

15. David Harvey, *The Limits to Capital* (London: Verso, 2006 [1982]); *The
Condition of Postmodernity* (London: Blackwell, 1990).

16. Manuel Castells, *The Rise of the Network Society, Vol. I: The Information Age: Economy, Society, Culture* (Oxford: Blackwell, 1996); Anthony Giddens, *The Consequences of Modernity* (Cambridge: Polity, 1990).

17. Harvey, *The New Imperialism*, 106.

18. Harvey, *The New Imperialism*, 32.

19. John Bellamy Foster, "The New Age of Imperialism," *Monthly Review* 55, no. 3 (2003): 13.

20. Henwood, *After the New Economy*.

21. Wood, *Empire of Capital*, 156.

22. Rhodium Group and National Committee on U.S.–China Relations, "Two-Way Street: 25 Years of US–China Direct Investment," Washington, DC, 2016.

23. See, inter alia, William I. Robinson, "China and Trumpism," *Jacobin*, February 24, 2017; William I. Robinson, "What Is Behind the Renegotiation of NAFTA? Trumpism and the New Global Economy," *Truthout*, July 24, 2017.

24. U.S. Department of the Treasury, as cited in Tom Murse, "How Much U.S. Debt Does China Really Own?" *ThoughtCo.*, March 18, 2017.

25. See, inter alia, William I. Robinson, *Global Capitalism and the Crisis of Humanity* (New York: Cambridge University Press, 2014).

26. Isabelle Delforge, "Thailand: the World's Kitchen," *Le Monde Diplomatique*, July 2004; International Monetary Fund, "Independent Evaluation Office (IEO) of the IMF, Report on the Evaluation of the Role of the IMF in Argentina, 1999–2001," June 30, 2004, www.imf.org/external/np/ieo/2004/arg/eng/index.htm.

27. "An Increasingly Precious Metal," *The Economist*, January 16, 2016, 69–70.

28. For details, see inter alia, the Tata Group's web page, www.tata.com/aboutus/index/About-us

29. Kees Van der Pijl, "A Theory of Global Capitalism: Feature Review," *New Political Economy* 10, no. 2 (2005): 276.

30. Yousef Baker, "Global Capitalism and Iraq: The Making of a Neoliberal Republic," paper presented at the international conference *Global Capitalism and Transnational Class Formation*, Center of Global Studies, Czech Academy of Sciences, September 16–18, 2011.

31. Naomi Klein, *The Shock Doctrine: The Rise of Disaster Capitalism* (New York: Metropolitan Books, 2007), 327.

32. See, e.g., Joseph Stiglitz, *Globalization and its Discontents* (New York: W.W. Norton, 2003).

33. By *overdetermination*, I mean that an event or process—in this case renewed US interventionism and militarization—is determined by multiple causes or conditions (determinations); the overdetermining condition is that which is singled out in concrete historical circumstances as an analytical explanandum.

34. Dan Briody, *The Iron Triangle: Inside the Secret World of the Carlyle Group* (Hoboken, NJ: John Wiley and Sons, 2003). See also the Carlyle web page: www.carlyle.com/about-carlyle.
35. David Rothkopf, *Superclass: The Global Power Elite and the World They Are Making* (New York: Farrar, Straus and Giroux, 2008), 207.
36. As cited in "Note from the Editors," *Monthly Review* (November 2004), inside front cover and 64–65; cite on 64.
37. David Phinney, "Blood, Sweat and Tears: Asia's Poor Build U.S. Bases in Iraq," *CorpWatch* (October 3, 2005).
38. I have not discussed here uneven development in the global age, including Leon Trotsky's particular theory of "combined and uneven development." However, I have discussed it at considerable length in Chapter 4 of my *Global Capitalism and the Crisis of Humanity*.

6: GLOBAL CAPITALISM, MIGRANT LABOR, AND THE STRUGGLE FOR SOCIAL JUSTICE

1. A superb study on the creation of a world market in labor is Lydia Potts, *The World Labor Market: A History of Migration* (London: Zed, 1990).
2. International Labor Organization, "Labour Migration," www.ilo.org /global/topics/labour-migration/lang--en/index.htm
3. United Nations Department of Economic and Social Affairs, *International Migration Report 2017* (New York: United Nations, 2017), 1.
4. See, e.g., Kam Wing Chan, "China: Internal Migration," in *The Encyclopedia of Global Human Migration*, Immanuel Ness and Peter Bellwood, eds. (Hoboken, NJ: Wiley-Blackwell, 2013).
5. See Robyn Magalit Rodriguez, *Migrants for Export: How the Philippine State Brokers Labor to the World* (Minneapolis: University of Minnesota Press, 2010).
6. On the new global capitalism, see in particular, William I. Robinson, *A Theory of Global Capitalism: Production, Class, and State in a Transnational World* (Baltimore: Johns Hopkins University Press, 2004), and *Global Capitalism and the Crisis of Humanity* (New York: Cambridge University Press, 2014).
7. See my *A Theory of Global Capitalism* and *Global Capitalism and the Crisis of Humanity*; also, inter alia, David Harvey, *A Brief History of Neoliberalism* (New York: Oxford University Press, 2005).
8. See, inter alia, William I. Robinson, *Transnational Conflicts: Central America, Social Change, and Globalization* (London: Verso, 2003) and *Latin America and Global Capitalism* (Baltimore: Johns Hopkins University Press, 2008).
9. Guy Standing, *The Precariat: The New Dangerous Class* (New York: Bloomsbury Academic, 2014 updated edition).
10. The International Labor Organization reported that in the late twentieth century, some one-third of the global labor force was unemployed.

International Labor Organization, *World Employment Report 1996–97* (Geneva: Author/United Nations, 1997).

11. See these two 2006 articles: Southern Poverty Law Center, "Center Exposes Exploitation of Immigrant workers" and "Rebuilding New Orleans," both on www.splcenter.org/. There is evidence that, as Latinos came to constitute the principal labor force for the reconstruction of New Orleans in the wake of the destruction wrought by Hurricane Katrina in 2005, employers turned to such practices as refusing to pay immigrant workers after they had rendered services, turning them over to immigration authorities for deportation, and employing them in an array of slave labor-like conditions.

12. For details, see inter alia, Joseph Nevins, *Operation Gatekeeper: The Rise of the "Illegal Alien" and the Making of the U.S.–Mexico Boundary* (New York: Routledge, 2002).

13. For example, in 1994, the US government launched "Operation Gatekeeper," which accelerated militarization of the US–Mexico border (see Nevins, *Operation Gatekeeper*). Two years later, the Clinton administration passed the Illegal Immigration Reform and Immigrant Responsibility Act, which tightened asylum claims, increased penalties on undocumented immigrants, and led to a massive increase in deportations.

14. Supplying global capital with immigrant labor is now a multibillion dollar industry. Globally organized networks of "migration merchants," or usurious middlemen, provide a full range of legal and illegal services needed for migration, including the supply of passports, visas, work permits, cash advances, safe houses, above ground and clandestine transport, border crossing by *coyotes*, and employment opportunities in countries of destination, all for fees that can add up to tens of thousands of dollars and, in many cases, place the transnational migrant in a situation of indentured servitude for many years. But these illicit and often underground profit-making ventures are dwarfed by the accumulation opportunities opened up to transnational corporate capital by the war on immigrants.

15. As cited in David Bacon, "Debunking 8 Myths About Why Central American Children Are Migrating," *In These Times*, July 8, 2014.

16. For an excellent brief documentary on the American Legislative Exchange Council, anti-immigrant legislation, and the vested corporate interest in the war on immigrants, see "Immigrants for Sale," youtube.com and www.mycuentame.org/immigrantsforsale.

17. For these details, see Laura Sullivan, "Prison Economics Help Drive Ariz. Immigration Law," National Public Radio, October 28, 2010, and Ian Gordon, "The Immigration Hardliner Family Tree," *Mother Jones* magazine, March/April 2012. Note that after a number of media exposés of the American Legislative Exchange Council in 2012, some forty of these corporations withdrew their funding. The list of those corporations that withdrew as well as more details on the council can be found at the Source-

watch website, www.sourcewatch.org/index.php/ALEC_Corporations.

18. See Gordon, "The Immigration Hardliner Family Tree."

19. See, inter alia, "Immigrant Detention Map and Statistics," *CIVIC*, www.endisolation.org/resources/immigration-detention/

20. Michelle Alexander, *The New Jim Crow: Mass Incarceration in the Age of Colorblindness* (New York: The New Press, 2012), 231.

21. Jeff Sommer, "Trump's Win Gives Stocks in Private Prison Companies a Reprieve," *New York Times*, December 3, 2016.

22. See, among other items, David Bacon, "Immigrant Labor, Immigrant Rights," *NACLA Report on the Americas* 47, no. 1 (2014): 64–69, 64; David Bacon, *Illegal People: How Globalization Creates Migration and Criminalizes Immigrants* (New York: Beacon Press, 2009); David Bacon, *The Children of NAFTA: Labor Wars on the U.S./Mexico Border* (Berkeley: University of California Press, 2004).

23. On the spring 2006 immigrant uprising and its aftermath, see Alfonso Gonzales, *Reform Without Justice: Latino Migrant Politics and the Home-land Security State* (New York: Oxford University Press, 2014).

24. For a discussion, see William I. Robinson and Xuan Santos, "Jess Diaz and Javier Rodriguez: Undocumented in America," *New Left Review* 47 (September–October 2007): 93–106.

25. Bacon, "Immigrant Labor, Immigrant Rights," 65.

26. For a good summary, see Aviva Chomsky, "The United States' Continuing Border Crisis: The Real Story Behind the 'Invasion' of the Children," *TomDispatch*, August 25, 2014.

27. David Bacon, "Tea Party and Border Patrol Spin the Story of Children in Detention," *Counterpunch*, June 26, 2014.

28. Geoffrey Mohan, "To Keep Crops from Rotting in the Field, Farmers Say They Need Trump to Let in More Temporary Workers," *Los Angeles Times*, May 25, 2017.

29. On these points, see William I. Robinson, *Global Capitalism and the Crisis of Humanity*.

7: GLOBAL CAPITALISM AND THE RESTRUCTURING OF EDUCATION: PRODUCING GLOBAL ECONOMY WORKERS AND SUPPRESSING CRITICAL THINKING

1. Antonio Gramsci referred to *organic intellectuals* as those who are attached to political projects, whether of the dominant or the subordinate classes. This is a critically important conception. But in this sentence, I use the term *organic intellectual* simply to mean the intellectual whose scientific labor objectively serves the strategic aims of the global capitalist system.

2. Robert B. Reich, *The Work of Nations* (New York: Vintage, 1992).

3. Oxfam, "Wealth: Having It All and Wanting More," January 19, 2015.

4. Thomas Piketty, *Capital in the Twenty-First Century* (Cambridge: Harvard University Press, 2014). For my critique of Piketty and the

newfound concern for inequality by the transnational elite, see my article "Reform Is not Enough to Stem the Rising Tide of Inequality Worldwide," *Truthout*, January 1, 2016.

5. This essay is a revised version of the presentation I gave to the conference, "Researching Elite Education," held at York University in Toronto, Canada, June 28–30, 2015.

6. There has been a rebirth of interest in crisis as a critical theme in Marxist and radical political economy since the 2008 global financial collapse. My analysis is laid out in Robinson, *Global Capitalism and the Crisis of Humanity* (New York: Cambridge University Press, 2014). See also, inter alia, Martins Konings, ed., *The Great Credit Crash* (London: Verso, 2010); Chris Harman, *Zombie Capitalism: Global Crisis and the Relevance of Marx* (Chicago: Haymarket, 2010); David Harvey, *Seventeen Contradictions and the End of Capitalism* (New York: Oxford University Press, 2015).

7. On this point, see for example, William I. Robinson, *Promoting Polyarchy: Globalization, U.S. Intervention, and Hegemony* (Cambridge: Cambridge University Press, 1996); Vijay Prashad, *The Darker Nations: A People's History of the Third World* (New York: The New Press, 2008).

8. This term was popularized (but not coined in) Guy Standing, *The Precariat: The New Dangerous Class* (New York: Bloomsbury, 2011). But Standing's social democratic conception is seriously flawed. He suggests that the precariat is "a new class" rather than part of the working class experiencing a condition faced by expanding sectors of the working class. He does not conceive of this condition as an instance of the capital–labor relation. He takes a First World/Eurocentric view of the global precariat—what we could call "methodological Westernism" —and appears unable to combine class with racial, ethnic, and cultural analysis. His liberal orientation does not critique *capital* as a relation causal to the rise of the precariat as much as the state as an inadequate regulator of the market and its social consequences.

9. On the social structure of accumulation, see Terrence McDonough, David M. Kotz, and Michael Reich, eds., *Social Structures of Accumulation Theory, Volumes I and II* (Northampton, MA: Edward Elgar, 2014).

10. Jürgen Habermas, *The Theory of Communicative Action, Vol. I: Reason and the Rationalization of Society* (Boston: Beacon Press, 1985).

11. In my *Global Capitalism and the Crisis of Humanity*, I make reference to a vast body of literature on the transnationalization of capital and the transcapitalist class beyond my own work.

12. Samuel Bowles and Herbert Gintis, *Schooling in Capitalist America: Educational Reform and the Contradictions of Economic Life* (New York: Basic Books, 1976).

13. See also the classic by Paul Willis, *Learning to Labor: How Working Class Kids Get Working Class Jobs* (New York: Columbia University Press, 1981).

14. Harry Braveman, *Labor and Monopoly Capitalism: The Degradation of Work*

in the Twentieth Century (New York: Monthly Review Press, 1974).

15. Jeremy Rifkin, *The End of Work: The Decline of the Global Labor Force and the Dawn of the Post-Market Era* (New York: Putnam, 1995); Stanley Aronowitz and William DiFazio, *The Jobless Future*, 2d ed. (Minneapolis: University of Minnesota Press, 2010).

16. On the fourth industrial revolution, see Klaus Schwab, *The Fourth Industrial Revolution* (Geneva: World Economic Forum, 2016) and Martin Ford, *The Rise of the Robots: Technology and the Threat of a Jobless Future* (New York: Basic Books, 2016).

17. Elise S. Brezis, "Globalization and the Emergence of a Transnational Oligarchy," United Nations University–World Institute for Development Economics Research, Conference on the Role of Elites in Economic Development, June 12–13, 2009, Helsinki, Finland.

18. Barbara Bruns, Alain Mingat, and Ramahatra Rakotomalala, *Achieving Universal Primary Education by 2015: A Chance for Every Child* (Washington, DC: The World Bank, 2003).

19. For discussion, see Samir Amin, "The Millennium Development Goals: A Critique from the South," *Monthly Review* 57, no. 10 (2006).

20. Bruns et al., *Achieving Universal Primary Education by 2015*, 1.

21. Stephen J. Ball and Deborah Youdell, "Hidden Privatization in Public Education," Preliminary Report presented to 5th World Congress of Education International, July 2007, pages.ei-ie.org/quadrennialreport/2007/upload/content_trsl_images/440/Hidden_privatisation-EN.pdf.

22. Some of these "guidelines" referred specifically to its recommendations for reform of the Mexican university system. For an excellent analysis, see Gian Carlo Delgado-Ramos and John Saxe-Fernández, "The World Bank and the Privatization of Public Education: A Mexican Perspective," *Journal for Critical Education Policy Studies* 3, no. 1 (2015).

23. D. Bruce Johnstone, *The Financing and Management of Higher Education: A Status Report on Worldwide Reforms* (Buffalo: World Bank/SUNY Buffalo, 1998), published as an addendum to the World Bank 1998 report, *Higher Education Financing Project*, Report No. 17174 (Washington, DC: World Bank, 1998).

24. On the matter of student loans, see Susanne Soederberg, "The Student Loan Crisis and the Debtfare State," *Dollars and Sense*, May–June 2015.

25. Sheila Slaughter and Larry L. Leslie, *Academic Capitalism: Politics, Policies, and the Entrepreneurial University* (Baltimore: Johns Hopkins University Press, 1999). Brendan Cantwell and Ilkka Kauppinen, eds., *Academic Capitalism in the Age of Globalization* (Baltimore: Johns Hopkins University Press, 2014).

26. Adrianna Kezar and Daniel Maxey, "The Changing Academic Workforce," *AGB Trusteeship Magazine*, May/June, 2013.

27. Chris Denhart, "How the $1.2 Trillion College Debt Crisis is Crippling Students, Parents and the Economy," *Forbes*, August 7, 2013.

28. National Center for Education Statistics, "Undergraduate Enrollment," *IES/NCES*, May 2016, nces.ed.gov/programs/coe/indicator_cha.asp.
29. See, inter alia, Robinson, *Global Capitalism* and the *Crisis of Humanity*; Stephen Graham, *Cities Under Siege: The New Military Urbanism* (London: Verso, 2010); John Gilliom and Torin Monahan, *SuperVision: An Introduction to the Surveillance Society* (Chicago: University of Chicago Press, 2012).
30. There is growing recognition that these "wars" are all about defending and advancing global capitalism, controlling the popular and working classes, and repressing social movements. See, inter alia, the critically important study by Dawn Paley, *Drug War Capitalism* (Oakland: AK Press, 2014), and with regard to the United States, Michelle Alexander, *The New Jim Crow: Mass Incarceration in the Age of Colorblindness* (New York: The New Press, 2012).
31. See, inter alia, Victor Rios, *Punished: Policing the Lives of Black and Latino Boys* (New York: New York University Press 2011).
32. Joaquin Sapien, "Texas Students Thrown in Jail for Days … as Punishment for Missing School?" ProPublica, June 13, 2013, published at alternet.org; Annette Fuentes, "The Truancy Trap," *The Atlantic*, September 5, 2012.
33. Andrew Emett, "Pentagon Supplies School Districts with Assault Rifles and Grenade Launchers," *Nation of Change*, September 22, 2014.
34. Teresa Masterson, "School Spies on Students at Home with Webcams: Suit," *NBC*, February 18, 2010; Bianca Bosker, "School Administrator Boasts About Spying on Students Using Laptop Webcams," *Huffington Post*, May 25, 2011.
35. See, inter alia, Kathleen Nolan, *Police in the Hallways: Discipline in an Urban High School* (Minneapolis: University of Minnesota Press, 2011); Derek W. Black, *Ending Zero Tolerance: The Crisis of Absolute School Discipline* (New York: New York University Press, 2016).
36. Ruth Wilson Gilmore, *Golden Gulag: Prisons, Surplus, Crisis, and Opposition in Globalizing California* (Berkeley: University of California Press, 2007).
37. Motoko Rich, "Grading the Common Core: No Teaching Experience Required," *The New York Times*, June 22, 2015.
38. Karl Marx, "The German Ideology," in *The Marx-Engels Reader*, 2d ed., ed. Robert C. Tucker (New York: W.W. Norton, 1978), 172–73.
39. Atilio Boron, *Consolidando la Explotacion: La Academia y el Banco Mundial Contra el Pensamiento Critico* (Cordoba [Argentina]: Editorial Espartaco, 2008), 12.
40. Boron, *Consolidando la Explotacion*, 36–37.
41. Boron, *Consolidando la Explotacion*, 37.
42. For discussion, see Robinson, *Latin America and Global Capitalism* (Baltimore: Johns Hopkins University Press, 2008).
43. Aviva Chomsky, "The Battle for the Soul of American Higher Education," *Common Dreams*, May 23, 2016.

8: DAVOS MAN COMES TO THE THIRD WORLD:
THE TRANSNATIONAL STATE AND THE BRICS

1. See, for instance, Radhika Desai, "The BRICS Are Building a Challenge to Western Economic Supremacy," *The Guardian*, April 2, 2013; Pepe Escobar, "Brazil, Russia, India, China and South Africa: BRICS Go Over the Wall," *Asia Times*, March 27, 2013; William Tabb, "Globalization Today: At the Borders of Class and State Theory," *Science and Society* 73, no. 1 (2009): 41–42; various contributions in the Third World Network's journal *Third World Resurgence*, special issue, "Whither the BRICS," no. 274, June 2013, www.twn.my/title2/resurgence/2013/pdf/274.pdf. On a related note, some of the BRICS literature is swayed by poststructural and postcolonial literature that posits a distinct "Southern epistemology." Bob Jessop has observed, in critiquing these claims: "While Eurcentrism and a metropolitan bias must be rejected, this does not justify other essentialist forms of analysis such as 'Southern Theory', 'indigenous social science', 'epistemologies of the South', or 'subaltern studies'." Jessop, "The World Market, 'North–South' Relations, and Neoliberalism," *AlternateRoutes: A Journal of Critical Social Research* 29 (2018).

2. Desai, "The BRICS Are Building a Challenge to Western Economic Supremacy."

3. Roberto Mangabeira Unger, *La Alternativa de la Izquierda* (Mexico, D.F.: Fondo de Cultura Economica, 2011).

4. See, for instance, various entries in Patrick Bond and Ana Garcia, eds., *BRICS: An Anti-Capitalist Critique* (London: Pluto, 2015); Matthew D. Stephen, "Rising Powers, Global Capitalism and Liberal Global Governance: A Historical Materialist Account of the BRICs Challenge," *European Journal of International Relations* 20, no. 4 (2014): 912–38.

5. Jim O'Neill, "Building Better Global Economic BRICs," Global Economics Paper No. 66 (New York: Goldman Sachs, 2001), pro790512df. pic10.websiteonline.cn/upload/building-better-pdf_geEM.pdf.

6. "Editors Note," *Third World Network, Third World Resurgence*, 1.

7. Vijay Prashad, *The Poorer Nations* (London: Verso, 2012). See also Prashad's other important study, *The Darker Nations* (New York: The New Press, 2007).

8. William I. Robinson, "Global Capitalism and the Emergence of Transnational Elites," *Critical Sociology* 38, no. 3 (2012): 349–64, and "Capitalist Globalization as World Historic Context: A Response," *Critical Sociology* 38, no. 3 (2012): 405–16; Vijay Prashad, "World on a Slope," *Critical Sociology* 38, no. 3 (2012): 401–4.

9. Patrick Bond, "BRICS and the Tendency to Sub-Imperialism," *Pambazuka News*, no. 673, April 10, 2014.

10. See the discussion in Patrick Bond, "Global Financial Governance and the Opening to BRICS Banking," in *South Africa: The State of the Nation*, ed. Gerard Hagg (Pretoria: Human Sciences Research Council,

2013–14), 442–463. In a very revealing passage, Bond notes that the very idea of a BRICS development bank originally came from former World Bank vice president Joseph Stiglitz, former World Bank chief economist Nick Stern, and now-deceased president of Ethiopia Meles Zenawi (who took his country down a neoliberal path). Stern explained at a London conference in 2013 that "if you have a development bank that is part of a [major business] deal then it makes it more difficult for governments to be unreliable.... What you had was the presence of the European Bank for Reconstruction and Development (EBRD) reducing the potential for government-induced policy risk, and the presence of the EBRD in the deal making of government of the host country more confident about accepting that investment. And that is why Meles Zenawi, Joe Stiglitz and myself, nearly three years ago now, started the idea .... We started to move the idea of a BRICS-led development bank for those two reasons" (as cited in Bond, "Global Financial Governance," 452).

11. For the integration of BRICS countries into transnational capital, see Stephen, "Rising Powers, Global Capitalism and Liberal Global Governance." For the integration of capitalist groups in BRICS countries into the transnational capitalist class, see William I. Robinson, *Global Capitalism and the Crisis of Humanity* (New York: Cambridge University Press, 2014).
12. For a discussion, see William I. Robinson, *Transnational Conflicts: Central America, Social Change, and Globalization* (London: Verso, 2003).
13. "Yuan Small Step," *The Economist*, July 11, 2009, 71.
14. See William I. Robinson, "China and Trumpism," *Telesur*, February 14, 2017.
15. Stephen, "Rising Powers, Global Capitalism and Liberal Global Governance," 12.
16. Richard Gnodde, "New Actors Play a Vital Role in the Global Economy," *Financial Times*, November 12, 2017, 11.
17. "South–North FDI: Role Reversal," *The Economist*, September 24, 2011, 19.
18. Lihuan Zhou and Denise Leung, "China's Overseas Investments, Explained in 10 Graphics," *World Resource Institute*, January 28, 2015.
19. United Nations Conference on Trade and Development, *World Investment Report* (Geneva: Author, 2017), Annex, Table 04.
20. "The Challengers: A New Breed of Multinational Company Has Emerged," *The Economist*, January 12, 2008, 61.
21. David Rothkopf, *Superclass: The Global Power Elite and the World They Are Making* (New York: Farrar, Straus and Giroux, 2008), 42.
22. Alejandra Salas-Porras, "The Transnational Class in Mexico: New and Old Mechanisms Structuring Corporate Networks (1981–2010)," in *Financial Elites and Transnational Business: Who Rules the World*, eds. Georgina Murray and John Scott (Cheltenham, UK: Edgard Elgar, 2012), 173.
23. Raj Patel, *Stuffed and Starved: The Hidden Battle for the World Food System* (Brooklyn, NY: Melville House, 2007), 197–200.

24. Patel, *Stuffed and Starved*, 199.
25. In criticizing my global capitalist approach, this is the argument that Walden Bello makes in *Dilemmas of Domination: The Unmaking of the American Empire* (New York: Holt, 2006).
26. Jerry Harris, "Emerging Third World Powers: China, India, and Brazil," *Race & Class* 46, no. 3 (2005): 10–11.
27. Xinjua News Agency, "Lawmaker Says Monopolistic M&As Threaten China's Economic Security," cable dated March 10, 2008, www.gov.cn/english/2008-03/10/content_916121.htm.
28. Giovanni Arrighi, *Adam Smith in Beijing* (London: Verso, 2009).
29. UNCTAD, "World Investment Report 2005: Transnational Corporations and the Internationalization of R&D" (New York and Geneva: United Nations 2005).
30. Don Lee, "China Pushes for Bigger Role in Reshaping the World Economy," *Los Angeles Times*, April 2, 2009, A1.
31. For example, see James Cypher and Raúl Delgado Wise, *Mexico's Economic Dilemma: The Developmental Failure of Neoliberalism* (Lanham, MD: Rowman and Littlefeld, 2010).
32. Patel, *Stuffed and Starved*, 53.
33. Salas-Porras, "The Transnational Class in Mexico," 159.
34. Patel, *Stuffed and Starved*, 55.
35. I discuss this process in detail in *Transnational Conflicts: Central America, Globalization, and Social Change* (London: Verso, 2003).
36. See, for example, Luis Solano, "El Mercado de los Agrocombustibles," Guatemala City, 2011, www.albedrio.org/htm/otrosdocs/comunicados/issuus/Documentos-0011.htm; Richard Jonasse, ed., *Agrofuels in the Americas* (Oakland: Food First Books, 2009); Philip McMichael, "The Land Grab and Corporate Food Regime Restructuring," *The Journal of Peasant Studies*, 39, no. 3–4 (2012): 681–701.
37. Don Lee, "Era of Global Consumer May be Dawning," *Los Angeles Times*, October 4, 2009, A1.
38. For instance, see Third World Network, "Wither the BRICS."
39. Jerry Harris, "Statist Globalization in China, Russia and the Gulf States," *Science and Society* 73, no. 1 (2009): 6–33.
40. Yousef Baker, "Global Capitalism and Iraq: The Making of a Neoliberal Republic," *International Review of Modern Sociology* 4, no. 2 (2014): 121–48.
41. Bond, "Global Financial Governance."

9: GLOBAL POLICE STATE

1. John Bellamy Foster, Richard York, and Brett Clark, *The Ecological Rift: Capitalism's War on the Earth* (New York: Monthly Review Press, 2011).
2. Elizabeth Kolbert, *The Sixth Extinction: An Unnatural History* (New York: Henry Holt and Co, 2014).
3. On these matters, see, inter alia, Jared Diamond, *Collapse: How Societies*

Chose to Fail or Succeed, 2d ed. (New York: Penguin, 2011); Sing C. Chew, *The Recurring Dark Ages* (Lanham, MD: AltaMira Press, 2007). For theoretical discussion, see Foster et al., *The Ecological Rift,* and Jason W. Moore, *Capitalism and the Web of Life* (London: Verso, 2015).

4. Reports of slave labor around the world are now numerous. For the Brazilian case, for example, see Thais Lazzeri, "Investigation Reveals Slave Labor Conditions in Brazil's Timber Industry," *Mongabay,* March 13, 2017. On the seafood slaves, see the series of articles published in 2015 by a team of Associated Press investigative reporters, who broke the story, at interactives.ap.org/2015/seafood-from-slaves/.

5. Karl Marx and Frederick Engels, *The Communist Manifesto,* in *The Marx-Engels Reader,* 2d ed., ed. Robert C. Tucker (New York: W.W. Norton, 1978), 478.

6. General Accounting Office, "Federal Reserve System: Opportunities Exist to Strengthen Policies and Processes for Managing Emergency Assistance," GAO-11-696, July 2011, Washington, DC.

7. Federal Reserve Bank of St. Louis, graph on "Private fixed investment in information processing equipment and software," compiled from U.S. Bureau of Economic Analysis, fred.stlouisfed.org/series /A679RC1Q027SBEA.

8. See various websites for this data: www.investopedia.com/ask/answers/052715/how-big-derivatives-market.asp; databank.worldbank.org /data/download/GDP.pdf; www.dailyfx.com/forex/education/trading_tips /daily_lesson/2014/01/24/FX_Market_Size.html. The mind-boggling explosion of derivatives is a sure sign of the deep structural crisis of global capitalism. Marx noted in *Capital* (Vol. III) that an excess in fictitious capital signals the decoupling of finance and credit from the circuits of productive capital: "[A]ll connection with the actual expansion process of capital is thus completely lost, and the conception of capital as something with automatic self-expansion properties is thereby 'strengthened'." As cited in Bob Jessop, "The World Market, 'North–South' Relations, and Neoliberalism," *AlternateRoutes: A Journal of Critical Social Research* 29 (2018). Perceptively, Jessop notes that "derivatives as forms of financial innovation integrate production on a world scale, and, via their role in all the functions of money that Marx identified, they also contribute to market completion in real time. Yet derivatives represent a fetishized form of money as money and money as capital. Indeed, they reinforce the separation between (1) the general movement of capital based on valorization and the generation of surplus-value anchored in production and (2) the more superficial real-world appearances of money prices and profit, which nonetheless has consequences for all circuits of capital."

9. See "Household Debt" at the Organization for Economic Cooperation and Development webpage, data.oecd.org/hha/household-debt.htm

10. Akin Oyedele, "Americans Have $12.58 Trillion in Household Debt—

Here Is What It Looks Like," *Business Insider*, February 17, 2015; Mark Obryn, "$100 Trillion Global Bond Bubble Poses 'Systemic Risk' to Financial System," *GoldCore*, March 31, 2015.

11. "The Problem with Profits," *The Economist*, May 26, 2016.

12. Van Le, "Private Prisons Are Making Millions by Helping to Deport Longtime Immigrant-Americans—And They're Positively Gleeful About it," *America's Voice*, August 9, 2017.

13. See William I. Robinson, "Global Capitalist Crisis and Trump's War Drive," *Truthout*, April 19, 2017.

14. As an aside, the language we use is part of the ideological and cultural dimension of struggles between oppressors and oppressed. It is now nearly universal to refer to the Pentagon and other military budgets as "defense spending." Yet there is nothing defensive about this spending. The US military is an *offensive* war machine employed against the world's people. The Israeli "defense" industry, which together with high-tech is the mainstay of that country's economy, launches *offensives* against Palestinians struggling for freedom and supplies dozens of governments around the world with weapons to repress their populations. And so on.

15. For these details, see Robinson, "Global Capitalist Crisis and Trump's War Drive."

16. Dawn Paley, *Drug War Capitalism* (Oakland: AKPress, 2014), 16.

17. For instance, the US government allocated $2.5 billion from 2008 to 2015 to the Merida Initiative, a program for assistance to the Mexican military allegedly to combat drug trafficking. Yet as one researcher pointed out, most of this money "does not even cross the border." Instead, it went directly from US state coffers into the accounts of Texas-based Fairchild Aircraft that makes the radar planes flown by the Mexican air force, of Connecticut company Sikorsky, which makes the Blackhawk helicopters used by the Mexican army, and to the California headquarters of General Atomics that makes the drones used to surveil the US–Mexico border. Christy Thornton, "Ending U.S. Support for Mexican Repression Starts at Home," *NACLA Report on the Americas* 18, no. 4 (2016): 322–23. In addition to Dawn Paley's brilliant study, *Drug War Capitalism* (Oakland: AK Press, 2014), see also among others, Jasmin Hristov, *Paramilitarism & Neoliberalism* (London: Pluto, 2014), and John Gibler, *To Die in Mexico* (San Francisco: City Lights, 2011).

18. Michelle Alexander, *The New Jim Crow* (New York: The New Press, 2012).

19. For discussion, see inter alia, Nick Srnicek, *Platform Capitalism* (Cambridge: Polity, 2017).

20. William I. Robinson, *Global Capitalism and the Crisis of Humanity* (New York: Cambridge University Press, 2014); see in particular Chapter 5, "Policing Global Capitalism."

21. I wrote two articles in 2017 that summarize my thinking on Trumpism and twenty-first-century fascism: "The Battle Against Trumpism and the

Specter of 21st Century Fascism," *Telesur*, January 21, 2017; "From Obama to Trump: The Failure of Passive Revolution," *Telesur*, January 13, 2017.

22. *The Intercept* revealed the counterinsurgency operation. See Alleen Brown, Will Parrish, and Alice Speri, "Leaked Documents Reveal Counterterrorism Tactics Used at Standing Rock to 'Defeat Pipeline Insurgencies'," *The Intercept*, May 27, 2017.

23. In the aftermath of Trump's electoral victory, there was heated debate in the United States with regard to Trump's social base in the working class. Some pointed to the fact that Trump voters had higher than average incomes (two-thirds of Trump supporters earned over $50,000 a year) to argue that his actual social base was among the "middle class" or petty-bourgeoisie, while others pointed to the fact that the small business class and professional strata gave significant electoral support to Trump. However, *the conclusion that Trump's social base was not in the white sectors of the US working class is fundamentally flawed*. In the first instance, income is not an indication of class, which is a structural relation to the process/relations of production. Some of the reports on the "middle class/petty-bourgeoisie" thesis simply alternate the word "middle income" with "middle class" to reach their conclusions. That Trump's working class base earned above-average wages or salaries actually supports my argument that this base represents those more privileged strata of the working class now facing heightened insecurity and downward mobility (this includes, especially, professional strata that have become increasingly precariatized and who face the specter of deskilling; precariatization through contract, outsourced, part-time, and temporary forms of employment; or replacement by technology). In addition, if we are to take income levels as some indication of class affiliation, then one-third of Trump supporters earned less than $50,000 per year, which should indicate that Trump could not possibly have won without significant working class support.

Second, Trump won nearly 50 million votes. There are simply not that many adults in the United States that belong to the petty-bourgeoisie, understood as the class that owns its own means of production yet works those means, so that it does not live off the exploitation of labor but neither is it alienated and exploited directly by capital through wage employment. (Indirectly, it is in several ways.)

It seems to me as I read over various reports that they reflect a great deal of Leftist angst at having to acknowledge that tens of millions of US workers did vote for Trump. And to be sure, Trump's victory was also a result of significant support for him among sectors of the capitalist class and the political elite.

For the "middle class"/petty-bourgeoisie argument, see, inter alia, Charlie Post, "The Specter of Trump," *Jacobin*, October 1, 2015; Sharon Smith, "States of Inequality: Political Polarization and the US Working Class," *International Socialist Review*, no. 107 (Spring 2017); Lauren Kaori

Gurley, "7 Pundits Who Spread the Myth of Trump's Working-Class Voter Base," *Alternet*, July 19, 2017; Lance Selfa, "Trump's Middle-Class Army," *Jacobin*, September 7, 2016.

10: REFLECTIONS ON A BRAVE NEW WORLD

1. This is a revised version of an essay originally published by the Great Transition Initiative (GTI) run by the Tellus Institute in Cambridge, Massachusetts, as "an international network for the critical exploration of concepts, strategies, and visions for a transition to a future of enriched lives, human solidarity, and a resilient biosphere." According to the GTI, the Initiative asks "where we [humanity] are?, where we are headed?, where do we want to go?, how to we get there?"

2. By *circuit of accumulation*, I mean the process by which the production of a good or a service is first planned and financed (by capitalists), followed by attaining and then mixing together the component parts (labor, raw materials, buildings and machinery, etc.) in production sequences, and then by the marketing of the final product. At the end of this process, the capitalist recovers his initial capital outlay as well as profit and has thus "accumulated" capital. This is what Karl Marx referred to as the "circuit of capital." In earlier epochs much of the circuit was "self-contained" within a single country.

3. Stefania Vitali, James B. Glattfelder, and Stefano Battiston, "The Network of Global Corporate Control," *PLOS ONE* 6, no. 10 (October 2011): 1–36.

4. "Special Report," *The Economist*, September 17, 2016, 4–6.

5. A. Sivanandan, in *Communities of Resistance: Writings on Black Struggles for Socialism* (London, Verso, 1990), states (p. 27) that the IT revolution enhanced productivity by a factor of a million, but this seems exaggerated. For a review of the literature on IT and productivity, see Erik Brynjolfsson and Shinkyu Yang, "Information Technology and Productivity: A Review of the Literature," *Advances in Computers* 43 (1996): 179–214.

6. See inter alia, William I. Robinson, "The Battle Against Trumpism and the Specter of 21st Century Fascism," *Telesur*, January 21, 2017; William I. Robinson, "Trumpism, 21st Century Fascism, and the Dictatorship of the Transnational Capitalist Class," *Social Justice*, January 20, 2017; William I. Robinson, "What Is Behind the Renegotiation of NAFTA? Trumpism and the New Global Economy," *Truthout*, July 24, 2017.

7. For more detail, see William I. Robinson, "Reform Is Not Enough to Stem the Rising Tide of Inequality Worldwide," *Truthout*, January 1, 2016.

8. Klaus Schwab, "Global Corporate Citizenship: Working With Governments and Civil Society," *Foreign Affairs* (January–February 2008): 108–109.

9. Richard Samans, Klaus Schwab, and Mark Malloch-Brown, eds., *Everybody's Business: Strengthening International Cooperation in a More Interdependent World* (World Economic Forum: Geneva, 2010).

260 Into the Tempest

10. Oxfam, *An Economy for the 1%* (Oxford, UK: Author, 2016).
11. International Labor Organization, *World of Work Report 2014: Developing Without Jobs*, Executive Summary, International Labor Organization Research Department, 2014.
12. The phrase is from Mike Davis, *Planet of Slums* (London: Verso, 2006). The International Labor Organization reported that in the late twentieth century some one-third of the global labor force was unemployed. International Labor Organization, *World Employment Report 1996–97* (Geneva: Author/United Nations, 1997).
13. Russ Mitchell and Tracey Lien, "Rides in Uber Robot Vehicles at Hand," *Los Angeles Times,* August 19, 2016, A1.
14. "A Giant Problem," *The Economist*, September 17, 2016, 9.
15. See various websites for this data: https://en.wikipedia.org/wiki/Gross_world_product; www.investopedia.com/ask/answers/052715/how-big-derivatives-market.asp; databank.worldbank.org/data/download/GDP.pdf; www.dailyfx.com/forex/education/trading_tips/daily_lesson/2014/01/24/FX_Market_Size.html.
16. Akin Oyedele, "Americans Have $12.58 Trillion in Household Debt—Here Is What it Looks Like," *Business Insider*, February 17, 2015; Mark Obryn, "$100 Trillion Global Bond Bubble Poses 'Systemic Risk' to Financial System," *GoldCore*, March 31, 2015.
17. Jen Wieczner, "Donald Trump's Election Win Is Making This Stock Soar," *Fortune*, November 9, 2016.
18. Paul La Monica, "Defense Stocks Up as Big as ISIS Crisis Escalates," *CNN*, September 22, 2014.
19. *The Economist* noted as far back as 2000 that "any distinction between the corporate and the NGO worlds is long gone." See "Sins of the Secular Missionaries," *The Economist*, January 29, 2000, 26.
20. Much has been written about this and the discussion is necessarily limited here. See William I. Robinson, *Promoting Polyarchy: Globalization, U.S. Intervention, and Hegemony* (Cambridge, UK: Cambridge University Press, 1996), and INCITE! Women of Color Against Violence, *The Revolution Will Not be Funded: Beyond the Non-Profit Industrial Complex* (Boston: South End Press, 2009).
21. These scenarios are described in Paul Raskin, *Journey to Earthland: The Great Transition to Planetary Civilization* (Boston: Tellus Institute, 2016).
22. See Raskin, *Journey to Earthland*, for an explication of his Earthland vision along these lines.

INDEX

"Passim" (literally "scattered") indicates intermittent discussion of a topic over a cluster of pages.

academia. *See* universities and colleges
accumulation, social structure of. *See* "social structure of accumulation" (term)
accumulation of capital, 61, 65, 69, 85, 87. *See also* overaccumulation; militarized accumulation; primitive accumulation of capital
acquisitions and mergers. *See* mergers and acquisitions (M&As)
adjunct faculty, 156
agribusiness, 171–72, 176–77, 178
agricultural subsidies. *See* subsidies, agricultural
Albemarle, 111
Amelio, William J., 49–50
American Legislative Exchange Council (ALEC), 133–34
Annan, Kofi, 92
anti-immigrant laws, 134, 139
Argentina, 109
Arizona, 134
Aronowitz, Stanley: *Jobless Future*, 153
assembly industry, 173, 179, 209, 218
automobile industry, 55–56, 58, 209, 218–19

Bacon, David, 136, 138, 139
Baker, Yousef, 116

banks and banking, 82, 89, 108; bailouts, 114, 189–90; BRICS, 163; Dakota Access Pipeline and, 201; regional, 243n10, 254n10. *See also* World Bank
Bello, Walden, 100–101
"biopolitics," 131
Bond, Patrick, 167, 182, 230–31, 254n10
bond market, 109, 110, 191, 219
borders, 141; militarization, 129–30, 133, 135, 137, 138; US-Mexico, 130, 135–41 passim, 193
Boron, Atilio, 159, 160
bourgeoisie, 14, 52, 67; national, 14, 62; transnational/global, 14, 25, 27, 66–68 passim, 91, 98; Trump election and, 258n23. *See also* transnational capitalist class (TCC)
Bowles, Samuel: *Schooling in Capitalist America*, 152
Braverman, Harry: *Labor and Monopoly Capital*, 153
Brazil, 171–72, 176, 180, 187
Bretton Woods system, 89, 92
Brewer, Jan, 134
BRICS bloc, 163–75, 179–82, 230, 231. *See also* Brazil; China; India; Russia; South Africa
Britain. *See* United Kingdom
Buffet, Warren, 145, 181
Bukharin, Nikolai, 245n3
Burawoy, Michael, 42
Bush, George W., 101, 117, 215

SELECTED WORKS BY WILLIAM I. ROBINSON ON GLOBAL CAPITALISM

BOOKS ON GLOBAL CAPITALISM

Global Capitalism and the Crisis of Humanity. Cambridge University Press, 2014

Latin America and Global Capitalism. Johns Hopkins University Press, 2008

A Theory of Global Capitalism: Production, Class, and State in a Transnational World. Johns Hopkins University Press, 2004

Transnational Conflicts: Central America, Globalization, and Social Change. Verso Press, 2003

Promoting Polyarchy: Globalization, U.S. Intervention, and Hegemony. Cambridge University Press, 1996

SELECT ESSAYS NOT INCLUDED IN *INTO THE TEMPEST*
(available at http://www.soc.ucsb.edu/faculty/robinson/articles.shtml)

"The Transnational Capitalist Class," in Mark Juergensmeyer, Saskia Sassen, and Manfred Steger, eds., *Oxford Handbook of Global Studies*, Oxford University Press, 2018

"Capitalism in the Twenty-First Century: Global Inequality, Piketty, and the Transnational Capitalist Class," in Lauren Langman and David A. Smith (eds), *Piketty, Inequality and 21st Century Capitalism*, Brill, 2018

"Capitalist Crisis and Twenty-First Century Fascism: Beyond the Trump Hype," *Science and Society*, Winter 2019.

"Debate on the New Global Capitalism: Transnational Capitalist Class, Transnational State Apparatuses, and Global Crisis," *International Critical Thought*, 7(2):171-189, 2017.

"What is Behind the Renegotiation of NAFTA: Trumpism and the New Global Economy," *Truthout*, 24 July 2017

"China and Trumpism: The Political Contradictions of Global Capitalism," *Jacobin*, 4 February 2017

"The Fetishism of Empire: A Critical Review of Panitch and Gindin's *The Making of Global Capitalism*," *Studies in Political Economy*, 93 147-165, 2014.

"The Political Economy of Israeli Apartheid and the Specter of Genocide," *Truthout*, September 19, 2014.

"Global Capitalism and the Emergence of Transnational Elites," *Critical Sociology*, 38(3):349-364, 2012, together with, "Capitalist Globalization as World Historic Context: A Response," *Critical Sociology*, 38:405-416, 2012

"Global Capitalism and Twenty-First Century Fascism: A U.S. Case Study" (coauthored with Mario Barrera) *Race and Class*, 53(3):4-29, 2012

"The Pitfall of Realist Analysis of Global Capitalism: A Critique of Ellen Meiksins Wood's *Empire of Capital*," *Historical Materialism*, 15:71-93, 2007.

"Gramsci and Globalization: From Nation-State to Transnational Hegemony," *Critical Review of International Social and Political Philosophy*, 8(4): 1-16, 2005.

"Remapping Development in Light of Globalization: From a Territorial to a Social Cartography," *Third World Quarterly*, 23(6): 1047-1071, 2002

"Social Theory and Globalization: The Rise of a Transnational State," *Theory and Society* 30(2): 157-200, together with "Response to MacMichael, Block, and Goldfrank": 223-236, 2001.

CPSIA information can be obtained
at www.ICGtesting.com
Printed in the USA
LVHW091948080219
606911LV00009B/268/P

9 781608 465460